After Europe

After Europe

Critical Theory and Post-Colonial Writing

Edited by

Stephen Slemon and Helen Tiffin

Dangaroo  Press

ACKNOWLEDGEMENTS

Cover: Painting by the Haitian artist, Edouard Duval of the vodun farmer-god, Zaka. Every attempt has been made to trace the holder of the copyright for this painting but we have up to date been unsuccessful. If anyone has this information we would be grateful if they would notify us.

11403675 - 3

Learning Resources
Centre

First published in 1989 by Dangaroo Press
Reprinted in 1992
Australia: G.P.O. Box 1209, Sydney, New South Wales, 2001
Denmark: Pinds Hus, Geding Søvej 21, 8381 Mundelstrup
UK: P.O. Box 186, Coventry CV4 7HG

ISBN 1 871049 71 7

But the mystery of the colonial is this; while he remains alive, his instinct, always and forever creative, must choose a way to change the meaning and perspective of this ancient tyranny.

George Lamming *The Pleasures of Exile*

Contents

Introduction

[W]e ... have been blandly invited to submit ourselves to a second epoch of colonisation – this time by a universal-humanoid abstraction defined and conducted by individuals whose theories and prescriptions are derived from the apprehension of *their* world and *their* history, *their* social neuroses and *their* value systems. It is time, clearly, to respond to this new threat ...

Wole Soyinka
Myth, Literature and the African World

'A second epoch of colonisation' – this is how Wole Soyinka characterises Western theoretical practice as it applies itself, even with the best of intentions, to the cultural productions of the non-Western world. And it would be fair to say that post-colonial writing – by which we mean writing that is grounded in the cultural realities of those societies whose subjectivity has been constituted at least in part by the subordinating power of European colonialism – contains hundreds of such statements: statements which lay bare the material, often devastating, consequences of a centuries-long imposition of Euro-American conceptual patterns onto a world that is at once 'out there' and yet thoroughly assimilable to the psychic grasp of Western cognition. But even within the mainstream of First World academic activity, it is scarcely news that 'theory' – and especially the various modes of Western 'literary' or 'critical theory' – exerts a disempowering energy against other forms of registering experience and of interpreting artistic expression. As Hayden White observes in *Tropics of Discourse*: 'The contours of criticism are unclear, its geography unspecified, and its topography therefore uncertain. As a form of intellectual practice, no field is more imperialistic.'[1] What then might this present collection of essays, which focuses specifically on the intersection between some of the dominant forms of critical theory and a wide variety of post-colonial literary practices, have to contribute to an increasingly familiar debate over the proper uses and possible locations of theory? How does this collection differ from other 'theoretical' ventures into this terrain? And how might the *problem* of this collection inform the astonishingly difficult question: how can our reading of post-colonial literary texts – in their cultural specificity *and* in their post-European commonality – issue productively into a genuinely post-colonial literary criticism?

Perhaps the best way to address these questions is to begin with Derrida's famous critical dictum *'Il n'y a pas de hors-texte'*: a statement which, whatever its own genealogy, stands at the headwaters of Euro-American post-structuralist thinking. '[T]here has never been anything but writing', Derrida continues; 'there have never been anything but supplements, substitutive significations which could only come forth in a chain of differential references, the "real" supervening, and being added only while taking on meaning from a trace and from an invocation of the supplement, etc. ... [W]hat opens meaning and language is writing as the disappearance of natural presence.'[2] It is by now generally recognised that this argument is in no way *theoretically* constrained to occlude social materiality – that is, to the wilful erasure of the actual determinants of gender, race, class, and cultural difference – in literary production and consumption. As Barbara Johnson explains, it is in fact 'the claim to unequivocal domination of one mode of signifying over another' which such a critical insight would call down,[3] not the claims of social consciousness or the recognition of the inflections of power in how literary meaning is produced and circulated.

In practice, however, this 'suspension' of the referent in the literary sign, and the 'crisis of representation' which has followed in its wake, has effected within the dominant forms of Anglo-American post-structuralist theory a wholesale retreat from geography and history into a domain of pure 'textuality' in which the principle of indeterminacy smothers the possibility of social or political 'significance' for literature. Within this domain, as Kum Kum Sangari puts it, history is refigured as an apparatus of collage; and as for social contradiction, it is simply deflated into a rhetoric of ambiguity and endless deferral.[4]

Obviously, such a reading practice could only have gained credence within a dominant segment of a dominant culture. For more than anything, this ostensibly apolitical script for reading functions as an apparatus of cultural authorization. Under the hegemony of Anglo-American 'theoretical' methodology, we now read critical texts – we probably even write them – from the footnotes backwards; and the paradoxical result is that even as the theoretically vigilant critical work establishes its autonomous grounding by ploughing under the now debunked thematics of the *literary* text, it also initiates an astonishingly filiative network of semantic and citational obedience towards the master-texts and master codes of 'theory' itself. One of the most ironic developments of what began as revolutionary scepticism has been the production of an institutionalised army of ridiculously credulous readers – 'critics' who systematically shut out the world in order to practice what Frank Lentriccia accurately depicts as a textual form of interior decoration.[5]

What is less obvious, however, are the ways in which this overarching extolling of the crisis of representation functions as a technology of containment and control within the cross-cultural theatre of neo-colonial relations. As Barbara Christian point out, post-structuralism's technical language – its graphs, its algebraic equations, its exegetical drive – has often at least one immediate effect upon Third World readers for whom the latinate compounds of deconstructive terminology evoke the horrors of missionary education and its interpellation of subordinate subjectivity: and that is to silence them in their work *as theorists.*[6] In another vector, post-structuralism's critique of the 'centred subject' has for many critics taken on a thoroughly displacive function in relation to the project of historically specific, culturally grounded critique, with the result that some potentially crucial work on colonialist power has been lost to a flabby subsumation of real social difference into a Western obsession with epistemological legitimation.[7] More visibly damaging, however, is the way in which a post-structuralist refutation of the referent can underscore a theoretical dismissal of some of the basic survival strategies of subordinated and colonised peoples. As Craig Tapping has noted – and it is a theme he returns to in his essay for this collection:

> despite theory's refutation of such absolute and logocentric categories as these – 'truth' or 'meaning', 'purpose' or 'justification' – the new literatures ... are generated from cultures for whom such terms as 'authority' and 'truth' are empirically urgent in their demands. Land claims, racial survival, cultural revival: all these demand an understanding of and response to the very concepts and structures which post-structuralist academicians refute in language games, few of which recognize the political struggles of real peoples outside such discursive frontiers.[8]

The dominant element here, of course, is the Western propensity for universalising and its radical fear of cultural relativity. For although the interests of Western theory are not – as Homi Bhabha has recently argued – *necessarily* 'collusive with the hegemonic role of the West as a power block', not necessarily 'freighted with Western "symbolic capital" ',[9] the practical force of theory's ranging zeal is to assimilate the literary or social 'text', wherever it is found, into a set of philosophical questions whose cultural and historical specificity within postmodern Anglo-American culture is rarely admitted, let alone significantly addressed. Sangari fixes with telling accuracy the political implications of this universalising impulse in poststructuralist methodology when she notes how on the one hand, the world contracts into the West; a Eurocentric perspective ... is brought to bear upon 'Third World' cultural products; a 'specialized' skepticism is carried everywhere as cultural paraphernalia and epistemological apparatus, as a way of seeing; and the postmodern problematic becomes *the* frame through which the cultural products of the rest of the world are seen. On the other hand, the West expands into the world; late capitalism muffles the globe and homogenizes (or threatens to) all cultural production – this, for some reason, is one 'master narrative' that is seldom dismantled as it needs to be if the differential economic, class, and cultural formation of 'Third World' countries is to be taken into account. The writing that emerges from this position, however critical it may be of colonial discourses, gloomily disempowers the 'nation' as an enabling idea and relocates the impulses for change as everywhere and nowhere ... Such skepticism does not take into account either the fact that the postmodern preoccupation with the crisis of meaning is not everyone's crisis (even in the West) or that there are different modes of de-essentialization which are socially and politically grounded and mediated by separate perspectives, goals, and strategies for change in other countries.10

For Edward Said, this intransigence in 'theory' amounts to no less than a complete evacuation of what he considers to be genuine *critical* consciousness – consciousness, that is, which is responsive to concrete experience and which is cognizant of human activity beyond the reach of dominating social and cognitive systems. As Said sees it, 'critical' consciousness always emerges as a resistance to theory, even in those moments when 'theory' is being employed. But when this critical consciousness is missing – and within Western institutions this is so often the case – critical theory goes 'travelling':[11] a 'eurovision'[12] set loose upon a field of difference, and one which fixes its exoticising, objectifying, knowledge-producing gaze wherever and whenever it pleases. It thus becomes clear just how it is that certain modalities of contemporary Western theory return to source as a colonising technology, for in their assimilation of Europe's Others to a Euro-American problematic – the question of representation – these methodological apparatuses reconstitute colonial and post-colonial subjects, and the texts they produce, as useful workers in an on-going Western industry: namely, the development of intellectual strategies for understanding and locating the agency and the specificity of the metropolitan imperial Self.

As an exemplum of this practice, it might be useful to consider the figure of Benjamin Disraeli's Tancred, whose burning desire it is 'to penetrate the great Asian mystery'.[13] '[I]t is very easy now to get to Jerusalem', notes Tancred; 'the great difficulty ... is to know what to do when you are there' (p. 136). And so, as Rana Kabbani retells the story, Tancred

... starts out from his parental estate armed with that locations' code of conduct and outlook. He heads for the East in order to become enlightened, but as his journey progresses, he gradually becomes an enlightener instead. He imports to the chaotic and emotive landscape that he travels through the restraint and the authoritative morality of his upbringing. He emerges from the East mellowed, but virtually unchanged. He has endured the alien without suffering any fragmentation of his being.[14]

Tancred stakes his claim to the 'East' on the astonishing argument that since the social and moral codes of Palestine are in fact the foundational principles of the Christianised 'West', the true contemporary home of this Other world he explores is therefore precisely that ethical dilemma he is attempting to solve for English imperial culture (pp. 272-75). Tancred already possesses 'theory', but what he needs is a figural location for its seamless application. And at the end of the novel, as he stands in full possession of both the land and the woman who constitutes its allegorical emblem, Tancred asks a question which still has resonance for Western theory and its interloping practitioners: 'I am here', says Tancred, as he rises from his kiosk to greet a second wave of Western travellers to the East, 'Why am I wanted?' (p. 501).

Why indeed? A rather cynical answer is that 'theory' has paid off its mortgage on the critical academy and now owns it outright; that therefore, if the post-colonial literatures are to have any real effect on the literary canon and on mainstream pedagogical practice, post-colonial critics will simply have to 'master the discourse of contemporary literary theory'.[15] This argument proves fairly easy to dismiss on ideological grounds – after all, why should First World tertiary institutions be so thoroughly privileged as *the* site of meaning-production? And why should post-colonial critics care if the post-colonial literatures fail to play up squarely on the green summer pitches of the Imperium in its neo-colonialist phase?

Tzvetan Todorov has demonstrated that one of colonialism's most supple strategies of control is to extend the principle of equality only when it withholds from its Others the principle of difference.[16] This argument for the parity of post-colonial literatures in a First World literary and critical canon is thus a heavily problematical one – it reinscribes, at least in part, precisely that tropological apparatus which helps to effect the subordination of colonial Others in the first place. Nevertheless, the Western critical industry does exert enormous hegemonic power over the reading practices of literatures written in a language whose original provenance is Europe; and as is always the case with power, the institutional purchase of the West's dominant cognitive principles is never simply going to go away. And so this argument *for* 'theory' on behalf of post-colonial writing does – at least in a practical sense – make clear that institutional apparatuses for cultural authority continue to govern and to naturalise the field of 'literature'. If the post-colonial literatures are to have an impact on Western thinking, even if only as a by-product, 'critical theory' can provide one of the vehicles through which post-colonial voices, however distorted, can be made audible.

More importantly, however, post-structuralist literary theory offers post-colonial criticism an important mechanism for making what Bhabha calls 'the historical connectedness between the subject and object of critique' thoroughly, and usefully, visible. 'It makes us aware', writes Bhabha,

> that our political referents and priorities – the people, the community, class struggle, anti-racism, gender difference, the assertion of an anti-imperialist, black or third perspective – are not 'there' in some primordial, naturalistic sense. Nor do they reflect a unitary or homogeneous political object. They 'make sense' as they come to be constructed in the discourses of feminism or Marxism or the Third Cinema or whatever, whose objects of priority – class or sexuality or 'the new ethnicity' ... – are always in historical and philosophical tension, or cross-referenced with other objectives.[17]

Bhabha's stress upon the *constructed* nature of all theoretical discourse is an important one, for this perception – made possible by post-structuralism's suspension of the referent – opens the door to an enormously enabling critique of power in all of its social locations.[18] It is therefore hardly surprising that much of the most interesting, avowedly post-structural, work to date on the question of colonialism takes as its object of study not the 'literary' texts of colonised or post-colonial peoples but rather the inescapably fractured, self-betraying 'texts' of imperial culture itself.

This project – of 'theoretically' sophisticated, anti-colonial critique – is fostering a growth industry within the Western academy, and its two major methodologies tend to classify themselves under the rubric 'deconstructive' or 'new historicist'. There are important differences between these two forms of theoretical practice (not to mention important differences within each of them); but what they share is an attempt to carry a critique of 'the imperialism of the signifier'[19] forward towards – to use Gayatri Chakravorty Spivak's words – a 'disclosure of complicities where a will to knowledge would create oppositions'.[20] Homi Bhabha's deconstructive 'commitment to theory' is thus predicated upon the possibility of exposing, through the 'translation' of mainstream post-structuralism, a 'contradictory and ambivalent space of enunciation' within the discourse of colonialism – an ambivalence, that is, which circles upon itself to disclose a radical, fissuring hybridity at the heart of colonialist 'desire' and thus a self-alienating energy within imperial authority which affords the strategic displacement of colonial discourse itself.[21] And Stephen Greenblatt's new historicism – 'new' because it eschews the univocal assumptions of historical coherence in the 'old' historicist claim – aspires to locate within colonialist documents the presence of subversive inquiries, of transgressions of authority, and to demonstrate how colonialism in fact depends upon such presences within the field of its power.[22]

Both of these theoretical methodologies *require* post-structuralist scepticism, and both of them provide post-colonial critical practice with an important answer to Tancred's question of why we might want to use 'critical theory' in our reading and teaching, despite its unacknowledged grounding in and implicit privileging of First World cultural concerns. But at the same time, both of these methodologies for 'theory' have come in for harsh criticism from scholars who attempt to speak on behalf of historically subordinated peoples. Benita Parry, for example, has argued that although deconstructive work on the discourse of colonialism has succeeded in reversing an implicit collusion between criticism and colonial power – a collusion she rather problematically locates in 'Commonwealth' literary studies and its alleged sublimation of the political into the moral or metaphysical sphere – deconstruction's necessary privileging of the colonialist text as the object of critical attention amounts, discursively, to an erasure of the anti-colonialist 'native' voice and a limiting of the possibility of 'native' resistance.[23] And in response to the anti-colonialist practice of the new historicist theory, Carolyn Porter has questioned the implicit politics of any reading strategy which seeks, first, to position resistance as already present within the domain of power, and secondly, to envision subversion as a necessary consequence of power, an 'opposition' which actually functions to serve the hegemonic interests of dominant culture itself.[24]

The key point in these objections to anti-colonialist 'theory' as it is most commonly being practised within the academy is that the cultural, historical *agency* of colonised and of post-colonial peoples is simply written out of the equation of power. Alongside – necessary to – 'theory's' abandonment of a reflective or mimetic purchase to literary writing comes the suspension of an operative *lived* experience under colonial power: a dimension in writing, that is, which surfaces in *thematic* contestation, in a socially *practised* linguistic rupture, and above all in the *expressive* representation of other codes of apprehending 'reality', other structures for disclosing resistance. For in reifying power and its oppositions to a specifically 'textualised' domain of inscription and its reading, deconstructive or new historicist theoretical practice, in its anti-colonialist vector, *also* forecloses on the social field as an extratextual arena of struggle and thus inscribes what Porter calls 'colonialist formalism'[25] onto the terrain of neo-colonial international relations. As critics such as Parry and Porter see it, contemporary anti-colonialist critical theory – at least of this kind – again carries that foundational dictum of

Derrida's, *il n'y a pas de hors-texte*, directly towards the ungrounded pole in its bifurcated potentiality. And thus this particular manifestation of 'theory', they argue, rather than arriving at a *material* critical practice which locates the 'literary' as a culturally significant dimension within the specifics of history and geography, transports colonialist 'history' and post-colonial 'society' directly into the theatre of the unrelievedly 'literary', where they function simply as semiotic figures, rhetorical presences in an endlessly self-disclosing 'text'.[26]

And so mainstream 'critical theory', even in its more politically vigilant manifestations, locks into an ironic relation with post-colonial critical practice. Although it offers the critical project an important set of strategies for challenging Western 'textualised' hegemony and for disrupting the univocal power and 'presence' of a naturalised neo-colonialist script, it also betrays a displacive purchase against the agency of marginalised and subordinated groups. Homi Bhabha points out that there is always within critical theory a 'tension ... between its institutional containment and its revisionary force',[27] and quite clearly this tension plays itself out in spectacular form when 'theory' turns its travelling eye towards the Others of Empire and baldly appropriates their cultural labour to its own cognitive uses. The scarifications of 'theory' become even more painful, however, when this tension, this irony, surfaces as an Anglo-American retooling enterprise whose anti-colonialist or anti-imperialist activity proceeds in its decentering work completely without reference to the oppositional, subversive cultural activity of colonised and post-colonial peoples. When theoretical practice amounts, in Parry's words, to the obliteration of 'the role of the native as historical subject and combatant, possessor of an-other knowledge and producer of alternative tradition',[28] it inherently joins hands with that neo-colonising apparatus which post-colonial criticism – whatever else it does – always sets out to subvert. 'Theory' – after Europe – becomes a discursive tool by which dominant culture ideologically reinscribes its imperial centrality; and yet, for all of that, 'theory' remains a potentially enabling mechanism for furthering the continuing practice of post-colonial critical resistance into new vectors.

In the early stages of our thinking about this collection, and while we were working with Anna Rutherford to formulate the intellectual 'project' that the conjunction between the two terms in our sub-title announces, we envisioned a rather different set of critical essays, a different kind of critical practice, than what this volume now offers. Specifically, we had in mind a set of papers which took on, in very direct ways, some of the more egregious theoretical engagements within the Western universalist project. Our own paradigmatic theoretical 'text', much in need of a post-colonialist critique, was Deleuze and Guattari's appropriative subsumation of what they wanted to call 'minor literature' to an ungrounded or 'deterritorialised', anti-referential writing practice, and their bald exhortation to the First World writer simply to 'become' minor – as though the experience of physical subordination had nothing whatever to do with the formulation of literary resistance.[29]

As we proceeded, however, we learned that for most post-colonial literary critics, a return to – a grounding in – the post-colonial literary text itself comprised an absolutely crucial gesture within the politics of critical writing and the *sine qua non* of a literary critical engagement with the structures of neo-colonialist power. This is not to say that we did not receive papers which engaged in direct confrontation with the practices of contemporary critical theory. Diana Brydon's argument for the preservation of a 'common *wealth*' criticism grounded in 'the voices of the colonised' locates the hegemonic impulses behind mainstream theoretical practices with great precision, for example. Graham Huggan's call for 'a post-colonial poetics of disturbance' takes on the global appropriations of postmodernist discourse in its specific institutional purchase. Meenakshi Mukherjee's analysis of Eurocentric educational apparatuses sets a discourse of personal, post-colonial witness against the interpellative power of both colonialism and patriarchy. Bill Ashcroft's positioning of post-colonial writing at the 'intersection' of language carries with it an explicit critique of Derrida's notion of 'infinite transmissibility' in writing. And Gareth Griffiths' and David Moody's call for a revaluation of Wole Soyinka's cultural and literary criticism makes a specific, detailed argument for the supplementation of European structural Marxism with the post-colonial theoretical analysis of Frantz Fanon.

Nevertheless, the commanding critical assumption of the essays collected in this volume is that post-colonial literary texts are *themselves* 'theoretical' documents – narratives, that is, which, whatever their expressive or reflective purchase in the heterodox realities of colonial or post-colonial societies, *also* provide detailed counter-discursive 'readings' of the 'master works' of imperial culture as it attempts to settle itself, discursively, upon an exoticised, colonised terrain. For J. Michael Dash, this 'always already' imperial inscription upon Caribbean society means that the Martinican writer Edouard Glissant's literary texts *necessarily* foreground a culturally specific 'terrain of the unspeakable' in their reflective operations, and that as they do so they implicitly mobilise a 'natural' deconstructive energy against the sign-systems of dominant culture. For Craig Tapping, colonialism's imposition of a self-privileging representational hierarchy, in which 'writing' arrogates to itself the only grounding for cultural 'authority', means that the Australian Aboriginal writer Mudrooroo Narogin's (Colin Johnson's) textual practice implicitly interrogates the semiotic machineries of Empire as it negotiates for an orally-grounded culture the empire of the written word.

This strategy of according to post-colonial 'literary' texts that 'interpretive' power which dominant theoretical practice would normally arrogate to the literary critic has an important ramification: and that is that post-colonial criticism, at least as it is practised here, requires a conscious ideological rejection of criticism's habitual 'heroic ethnocentrism' and a much humbler self-positioning than is usually operative in First World 'strong' critical readings. When reading for textual resistance becomes entirely dependent on a 'theoretical' disentanglement of contradiction or ambivalence within the colonialist text – as it does in deconstructive or new historical readings of colonialist discourse – then the actual locus of subversive agency is necessarily wrenched away from colonised or post-colonial subjects and resituated within the textual work of the institutionalised western literary critic; and this is a form of cultural self-privileging that the contributors to this collection consciously want to avoid. This does not mean that the essays collected here refuse the critical work of reading 'against' the text or 'for' the presence of ideological contradiction within it: Vijay Mishra's analysis of social contradiction within one of the 'Bombay Cinema's' most popular cultural 'texts' is a case in point. But in Mishra's reading, the theoretical principles which permit criticism to locate within the Bombay Cinema a filmic interpellation of anti-revolutionary values emerge directly from 'the base culture' or 'deep structure' of Indian society itself, and *not* from an unassimilated application of Western cultural or film theory. 'Critical theory' here – as elsewhere in this volume – has to be *negotiated*; and what this double movement in methodology produces is a critical practice which is neither self-privilegingly autonomous in agency nor excessively affiliative in citation.

One of the immediate implications of such a critical self-positioning is that several of the textual readings that this volume offers accept the theoretical 'risk' of an intentional assumption. Generally, this recuperation of intentionality in the production of textual meaning is not, in these essays, narrowly located in the name of the 'author'. Rather, it is fastened to an anterior, though not determining, cultural dimension to writing: a grounding – as Mark Williams and Alan Riach explain – of post-colonial representation in an on-going cultural refiguration of 'the various inheritances, traditions, cultural memories ... which make up the post-colonised world'.

Another implication of this critical self-positioning is that few of the papers collected in this volume 'speak' dynastically within the customary 'language' of 'theory'. There is little here of the filiative footnoting enterprise, little of 'theory's' linguistic obliquities, little in the way of those covert signs of post-structural 'belonging' which have become *de riguer* in essays that wish to announce the presence of a 'serious' theoretical dimension in their plan. The reasons for why this is so are everywhere in evidence, but noone here makes the point more forcefully than does Carolyn Cooper, who challenges 'the authority of English as our exclusive voice of scholarship' through an astonishingly subversive theoretical praxis. Cooper's project finds an immediate explanatory echo in Derek Walcott's injunction to the post-colonial critic to eschew the voice that speaks in the name of 'the dead fish of French criticism', and *never* to surrender the agency of resistance to the power of Western intellectual systems. It would therefore be a gross mistake to assume that because many of these essays refuse an overtly 'theoretical' stance they necessarily fall back upon an unproblematised critical formalism or that they languish in passé theoretical assumptions. There remains a dominant 'developmental' model to critical language within the mainstream Western academy, a 'theorised' versus 'pre-theorised' binary assumption which ethnocentrically consigns disobedient critical practice to that discursive dead-zone in which writing remains cognitively unable to interrogate its own social and philosophical pre-conditions. But if anything, the papers collected in this volume keep squarely in view the principle that theory is always grounded to a cultural specificity, and that both 'theory' and 'criticism' – in the *first* instance – are always material practices that are ideologically motivated and historically positioned.

A third implication of this critical self-positioning is that the idea of the 'post-colonial' itself is broadened out in the essays that follow to include a wide range – and often a conflation – of all three of its possible meanings. 'Post-colonial' most commonly refers to formerly colonised Third- and Fourth-World peoples who have gained a measure of political – though not economic – independence from empire; for some critics it also refers to white settler cultures whose ambivalent location within the structures of imperial authority offers an important – though often highly ambivalent – grounding for discursive interrogations of imperialism's centralising power. The conjunction of these two variant concepts of the 'post-colonial' thus produces a third modality of signification: a 'horizon of expectation' for literary production and consumption wherein the term 'post-colonial' nominates the actuations of a specific form of discursive resistance to colonialist power – a resistance which is grounded in experience and which is set in train the moment that colonialist culture acts upon the body and space of its Others.

This conflation of all three concepts of the 'post-colonial' in many of the essays that follow derives from a recognition of collectivity in the *motive* of their writers – which is to open the field of marginalized literatures written in European languages to a reading and teaching practice that speaks directly to geographically, culturally, and economically marginalized peoples themselves. And because of this, it is important to recognise that while most of these essays hold the 'post-colonial' literary text before them as a *seemingly* naturalised object in an undeconstructed representational space, part of their collective project is to effect a specific post-colonial intervention into an on-going – often doubly hegemonic – critical debate over the use and location of 'theory' in the study of 'literary' documents. Liz Gross has noted that cultures which are dominated by Anglo-American intellectual imperialism, but which are also to some extent 'outside' the range of its interpellative ideological power, are ideally placed to interrogate the shibboleths of Western critical theory, and to *use* unslavishly whatever is valuable within it for their own culturally specific ends.[30] This, we should think, remains the collective critical 'problem' that the various modalities of post-colonial literary criticism, whatever their differences, must continue to negotiate; and to that end we might offer as a figural paradigm another exemplary image of cultural mobilisation, one which might yet supplant the imperial figure of Tancred, sign of neo-colonialism's 'travelling theory' and its appropriative, exoticising eye.

The cover illustration of this collection of essays shows the Haitian artist Edouard Duval's fantastic depiction of Zaka, or Cousin Zacca, or Azacca-Medé, 'farmer-god' in the Rada nanchon of Haitian *vodun* or voodoo, and *gros-bon-ange* of a once 'living' entity which has now, through ritual and purification, attained the special status of 'Loa' or divinity.[31] Within Euro-American popular culture, *vodun* ritual has been transmogrified into stereotypical horror – a site where a universe of cultural repression and disavowal returns to the scene of civilisation and flattens it into barbarity. But for post-colonial literary 'theorists' such as Wilson Harris and Edward Kamau Brathwaite, *vodun* figures the perpetual drive in colonial and post-colonial cultures to cross through the imperial territory of the given – the imposed and the 'certain' – into a primordial realm of broken recollection where 'community' can be recovered and brought back into 'possession'.[32] In vodun, the loa are often figured as horse riders, for their 'possession', through ritual, of a 'living' person seems absolute and unyielding – an animating force in control of a physical body, a rider in charge of a compliant mount. But when the *vodun* ritual is over, the Loa release the living body and turn it back to the community; and the community now finds itself instructed, assured of its inextricable connectedness to its own pre-colonial history.

For post-colonial cultures, literary writing too can initiate the riding down of colonised consciousness, and 'critical theory' can mark the always provisional, always temporary, purchase of that writing upon system and structure – a complex figuring energy which, as Wilson Harris comments,[33] strives through adversarial contexts and infinite 'rehearsals' to consume both its own biases and those of its always threatening Other. If the landscape of post-colonial literature is necessarily marked by the inscriptions of dominant Western critical practice and its technologies of interpretation and control, it is also infused with a pulsating, though often silenced, subterranean energy which speaks to the post-colonial reader of *another* realm of semiotic 'meaning', *another* ground of interpretive community. 'So on that ground...', Edward Brathwaite tells us,

> walk
> the hooves will come, welcomed
> by drumbeats, into your ridden head;
> and the horse, cheval of the dead
> charade of *la mort*
>
> tongued with the wind
> possession of the fire
> possession of the dust
> sundered from your bone
> plundered from my breast
>
> by ice, by chain, by sword, by the east wind,
> surrenders up to you the graven Word
> carved from Olodumare
> From Ogun of Alare, from Ogun of Onire
> from Shango broom of thunder and Damballa Grand Chemin
>
> For on this ground
> trampled with the bull's swathe of whips
> where the slave at the crossroads was a red anthill
> eaten by moonbeams, by the holy ghosts
> of his wounds
> the Word becomes
> again a god and walks among us ...[34]

NOTES

1. Hayden White, *Tropics of Discourse: Essays in Cultural Criticism* (Baltimore: Johns Hopkins Univ. Press, 1973), p. 281.

2. Jacques Derrida, *Of Grammatology*, trans. Gayatri Chakravorty Spivak (1967; Baltimore: Johns Hopkins Univ. Press, 1974), pp. 158-59.

3. Barbara Johnson, *The Critical Difference: Essays in the Contemporary Rhetoric or Reading* (Baltimore: Johns Hopkins Univ. Press, 1980), p. 5.

4. Kum Kum Sangari, 'The Politics of the Possible', *Cultural Critique*, 7 (Fall 1987), p. 181. See also Edward Said, *The World, the Text and the Critic* (Cambridge: Harvard Univ. Press, 1983), pp. 3-4, and Frank Lentriccia, *After the New Criticism* (Chicago: Univ. of Chicago Press, 1980), p. 186 ff.

5. Lentriccia, op. cit., p. 186. See also Said's 'Travelling Theory' in *The World, the Text and the Critic*, cited above, and Daniel O'Hara's argument in 'Criticism Worldly and Otherworldly: Edward W. Said and The Cult of Theory', *Boundary 2*, xii, 3 / xii, 1 (Sp.-Fall 1984), pp. 378-403 that the burgeoning of 'theory' within Western tertiary institutions responds to a specific pressure within late capitalism for career patterns marked by filiation.

6. Barbara Christian, 'The Race for Theory', in *Cultural Critique*, 6 (Spring 1987), pp. 51-63.

7. For an extended critique of this arrogation of theoretical terrain by the West, see Sangari, op. cit., pp. 157-86.

8. Craig Tapping, 'Literary Reflections of Orality: Colin Johnson's *Dr. Wooreddy's Prescription for Enduring the Ending of the World*', Paper presented at the Modern Language Association, New Orleans, December 1988.

9. Homi Bhabha, 'The Commitment to Theory', *New Formations*, 5 (Summer 1988), p. 7.

10. Sangari, pp. 183-84. For an analysis how Western universalism maps itself onto Latin American cultural difference, see Jean Franco's 'Beyond Ethnocentrism: Gender, Power, and the Third-World Intelligentsia', in *Marxism and the Interpretation of Culture*, ed. Cary Nelson (Urbana and Chicago: Univ. of Illinois Press, 1988), pp. 503-516.

11. Said, op. cit., pp. 242-47.

12. See Benita Parry, 'Problems in Current Theories of Colonial Discourse', *Oxford Literary Review*, 9, 1-2 (1987), p. 51.

13. Benjamin Disraeli, *Tancred, or The New Crusade* (1847; London: Peter Davies, 1927), p. 128. Further references are to this edition.

14. Rana Kabbani, *Europe's Myths of Orient* (Bloomington: Indiana Univ. Press, 1888), p. 87.

15. Michael Awkward, in 'Appropriative Gestures: Theory and Afro-American Literary Criticism', *Gender and Theory: Dialogues on Feminist Criticism*, ed. Linda Kauffman (London: Blackwell, 1989), pp. 238-48, makes this argument in response to Barbara Christian's dismissal of critical theory in the article cited above.

16. Tzvetan Todorov, *The Conquest of America: The Question of the Other*, trans. Richard Howard (1982; New York: Harper & Row, 1984).

17. Bhabha, op. cit., p. 11.

18. On the question of post-structuralism and its troubled relations with 'history', see Derek Attridge, Geoff Bennington, and Robert Young, eds., *Post-Structuralism and the Question of History* (Cambridge: Cambridge Univ. Press, 1987). Chris Weedon offers a useful account of 'theory's' intersection with the project of feminism in *Feminist Practice and Poststructuralist Theory* (Oxford: Blackwell, 1987). The most detailed exploration of post-structuralism's intersection with colonialism is provided by Gayatri Chakravorty

Spivak in her collection *In Other Worlds: Essays in Cultural Politics* (New York and London: Methuen, 1987), but see also Homi Bhabha's 'The Other Question: Difference, Discrimination and the Discourse of Colonialism' in *Literature, Politics and Theory: Papers from the Essex Conference, 1976-84*, ed. Francis Barker *et. al.* (London and New York: Methuen, 1986), pp. 148-73.

19. See Peter Dews, *Logics of Disintegration: Post-structuralist Thought and the Claims of Critical Theory* (London: Verso, 1988).

20. Spivak, *In Other Worlds*, p. 179.

21. See Homi Bhabha, 'Signs Taken for Wonders: Questions of Ambivalence and Authority under a Tree Outside Delhi, May 1817', *Critical Inquiry*, 12, 1 (Autumn 1985), 144-65 and 'The Commitment to Theory', *op. cit.*

22. Stephen Greenblatt, 'Invisible Bullets: Renaissance Authority and its Subversion, *Henry IV and Henry V*' in *Political Shakespeare: New Essays in Cultural Materialism*, ed. Jonathan Dollimore and Alan Sinfield (Ithaca and London: Cornell Univ. Press, 1985), pp. 18-47.

23. Parry, p. 34.

24. Carolyn Porter, 'Are We Being Historical Yet?', *South Atlantic Quarterly*, 87, 4 (Fall 1988), pp. 743-86.

25. Porter, p. 779.

26. The argument here follows Porter, p. 780: 'It is not only marginal groups and subordinated cultures that are occulted, whether by exclusion or incorporation, by effacement or appropriation, but the "social" itself as well. In other words, the "social text" remains a text in the formalist sense, rather than the literary being historicized as social discourse'.

27. Bhabha, 'The Commitment to Theory', p. 17.

28. Parry, p. 34.

29. See Gilles Deleuze and Felix Guattari, 'What Is a Minor Literature?', in *Kafka: Towards a Minor Literature*, trans. Dana Polan (1975; Minneapolis: Univ. of Minnesota Press, 1986), pp. 16-27. An extended discussion of this project is offered in *Cultural Critique*, 6 (Spring 1987) and ABD 7 (Fall 1987).

30. Liz Gross, 'Speculum Feminarum', *Southern Review*, 20, 1 (March 1987), pp. 99-100.

31. See Maya Deren, *Divine Horsemen: Voodoo Gods of Haiti* (New York: Chelsea House, 1970) and Claude Planson, *Vaudou: un initie paris...* (Paris: Jean Dullis, 1974).

32. See Wilson Harris, *Tradition, the Writer and Society: Critical Essays* (London and Port of Spain: New Beacon, 1967), pp. 48-54.

33. Wilson Harris, 'Adversarial Contexts and Creativity', *New Left Review*, 154 (Nov.-Dec. 1985), p. 127.

34. Edward Brathwaite, *The Arrivants* (Oxford: Oxford Univ. Press, 1967), pp. 265-66.

Commonwealth or Common Poverty?: the New Literatures in English and the New Discourse of Marginality

Margins are popular these days. Everyone is claiming them. But one thing remains the same. Colonial and post-colonial literatures remain on the margins. We were marginal to the old critical approaches and we are marginal to the new. The new literatures in English have been discovered as fit subject matter for journals that would never have considered them of interest a few years ago. My problem is with the nature of this interest. To what extent does it represent a genuine discovery of cultural differences and to what extent can it be seen as a new form of cultural imperialism that now appropriates instead of silencing post-colonial literary productions? I am inspired by the new avenues for rethinking the discipline opened up by the pioneering work of critics such as Edward Said and Gayatri Spivak. But I am also disturbed by the implications of some of the work that is now appearing. This paper deals with some of my reservations about the language and approach now being applied to marginal literatures by mainstream critics. It asks about the implications of their quick dismissals of work in the fields of Commonwealth literatures and national literatures and their quick claiming of what they call marginal, minority or third world literatures.

Homi K. Bhabha, for example, dismisses in a sentence and a half the discipline of Commonwealth literature as an 'expansionist epigone' whose 'versions of traditional academicist wisdom moralize the conflictual moment of colonialist intervention into that constitutive chain of exemplum and imitation, what Friedrich Nietzsche describes as the monumental history beloved of "gifted egoists and visionary scoundrels" '.[1] Nietzsche merits a footnote as the source of the dismissive phrases; those being dismissed do not. Bhabha lumps all practitioners of Commonwealth history and literature together as stereotypically nationalist, expansionist and moralising, denying them the very specificity he accuses them of suppressing, and without providing any evidence for his claims. Such an attitude enables him to concentrate his attention on the work of Europeans and a few privileged

Europe-acclaimed writers of colonial origins, such as V.S. Naipaul and Frantz Fanon. I will deal with the substance of his claims later. What interests me first is the lack of interest in the voices of the colonised – in their version of their experience – and the choice to focus instead on deconstructing the colonialist and neo-colonialist discourse of the oppressors.

Bhabha's article appears in a special issue of *Critical Inquiry* devoted to *'Race', Writing and Difference*, an issue that raises important questions but that ignores the contributions made to their consideration by the colonised themselves. In his response to this issue, Houston A. Baker, Jr. makes this point – 'For me, the signal shortcoming of *"Race", Writing and Difference* is the paucity of Caliban's sound'.[2] But Baker himself uses a metaphor that is drawn from European discourse. Despite Caliban's transformation by New World writers such as George Lamming and Aimé Césaire, Caliban remains an ambiguous symbol for the self-determination of the colonised. The claiming of Caliban was a necessary ideological step at a specific historical moment, but one could argue that that moment has now passed.[3] Furthermore, Caliban cannot simply be used as a synonym for black male: in post-colonial writing, s/he is sometimes white or aboriginal. Neither are 'black talk' or dialect the only speech writing variants that centralists have problems understanding. Ironically, Baker's intervention sounds as establishment-oriented in its concerns as the articles in the issue he criticises, but this irony does not invalidate his point. In fact, it makes it more urgent.

Henry Louis Gates, Jr.'s response to Baker is illuminating: 'No, Houston, there are no vernacular critics collected here; nor did you expect there to be.... Todorov can't even hear us, Houston, when we talk *his* academic talk; how he gonna hear us if we "talk *that* talk", the talk of the black idiom?'[4] Here the omission of black talk is a deliberate strategy of self-censorship in response to the perceived unreceptiveness of the establishment. I think this is a misguided strategy because it allows what should be a dialogue to remain a monologue: the discussion continues within the terms established by the dominant discourse, whether one characterises that as 'analytico-referential', with Timothy J. Reiss,[5] or as the 'marriage between Reason and capital', with Partha Chatterjee.[6] Such a strategy cripples at the outset the alleged goal of seeking 'to understand the ideological subtext which any critical theory reflects and embodies, and the relation which this subtext bears to the production of meaning'.[7] By not addressing the larger frame (of *Critical Inquiry's* assumptions about what can be said and how) within which they have agreed to allow discussion to take place, they have abandoned this goal before beginning to attempt it.

An acrimonious discussion in *New Literary History* (Winter 1987) takes up this problem, but inconclusively, allowing itself to be side-tracked into a discussion of theory versus advocacy instead of developing an inquiry into the kinds of theory most appropriate to understanding American black literature as another literature of the colonised. Here again, the implicit standard of reference is European. Henry Louis Gates, Jr. writes: 'Unlike almost every other literary tradition, the Afro-American literary tradition was generated as a response to allegations that its authors did not, and *could* not, create "literature" '.[8] If he had seen his own tradition as central to a larger struggle instead of marginal to the U.S. 'mainstream', he might have seen instead that the Afro-Americans shared this dilemma with most other colonised peoples. They too have faced the problem of how to dismantle the master's house when the master's tools are apparently the only ones available, and they have confronted it in a variety of ingenious ways. Joyce A. Joyce recognises these connections among the colonised, but assumes that 'the Black American critic – merely and significantly because he or she lives in a powerful country – should be at the vanguard of a world-wide Black intellectual movement'.[9] There are two problems with this argument, both connected to power. Joyce makes shared ethnicity, rather than the relation to power, her criterion for solidarity, and she assumes that the foundations on which power are based are irrelevant to its exercise. But why should Black U.S. imperialism be any more palatable than White U.S. imperialism?

The challenge for the critic is to find an alternative power base to that which has traditionally fueled imperialist academic endeavour. That base lies in recognising the potential power of comparative post-colonial studies to pose an alternative to traditional English studies. Despite their disagreements, Joyce A. Joyce, Henry Louis Gates, Jr. and Houston Baker, Jr., neglect this potential in their common quest for change, as they articulate it in *New Literary History*.

Elsewhere the omission of the perspective of the colonised comes, not from a misguided strategy, but from a wilful ignorance. I encountered this lack of interest in what the colonised had to say for themselves at a conference on 'The Colonial Mind' held at the Monterey Institute of International Studies in November, 1986. Several speakers from the United States lamented the absence of novels analysing American imperialism at work abroad. When I pointed out that there were many novels providing just such an analysis by writers in the countries affected by U.S. imperialism, I was told they were not interested in them. What they wanted were *American* (meaning U.S.) perspectives on American imperialism, not Trinidadian, Canadian or Fijian perspectives. Despite all the noise about revaluing the margins, those historically marginalised remain silent to those who do not know how to hear what they have to say.

The new discourse has been so constituted as to continue to ignore the contributions of the colonised. The interest is in how some of us have been silenced (those of us seen as sufficiently exotic), and not in what we have to say. Recognising this bias, Peter Hulme suggests that the model of 'radical history' contains 'two interdependent but separable moments: first, a critique of existing versions, partly dependent upon, second, the presentation of alternative and contradictory evidence'.[10] Much of the theorising to date has been excessively preoccupied with the first, perhaps because it has already been decided that this should be the first step. And why? Perhaps because of a continuing unquestioned assumption that Europe is the origin of discourse and the colonies merely the branches growing out from that source, perhaps because it seems the more familiar task to critics trained to see the English tradition as central. The post-colonial literatures, when looked at from within their own perspectives, however, do not justify such assumptions.

It is time to take up the challenge of what Hulme labels the second step, a challenge already met by many post-colonial writers, such as Fanon, Césaire, Retamar, C.L.R. James, Lamming, Harris, and Brathwaite, to list a few of the well-known Caribbean names. They provide the 'alternative and contradictory evidence' that we must now study more closely. Peter Hulme has brilliantly analysed the ways in which *The Tempest* inscribes the 'discursive conflict in which a Mediterranean discourse is constantly stretched by the novelty of an Atlantic world' (p. 3). We should be looking more closely at the ways post-colonial writers have re-written that conflict, not only to question the dominant culture's assumptions but also to reinscribe their own versions of possibility. Such a project should work comparatively, to avoid the narrowness that occasionally mars Rob Nixon's fine article, which by limiting itself to Africa and the Caribbean, misses resonances in the play that have been taken up by Canadian and Australian writers.[11]

Even worse, perhaps, than the continuing silence about post-colonial achievements in writing against colonialist discourse, is the temptation for those of us in the ex-colonies to allow ourselves to be lulled into accepting a definition of ourselves as marginalised – a definition which until now we have continued to resist. Now that the marginal is being revalued as the new source of authority in discourse, it is tempting to accept the imperial definition of the colonised as marginal. But this would be a mistake. As a colleague of mine exclaimed in response to a friend's lament over her marginality as a woman: 'Women aren't marginal. They're bloody well right down the centre of the page!' The same is true for the post-colonial literatures. From our perspective, we are central. We are where we must begin and we are not marginal to ourselves, however much others may marginalise us economically and politically. To assert our centrality in this way is not to revert to the nationalism Bhabha deplores in the Commonwealth literatures. It is an attempt to appropriate our own discourses as part of a larger attempt to determine the course of our own lives.

The same debate about the appropriateness of 'minority discourse' as yet another term for designating marginality occurs in two special 1987 issues of *Cultural Critique*, where Barbara Christian takes the position I advocate here. As she points out, 'many of us have never conceived of ourselves only as somebody's *other*'.[12] This question of language is important. We must refuse the neo-colonial interpellation that would name us as marginal. Recently, I heard the Trinidadian novelist and playwright Earl Lovelace argue against the use of the term 'slave' in relation to the history of the blacks in the Caribbean. They were enslaved, certainly, but they were never slaves, because they never accepted that naming or that condition. Rather, they lived a resistance

> all through slavery, carried on in their unceasing escape – as Maroons, as Runaways, as Bush Negroes, as Rebels: and when they could not perform in space that escape that would take them away from the scene of their brutalization they took a stand in the very guts of the slave plantation ... asserting their humanness in the most wonderful acts of sabotage they could imagine and perform.[13]

The word 'slave' already implies a dehumanisation and a resignation that accepts the slavemaster's view of the colonised. Lovelace's celebration of a history of resistance presents the self-determination of a people who refuse that interpellation

Marlene Nourbese Philip develops this point in an article entitled 'Women and Theft'.[14] Asked to speak on the theme 'women and poverty', Philip began to question 'how well the words went together', how they suggested a passive state, a natural condition, and how they tended to ignore how poverty came about. On the other hand, if we start talking about women and theft, she reasoned, 'we have to start asking questions like who did the stealing ... and what was stolen'. She concludes that

> even when we believe we are being objectively descriptive by using a word like poverty, or poor, we continue the myth that poor people are poor because they produce little: we have all, I'm sure, heard the modern variation of that argument about Blacks, native people, women and poor people.

Philip reappropriates the language to serve her interests. She writes that 'as a writer nurtured on the bile of a colonial language whose only intent was imperialistic, I see no way around the language, only through it, challenging the mystification and half truths at its core'. That is the post-colonial critic's task too. The theoretical analyses which construct that challenge come from the various Marxist reconsiderations of the role of ideology in shaping cultural experience.[15] But they themselves require transformation when transplanted to new settings.

Colonial and post-colonial writers have tended to ignore the 'wealth' hidden in 'Commonwealth' to focus on the poverty the imperialist would like us to see: the poverty of our indigenous cultures as well as the poverty resulting from imperialist thefts. In the past, literary critics have tended to focus on the negative aspects of the colonial mentality, seeing it as something inhibiting the creation or survival of an indigenous culture. Australians denigrated the 'cultural cringe', Canadians spoke of an 'inhibiting frost-bite at the roots of the imagination' and a 'deep-seated terror' in the face of nature, and West Indians deplored their symbolic 'castration'.[16] The new spokespeople for 'colonialist discourse', the new champions of the marginalised, continue to stress that poverty, either through directly addressing it as Naipaul does or through implying it as Bhabha does. In 'Some Problems in Nationalist Criticism', Bhabha sees that poverty as a myth, but as a very successful one. 'When V.S. Naipaul writes that "History is built around achievement and creation, and nothing was created in the West Indies", we become aware of the complete success of colonialist values and of the complete despair of the colonised'.[17] Yet one would not reach such a conclusion if one read Naipaul in context. Increasingly the post-colonial literatures themselves are celebrating the strengths of our differences. Our histories contain both oppression and resistance. We make a strategic choice when we choose to stress one above the other. To stress our helplessness and despair is to continue our oppression; to stress our power to effect change is the first step toward making change happen. As the Canadian writer Donna E. Smyth recognises, 'What I have to do, what we dispossessed have to do, is to take possession of what is rightfully ours: beauty, grace, and the power of articulation'.[18] The shift from 'I' to 'we' is deliberate. Perhaps it is also time to reclaim the commonality of that wealth, a trait the dominant ideology seeks to obscure. We colonised form a community, with a common heritage of oppression and a common cause of working toward positive social change. To recognise what we hold in common is not to underestimate our differences, but to provide us with a context for understanding them more clearly.

There is no shortage of critics to analyse the functions of colonialist discourse, while the various functions of post-colonial discourse continue to go unexamined. Caliban quickly tires of cursing Prospero. His speech is most compelling when he celebrates his own skills and love of place, and when he transforms himself from European creation into an autonomous indigene capable of astounding metamorphosis – into black nationalist or lesbian feminist. I would like to see post-colonial critics using the insights of contemporary theory to explore those of our indigenous/hybridised traditions that positively express our differences.

I do not recognise my work in Homi Bhabha's characterisation, but it is worth asking what we do when we teach 'Commonwealth Literature'. The name itself is problematic, carrying a weight of cultural accretion that works against the recognition of differences I am pleading for here. I would prefer to discuss the new Englishes or the post-colonial literatures in English to stress the fissures rather than the unity of the subject. But I do not share Henry Louis Gates Jr.'s reasons for rejecting the term. He writes:

> The sometimes vulgar nationalism implicit in would-be literary categories such as 'American Literature', or the not-so-latent imperialism implied by the vulgar phrase 'Commonwealth literature', are extraliterary designations of control, symbolic of material and concomitant political relations, rather than literary ones. We, the scholars of our profession, must eschew these categories of domination and ideology and insist upon the fundamental redefinition of what it is to speak of 'the canon'. ('What's Love Got To Do With It?', p. 351).

It is with the vulgar, in its original meanings of the common people and the vernacular, that I would like to see the discipline maintain its connections. Because I do not share Gates's belief that the 'extra-literary' can be separated from the literary, I value a descriptive term that draws attention to the connections between the two, connections too often obscured by traditional and experimental literary discourse alike. It is not 'the categories of domination and ideology' that we must eschew; on the contrary, we need the categories to help us understand the experiences. Domination and ideology are real; they exist, in life and in our discipline; and they are what we must combat.

A year after writing these confident remarks, I find Gates repeating his assertions in a new article within a different context and as a result I find myself taking these comments more seriously as a difference in categorising not easily resolved.[19] As Aijaz Ahmad reminds us: 'nationalism itself is not some unitary thing with some pre-determined essence and value. There are hundreds of nationalisms in Asia and Africa today; some are progressive, others are not'.[20] As a Canadian whose country is on the brink of making a free trade agreement with the United States in which everything, including culture, appears to be on the table, I put a positive value on nationalism. As an American whose nationality is assured, Gates obviously does not. All the more reason, then, for declaring our cultural baggage before crossing cultural borders into foreign territory. We all speak English, but we use it in very different ways. We, the scholars of our profession, cannot afford to ignore the categories of domination and ideology that Gates would have us eschew. In making and then reiterating this statement, Gates appears to be accepting an assumption that Said advises us to question, the assumption that '... the principal relationships in the study of literature – those I have identified as based on representation – ought to obliterate the traces of other relationships within literary structures that are based principally upon acquisition and appropriation'.[21] Formerly colonised peoples know that we ignore those traces at our peril.

As Ngugi wa Thiong'o points out in *Decolonising the Mind*, 'the physical violence of the battlefield was followed by the psychological violence of the classroom'.[22] While we readily accept such a statement in looking at African societies, many members of the so-called older Commonwealth – the settler colonies of Australia, Canada and New Zealand – have difficulty accepting its relevance to their lives. We too have been educated in the violence of those classrooms and continue, even despite our intentions, to perpetuate that violence ourselves. When we teach, we must fight against reinforcing the colonial's 'fundamental imaginative relationship with the Imperium'[23] to try instead to learn, together with our students, how to read and think and speak 'across and against it'.[24] Is the university's role to preserve cultural traditions or to question them? Must we choose between preserving and questioning? Whose cultural traditions are we discussing here? – Judging by curriculum requirements, our commitment to affirming the validity of the post-colonial perspectives is still a marginalised position. From that position, how do we make ourselves heard and how do we make ourselves understood? What is the theory of our practice? Does it differ from the Derridean and Lacanian models employed by the mainstream critics who are now staking out the marginalised as their territory? Or to paraphrase Flemming Brahms, do such ' "civilized distinctions" actually lead us into a state of "ignorance" with regard to crucial aspects of works from the Commonwealth'?[25] Much recent work suggests that they may.

As Gerald Graff and Reginald Gibbons define it, ' "theory" is simply a name for the questions which necessarily arise when principles and concepts once taken for granted have become matters of controversy'.[26] The centrality of the English canon has been questioned by Marxism, by

8

feminism and by a series of developing colonial literatures, beginning with American in the nineteenth century. Some of those excluded have now been included, but on what terms? Do we want to set up our own counter canons, or do we want to question the idea of canonicity itself? Are we searching for new ways of unifying our discipline or for ways of living with the fact of its fundamental disunity? What is our discipline?

I work in a university English department. Is my discipline English? I try to teach Canadian literature in terms of its historical, political, sociological and cultural contexts. Is my discipline Canadian Studies? I try to teach the post-colonial literatures, both in terms of their own local specifics, as I do Canadian literature, and in terms of their shared relations to the experience of imperialism. Is my discipline the discourse analysis of the processes of domination and resistance produced by imperialism? Obviously I think it is all of these, but how do I deal with the competing claims of each? Do I try to reconcile them or highlight them, fit them into ever larger patterns or use them to illuminate the contradictions we live with? In writing an article such as this, the temptation is always to synthesize and clarify, yet I believe we must trust the contradictions, allowing them to open up for us fresh ways of perceiving what is and imagining what could be.

In exploring these problems I draw on my experience teaching at the University of British Columbia because I believe we must begin with the local and specific if we are to fully grasp the implications of what we do. I teach in a place where both the local and national cultures are still undervalued, where the majority of professors, in Brian Fawcett's terms, 'retain a fundamental imaginative relationship with the Imperium' and therefore do not see the local culture as a fundamental starting point for thinking about literature. I live in a province where confrontation is the norm, where I am forced into the role of being an oppositional voice, automatically seen as the negative of the dominant culture's positive. In such a context, how can one speak to be heard, and still speak differently? How can one imagine a form of cultural autonomy that will elude the pervasive control from the United States?

In my own recent work I have turned to the analysis of Canadian ideologies, and particularly the distinctive 'Tory strain' as mediated through literature and the works acclaimed as part of a Canadian canon, in order to see how Canada both participates in larger North American ideological patterns and deviates from them. Such work requires an interdisciplinary context and begins to take on immediate practical implications at a time when the 'economic integration' of North America seems imminent.

At the moment, we have two parallel discourses for examining the relations between what Said has termed 'the text, the world and the critic' in the aftermath of the age of imperialism: the mainstream reconsiderations of colonialist discourse, which to a large extent continue imperialism's 'bracketing the political context of culture and history',[27] and Commonwealth literature, which is sensitive to such contexts but does not speak of them in ways that are accessible to its natural allies. In Baker's terms, these are the 'rationalists' and the 'debunkers'; in Said's they are the 'excluding insider[s] by virtue of method' and the 'excluding insider[s] by virtue of experience'.[28] The first tends to assume 'the unity of the "colonial subject" ' (JanMohamed, p. 59), the second to stress its specificities at the expense of any cross-cultural comparisons. The first privileges European views of the 'Third World', itself a term of European invention and limited usefulness, now being rejected by those it would seek to designate; the second privileges nationalist perspectives at the expense of a critique of imperialism as the logical extension of capitalism. Neither provides a way out of the dilemmas outlined above. Each reinforces in its own way the logic of the dominant discourse.

But we also have critics who seek a way out of this 'Manichean discourse' (JanMohamed) – through Baker's 'triple play', Hulme's 'radical history', Mocnik's 'materialist concept of literature',[28] and the reseeing of intelligibility as a problematic rather than a value.[29] Said's list of possible strategies at the end of 'Orientalism Reconsidered' could serve as a summary of many of the points made in this article:

> A need for greater crossing of boundaries, for greater interventionism in cross-disciplinary activity, a concentrated awareness of the situation – political, methodological, social, historical – in which intellectual and cultural work is carried out. A clarified political and methodological commitment to the dismantling of systems of domination which since they are collectively maintained must, to adopt and transform some of Gramsci's phrases, be collectively fought, by mutual siege, war of manoeuvre *and* war of position.[30]

What we must continue to fight are essentialising oppositions that pit a 'colonial mind' implicitly against an imperial mind, implying an equivalence that masks the real inequalities of power that determine these two states and implying that all colonial experiences are similar. If the sound of the black voice has been silenced in much of the new writing on race, the settler colonies, with their large immigrant populations and their native peoples, remain absent from discussions of colonialist discourse. It still seems easier for critics to discuss the cultural impositions of the British empire on civilisations established along lines recognised, if not admired, by European models – that is India and Africa – than it is to consider the transportation and transplantation of English in Australia, Canada, New Zealand and the Caribbean. We must ask why this should be so, while demonstrating that the post-colonial is not a uniform field.

In cultivating this uneven field, we must avoid the false universalisms of Nick Wilkinson's rationale for a method[31] and the false nationalisms that identify Britain, rather than the imperialist structure of capitalist relations, as the enemy. As Chatterjee points out, 'the political success of nationalism in ending colonial rule does not signify a true resolution of the contradictions between the problematic and thematic of nationalist thought' (p. 169). To understand these contradictions is our most important task. In recognising the asymmetry of domination, we can better understand how language and literature may be used to maintain dominance.

In the past, the universalising drive of traditional English studies appropriated or silenced the differences of the post-colonial literatures. The deconstructive strategies of many of the new experts on colonialist discourse appear to be continuing this process. If one asks to whom are the majority of these articles addressed, the answer seems clear. They address the other, the imperialist, the white liberals who wish to wallow in pleasurable feelings of guilt about their terrible past, while enjoying the memory that once they were all-powerful. As Gates admitted, they are writing for 'Todorov' and the establishment his name represents. If we wish to read writers who address themselves to the people in colonial and post-colonial situations, we must turn to Ngugi, Lamming, Lovelace, Fawcett, Smyth and all the other writers and critics who seldom receive notice beyond Commonwealth circles. It is our duty to publicise and continue their work, through questioning and challenging the mystifications that are used to oppress us.

At first I was puzzled by the seemingly gratuitous attacks on Commonwealth literature in the work of critics who would seem to share our goals of challenging the hegemony of an imperialist, universalising discourse. The questions, 'who writes?' and 'what is being written on whom?' have helped me focus the problem. While race is the highlighted difference in these writings, class remains the hidden difference. Gates's reply to Joyce makes this distinction clear. He proudly proclaims his blackness while defensively insisting that his class is none of her business. He implies that his authority to speak derives from his blackness (his participation in black culture, not his race, since race is an ideological construction rather than a biological fact), yet his rhetoric suggests otherwise. His rhetoric lays claim to the authority of the universities where he has studied and where he teaches (Cambridge and Yale) – an institutionally based authority independent of actual expertise (he admits that black literature was hardly recognised as an authentic object of study let alone understood at Cambridge). His rhetoric also lays claim to the authority of his maleness – a socially reinforced authority that allows him to patronise Joyce in ways he would never try with another man. Gates willingly uses the privileges of class and gender to silence opposition to his version of the difference of race. I think this violent reaction to Joyce and the quick dismissal of Commonwealth literature are related.

Race is rapidly becoming an academically respectable difference; class and national self-determination (except, of course, when it is American self-determination) have not yet been satisfactorily recuperated in the way that race – at least in the *Critical Inquiry* issue – has. It is useful here to remember Ernesto Laclau's distinction:

> A class is hegemonic not so much to the extent that it is able to impose a uniform conception of the world on the rest of society, but to the extent that it can articulate different visions of the world in such a way that their potential antagonism is neutralized.[32]

Judith Williamson expands on the implications of this insight:

> The whole drive of our society is toward displaying as much difference as possible within it while eliminating where at all possible what is different from it.... Our culture, deeply rooted in imperialism, needs to destroy genuine difference, to capture what is beyond its reach; at the same time, it needs *constructs* of difference in order to signify itself at all.[33]

The post-colonial literatures represent that genuine difference which an imperialist culture fears. The establishment must therefore ensure that post-colonial self-representations continue to be ignored, while representations of them are reconstructed within the academy as safe alternatives to their real threat. Bhabha's, Baker's and Gates's writing sometimes serves this function, however unwillingly and unwittingly. Gates's recent work suggests a shift in strategy: 'I once thought it our most important gesture to *master* the canon of criticism, to *imitate* and *apply* it, but I now believe that we must turn to the black tradition itself to develop theories of criticism indigenous to our literatures' ('Authority', p. 41). Nonetheless, the focus on race as an ideological construct and especially on the psychological roots of racism in the white psyche address a difference only to defuse its radical potential. The connections between race and class and access to power remain submerged. The discipline of 'Commonwealth literature' is potentially a threat because it tries to address these issues, however inadequately.

If our work is to be genuinely productive, we must see it as 'part of a larger political program of cultural transvaluation'.[34] As Mocnik points out, the contradictory task of bourgeois dominance '– a homogenization respectful of the regional discursive heterogeneities – is conveniently tackled by the imposition of the national language as the general matrix of the mutual translation of (heterogeneous) local discourse' (p. 175). If we do not wish to be part of that process, we must recognise that the new Englishes do not form one English, that they do not derive simply from one source, and that they are unlikely to form a unified whole for which a single theory could suffice. We are on the verge of something new, trying to rethink our assumptions at the same time as we rethink the boundaries of our work, the nature of our subject, and the nature of ourselves as subjects and the objects of our studies. Dieter Riemenschneider's reminder is timely:

> Only when comparative investigations into their historical context, which include an understanding of their differing aesthetic traditions, have reached a stage of information and thus critical awareness transcending by far our present knowledge, will there be a sound basis on which to erect a specific aesthetic of the 'new' English literatures.[35]

All the critics whose work I have discussed in this paper share this search for a 'sound basis'. Like Riemenschneider, I believe it must be found in the new literatures themselves. Like Bhabha, I believe we must reject 'traditional, academicist wisdom'. If my interest in how English has been transformed under various conditions of resistance to oppression around the world makes me 'vulgar', a 'gifted egoist' and 'visionary scoundrel' in the eyes of the new establishment, that is a price I am willing to pay. But I believe that if those of us who seek real changes in the organisation of knowledge can agree to explore the field cooperatively, we may discover other options.

NOTES

1. Homi K. Bhabha, 'Signs Taken for Wonders: Questions of Ambivalence and Authority under a Tree Outside Delhi, May 1817', *Critical Inquiry*, 12 (Autumn 1985), p. 147.

2. Houston A. Baker, Jr., 'Caliban's Triple Play', *Critical Inquiry*, 13 (Autumn 1986), p. 190.

3. See Rob Nixon, 'Caribbean and African Appropriations of *The Tempest*', *Critical Inquiry*, 13 (Spring 1987), p. 576, for the argument that '*The Tempest*'s value for African and Caribbean intellectuals faded once the plot ran out. The play lacks a sixth act which might have been enlisted for representing relations among Caliban, Ariel, and Prospero once they entered a post-colonial era....' While others might argue that this silence is

precisely where new appropriations might wish to begin, Nixon is correct in noting the 'declining pertinence' (p. 577) of the play to contemporary concerns.

4. Henry Louis Gates, Jr., 'Talkin' That Talk', in *Critical Inquiry*, 13 (Autumn 1986), p. 210.

5. Timothy J. Reiss, *The Discourse of Modernism* (Ithaca: Cornell University Press, 1982).

6. Partha Chatterjee, *Nationalist Thought and the Colonial World: A Derivate Discourse?* (London: Zed, for the United Nations University, 1986), p. 168.

7. Henry Louis Gates, Jr., 'Editor's Introduction: Writing "Race" and the Difference it Makes', in *Critical Inquiry*, 12 (Autumn 1985), 15.

8. _____, 'What's Love Got To Do With It?' in *New Literary History*, 18, 2 (Winter 1987), p. 347.

9. Joyce A. Joyce, '"Who the Cap Fit": Unconsciousness and Unconscionableness in the Criticism of Houston A. Baker, Jr. and Henry Louis Gates, Jr.', in *New Literary History*, 18, 2 (Winter 1987), p. 378.

10. Peter Hulme, *Colonial Encounters: Europe and the Native Caribbean 1492-1797* (London: Methuen, 1986), p. 8.

11. Rob Nixon concludes that 'Given that Caliban is without a female counterpart in his oppression and rebellion ... it follows that all the writers who quarried from *The Tempest* an expression of their lot should have been men' (p. 577). Such a statement ignores Lamming's recognition of Miranda as in many ways Caliban's counterpart, explicitly in *The Pleasures of Exile* and implicitly in *Water with Berries*. It also ignores Suniti Namjoshi's 'Snapshots of Caliban' from *The Bedside Book of Nightmares* (Fredericton: Fiddlehead & Goose Lane, 1984), where Caliban is feminised and develops a close relationship with Miranda, as well as Margaret Laurence's *The Diviners* and Audrey Thomas's *Munchmeyer and Prospero on the Island*, which develop Miranda's resistance to Prospero's oppression. For more on this issue see my 'Re-writing *The Tempest*' in *World Literature Written in English*, 23, 1 (1984), pp. 75-88. What Nixon mistakenly sees as problems in the source play, an ideologically-informed analysis would identify as characteristic of the society – of the choices it does and does not see – in its reading of the play. These choices become clearer when we see that other societies have indeed read them as options presented by *The Tempest*.

12. Barbara Christian, 'The Race for Theory', in *Cultural Critique* ['The Nature and Context of Minority Discourse I', ed. Abdul JanMohamed and David Lloyd], 6 (Spring 1987), p. 54.

13. Earl Lovelace, *The Dragon Can't Dance* (1979; London: Longman Drumbeat, 1981), p. 10.

14. Marlene Nourbese Philip, 'Women and Theft', in *Fuse*, 44 (April 1987), pp. 38-40.

15. A good example of what can be done in this area is David Maughan-Brown's *Land, Freedom and Fiction: History and Ideology in Kenya* (London: Zed, 1985). The theorist whose work I have found most useful for writing about ideology and literature is Goran Therborn, *The Ideology of Power and the Power of Ideology* (London: Verso, 1980).

16. For the origins of these phrases see A.A. Philips, *The Australian Tradition* (Melbourne: Cheshire, 1958), Northrop Frye, *The Bush Garden: Essays on the Canadian Imagination* (Toronto: Anansi, 1971), and George Lamming, *The Pleasures of Exile*, (1960; London & New York: Allison & Busby, 1984).

17. Homi K. Bhabha, 'Some Problems in Nationalist Criticism', in *Literature and History*, 5, 1 (Spring 1979), p. 110.

18. Donna E. Smyth, *Subversive Elements* (Toronto: Women's Press, 1986), p. 107.

19. Henry Louis Gates, Jr., 'Authority, (White) Power and the (Black) Critic; It's All Greek To Me', in *Cultural Critique* ['The Nature and Context of Minority Discourse II', ed. Abdul JanMohamed and David Lloyd], 7 (Fall 1987), p. 32.

20. Aijaz Ahmad, 'Jameson's Rhetoric of Otherness and the "National Allegory", in *Social Text*, 17 (Fall 1987), p. 8.

21. Edward W. Said, 'Secular Criticism', in *The World, the Text, and the Critic* (Cambridge, Mass: Harvard University Press, 1983), p. 23

22. Ngugi wa Thiong'o, *Decolonising the Mind: The Politics of Language in African Literature* (London: James Currey, 1986), p. 9.

23. Brian Fawcett, *Cambodia: a book for people who find television too slow* (Vancouver: Talon, 1986), p. 148. The full quotation reads: 'In the latter part of the twentieth century, a colonial is one who retains a fundamental imaginative relationship with the Imperium'.

24. Robert Bringhurst, *Pieces of Map, Pieces of Music* (Toronto: McClelland & Stewart, 1986), p. 102. The full quotation reads: 'So while most of my colleagues in the Canadian and American poetry racket devote themselves to speaking for and within the colonial culture to which they belong – and which, of course, contains a great deal of profundity and beauty – I have spent my own life learning to speak across and against it'.

25. Flemming Brahms, 'Entering Our Own Ignorance. Subject-Object Relations in Commonwealth Literature', in *World Literature Written in English*, 21, 2 (Summer 1982), p. 224.

26. Gerald Graff and Reginald Gibbons, Preface to *Criticism in the University*, ed. Gerald Graff and Reginald Gibbons (Evanston, Ill.: Northwestern University Press, 1985), p. 9.

27. Abdul R. JanMohamed, 'The Economy of Manichean Allegory: The Function of Racial Difference in Colonialist Literature' in *Critical Inquiry*, 12 (Autumn 1985), p. 59.

28. Rastko Mocnik, 'Toward a Materialist Concept of Literature', in *Cultural Critique*, 4 (Fall 1986), pp. 171-89

29. Helen Tiffin and I make a similar list in the Introduction to our forthcoming book *Decolonising Fictions* (Dangaroo Press), written in 1985. For further discussion of 'the ways in which a reconsidered, or revised notion of what might be called a post-colonial intellectual project is likely to expand the area of overlapping community between metropolitan and formerly colonized societies', see Edward W. Said, 'Intellectuals in the Post-Colonial World' in *Salmagundi*, 70-71 (Spring-Summer 1986), pp. 44-64.

30. Edward W. Said, 'Orientalism Reconsidered' in *Literature, Politics and Theory: Papers from the Essex Conference 1976-84*, ed. Francis Barker et al. (London: Methuen, 1986), p. 229.

31. Nick Wilkinson, 'A Methodology for the Comparative Study of Commonwealth Literature', in *The Journal of Commonwealth Literature*, 13, 3 (April 1979), pp. 33-42. This article may well represent the kind of 'traditional academicist wisdom' Bhabha has in mind. Wilkinson makes four pragmatic assumptions that have been undermined by both nationalist African critics such as Achebe and Chinweizu and by European theorists such as Foucault, Barthes, Derrida and Macherey. While sharing Wilkinson's desire for a clearer statement of the assumptions underlying what we do, I find his assumptions, as stated in this article, completely unacceptable, indeed, a perfect summary of everything I oppose.

32. Ernesto Laclau, *Politics and Ideology in Marxist Theory* (London: New Left, 1977), p. 161.

33. Judith Williamson, 'Woman is an Island: Femininity and Colonization' in *Studies in Entertainment: Critical Approaches to Mass Culture*, ed. Tania Modleski (Bloomington & Indianapolis: Indiana University Press, 1986), pp. 100-101. See also her statement: 'The need of our society both to engulf Others and to exploit "otherness" is not only a

15

structural and ideological phenomenon; it has been at the root of the very development of capitalism...' (p. 110).

34. John Carlos Rowe, ' "To Live Outside the Law, You Must Be Honest": The Authority of the Margin in Contemporary Theory', in *Cultural Critique*, 2 (Winter 1985-86), p. 67.
35. Dieter Riemenschneider, 'The "New" Literatures in Historical and Political Perspectives: Attempts toward a Comparative View of North/South Relationships in "Commonwealth Literature" ', in *New Literary History*, 18, 2 (Winter 1987), p. 433.

I would like to thank Lee Briscoe Thompson and Craig Tapping for providing me with my title during discussion following the meetings of the Canadian Association for Commonwealth Literature and Language Studies at the Learned Societies Meetings in Hamilton, Ontario, May 1987.

MICHAEL DASH

In Search of the Lost Body: Redefining the Subject in Caribbean Literature

> Nous sommes enfermé à l'extérieur
> de nous mêmes.
> Paul Valéry
>
> toute île appelle
> toute île est veuve
> Aimé Césaire

EX-ISLE

Master Prospero and slave Caliban, Robinson Crusoe and Man Friday, King Christophe and Fool Hugonin, the disincarnate ego and the incarnate other – the confrontation between the castaway subject and the cast-out other in the Caribbean makes these universal images of the divided self, the dissociated sensibility, more acute and pervasive. The Caribbean writer is haunted by the darker implications of these polarities. His imagination is constantly drawn to these contrastive mental spaces which symbolically reflect the relationship between power and the promise of its subversion, between spiritual pretence and its demonic underside, between the self-certain subject and the liberating thrust of Otherness. The individual artist's unsettling focus on these precarious dichotomies ultimately constitutes a tradition built around redefining the subject, reacting against cultural and psychological estrangement and, in its most visionary manifestation, creating a poetics of a fissured, constantly changing space.

In a region made ominously intelligible because of systems of domination, in which origins are obscured or degenerate into self-serving fictions, traumatised by dependency, the quest for self-formation is the only valid imaginative response. The task of consciousness becomes necessary in a world that is the product of others' dreams, where systems of knowledge and signification are enforced in order to produce docility, constraint and helplessness. Active self-formation or 'subjectification', a major concern of

17

modern critical theory (cf. Michel Foucault), is a phenomenon which occurs with obsessive frequency in Caribbean writing. Establishing a new authority or authorship is one of those vital continuities in Caribbean literature that has created the possibility of a redistribution of discourse, of re-presenting self. For instance, the Martinican novelist Edouard Glissant and the Guyanese novelist Wilson Harris, independently of each other, focus on the question of self-formation, the process of 'becoming' in terms of images of space, threatened but constantly reasserting itself. In Harris's imagination,

> Two oceans, symbolic and real, impinge on modern Guyana. The Atlantic has tested the coastland peoples for generations. They have fought a long battle with the sea to maintain their homes. The vast interior at their back is another, equally complex, ocean that rises into a 'sounding cliff' or majestic waterfall within rainforest, savannah, rock, river.[1]

For Glissant the dialectic between stable and unstable, real and unreal, voiced and unvoiced is equally inscribed in Caribbean space:

> The sea is always an envelope, something extra, that which is outside everything and which forms a definite border, but which has a shaping and defining power at the same time.... In this place of acceptance and denial, this line of trees contains the essentials of wisdom, it teaches moderation and at the same time inspires audacity.[2]

This view of the psyche as a constantly shifting site where the known or the knowable tentatively emerges from the world of flux, of latent possibilities, points to the special manifestation of self-definition in the Caribbean imagination. It is precisely this dialectic between said and not only unsaid but unsayable that dictates theme, technique and ideological orientation for the Caribbean writer. There are those who focus on the known and the real as an exclusive area of concern and who can explain all structures as part of rational knowable order. The self-certain subject, free to confer meaning on his or her world, to wrest the land from Prospero's signifying grasp, is the exemplary figure in this fiction. For other writers, the world exists prior to and independent of subject. They concentrate on that area of experience which exceeds explanation, on the deconstruction of the sovereign subject. The constructive subject's grasp of the world is always inadequate. There is always an irreducible unknown, a Derridean *différence*, those 'aporias' which resist systematic interpretation. In the first instance, the structuring ego longs for a world of alternative stable meanings, of fixed values. The second provides a radical critique of the privileged subject. In this view, the individual subject is simply the site, the threshold where collective subject finds articulation, where private and public, individual and group interact. The apotheosis of the subject and the decentred subject, the poetics of rupture and 'relation', are the determining factors in a Caribbean literary tradition.

The focus on the constructive subject in modernism and in Sartrean existentialism allows us insight into one of those imaginative structures. The post-modernist dismantling of the subject and insistence on the relation between humanity and cosmos provides the critical tools for examining the other direction taken by the creative imagination. This is what Glissant means when he points to the 'lived modernity' of the Caribbean. In *Le discours antillais* he examines the urgency with which the question of the problematics of the subject and the discourse of otherness is posed. He sees Caribbean writing as preoccupied with the issue of incompleteness and as a creative rupture with the petrified and alienated self of the colonial world.

> We need to develop a poetics of the 'subject', if only because we have too long been 'objectified' or rather, 'objected to'.... The text must for us (in our lived experience) be destablized because it must belong to a shared reality and it is perhaps at this point that we actually relate to those ideas that emerged elsewhere. The author must be demythified, certainly, because he must be integrated into a common resolve. The 'collective we' becomes the site for the generative system and the true subject.[3]

The demystification of the author as authoritarian voice is not a gratuitous devaluation of human agency but a refocussing of attention on the inescapable shaping force of otherness, of the collectivity. Similarly, Harris's view of structuralism is critical of its belief that all structures can be rationally defined. But he approves of its insistence on looking beneath the surface. He is concerned with deflating articulate consciousness, as Glissant is, and valorising the 'inarticulate'.

> What we can salvage from structuralism at its best, I think, is the descent it encourages the serious arts to make into 'inarticulate' layers of community beneath static systems whose 'articulacy' is biased. The 'inarticulate' layers may be equated with variables of the unconscious. (*Explorations*, p. 132)

Both Harris and Glissant are indicating in their assertion of the links between humanity and cosmos, in their demythification of omniscience and 'articulacy', the ways in which issues that have long preoccupied the Caribbean writer are now major philosophical issues in post-modernist thought. In this way, the radical scepticism of post-modernism overlaps with the creative intuition of Caribbean writing.

In the various readings and rewritings of the Prospero, Caliban and Ariel relationship in Shakespeare's *The Tempest*, we can trace the Caribbean preoccupation with the divided sensibility and gradual redefinition of the subject on the imaginative level. The conventional Caribbean re-reading of *The Tempest* asserts Caliban's right to power and repossession of the island. Caliban's structuring, sovereign subjectivity is opposed to Prospero's intrusive presence. The only example we have of a deconstructive reading of Shakespeare's play is Césaire's *Une tempête* which replaces the apotheosis of Caliban with a mysterious island-space which no one can possess. The island is full of noises, the discourse of otherness which falls into the zone of the unknowable, of a disconcerting elusiveness. At the end of Césaire's play both Prospero's reluctant appeal for human warmth and Caliban's aggressive songs of freedom are drowned by the sounds of the island. The only character who is not in a state of 'ex-isle' is Ariel, who represents an exemplary responsiveness to the landscape. In Ariel's *disponibilité*, the 'inarticulacy' of the island finds expression. The militant discourse of the self-assertive subject is replaced by a reticent, de-centred voice. The primacy of the Césairean imagination in the Caribbean is its capacity to conceive of the deconstructed subject, the abolition of all dualisms and the poetic expression of the unspeakable. In Césaire's work, Ariel represents an ideal moment of fusion, of androgynous wholeness, of the integrating capacity of the threshold sensibility.

The imaginative concern with the subject in the Caribbean is fundamental to the phenomenal reality of the text. It is responsible for a system of imagery in Caribbean literature whose centre is the body. The body is an endlessly suggestive sign through which the process of 'subjectification' is mediated and expressed. Corporeal imagery in the Caribbean indicates the tensions that underlie the process of self-characterisation, of the *récupération de soi* in the individual imagination. The ever shifting, unstable relationship between body and non-body, between dis-membering and re-membering, is a continuous aesthetic and thematic concern. The importance of this opposition in all cultures is noted by Octavio Paz:

> Whatever the word and the particular meaning of *body* and *non-body* within each civilisation, the relationship between these two signs is not, and cannot be, anything but unstable.[4]

The mediation between spirit and flesh, disincarnate subject and incarnate other, conservative denial of the body and its subverse resurrection, is particularly acute in the Caribbean because of the corporeal as well as psychic nature of alienation. The dual nature of repression in the Caribbean, both verbal and carnal, is the focus of Glissant's attention in *La discours antillais*:

... the alienated body of the slave, during slavery, is in fact deprived, as if to make the emptiness complete, of language.... When the body is liberated (when the day comes) it accompanies the shout, which is explosive. (p. 238)

In linking the frantic shout and the frenzied body, Glissant underlines the inextricable relationship between verbal and physical self-assertion, *cri* and *corps*. Similarly Harris points to the corrective and reconstructive potential that is released when possession in Haitian *vodun* liberates the individual body. At the beginning 'the dancer regards himself or herself as one in full command of two legs, a pair of arms', but when possessed he is drawn into 'the womb of space' as 'conventional memory is erased' and he becomes a 'dramatic agent of consciousness'.[5]

The use of corporeal imagery as an index to the process of self-formation is extensive in Caribbean literature. There are no chronological linguistic or ideological barriers to the Caribbean writer's use of the image of the body in dealing symbolically with the issue of 'subjectification'. Two areas of its use will constitute our short survey: *The Word Made Flesh* – the return of the ex-centric persona to the island-body in a Césairean poetics of the subject – and *Mutation, Metamorphosis and Androgyny* – images of the body that abolish or transcend all binary systems, in which an androgynous indeterminacy exists.

THE WORD MADE FLESH

In Césaire's writing the body has the last word. In his poetry and theatre he re-enacts the need to reintegrate the exiled subject in the lost body. In his epic poem *Cahier d'un retour au pays natal*, Césaire imagines the journey of the disembodied subject across the estranging waters and the eventual reintegration of the body with the *pays natal*. The need to undergo a sea-change is the dilemma of the Césairean subject but this journey is different from other journeys to the New World. Césaire's journey is not one of conquest, nor is the world 'new'. That fiction is part of the heroic mythification of Columbus, who conceived of the island as an empty vessel into which his fantasies could be poured.

The dream of the untouched, complete world, the thing for ourselves alone, the dream of Shangri-la, is an enduring human fantasy. It fell to the Spaniards to have the unique experience.[6]

Césaire's journey is not to a prelapsarian Eden but a fallen world, a defiled body. His is a voyage beyond illusion. To go forward is to return; the past holds the key to the future; retrospection is vision. Césaire's 'New World adventure' is a terrible ordeal since the object of the expedition is a malodorous, lacerated body silently suppurating in a sea of congealed blood.

In order to embrace this mutilated *pays natal*, the subject must overcome his or her initial revulsion. He or she must radically redefine notions of time, space, beauty and power before return becomes possible, and must strip away all illusions – whether that of heroic prodigal, solemn demiurge or New World African – empty consciousness of all pretensions ('overboard with alien riches/overboard with my real lies') in order to achieve reintegration.[7] The end of exile, the triumph over the estranging sea, is only possible when the subject feels his or her bonds with the lost body of the native land. The ego-centred attitude of saviour or reformer must yield to a humble realisation that the discourse of the island-body is more powerful. The *pays natal* is the realm of viscuous damp where familiar meanings dissolve, of the unspeakable that eludes the systematising word.

The importance of Césaire's contribution to a tradition of Caribbean writing is his passionate concern with psychic 're-memberment', with the successful incarnation of the displaced subject. Without reference to Césaire, Harris describes this concern as 'a new corpus of sensibility' which imaginatively releases the deep archetypal resonances of 'the theme of the phantom limb – the re-assembly of dismembered man or god' (*Explorations*, p. 27). The *Cahier* ends with a triumphant vision of sensory plenitude as the subject is possessed by the lost island-body. In the final movement of this poem, the 'wound of the waters' yields its secret as it becomes the pupil of the eye, the navel of the world, an integrating Omphalos. The dream of '*La Rencontre Bien Totale*' , the ecstatic abolition of all dualism, haunts Césaire's imagination. In Césaire's essay *Poésie et Connaissance* (1944) he describes the poetic ideal as a capacity to transcend oppositions, to achieve André Breton's vision of a 'certain point in mind' which could exist beyond contradictions. The dynamic image at the end of the *Cahier* – of the spiral, plunging in two directions – is an imaginative representation of the power of the reanimated body. The ideal of a restless, protean physicality is constantly invoked in his poetry. As *Intimité marine*, he states his poetic identity in terms of 'the neck of an enraged horse, as a giant snake. I coil I uncoil I leap'.

The images of dismemberment and reintegration so passionately stated in Césaire's epic poem recur throughout his poetic *oeuvre*. For instance the poem '*Corps perdu*' (which gives its name to the collection of poems) specifically deals with the retrieval of the lost body. Another poem that restates the theme of dismemberment is *'Dit d'errance'*, which does invoke 'archetypal resonances', in Harris's words, in its reference to the indestructibility of the Egyptian god Osiris. The poetic subject assumes all dismemberments which have existed.

> All that ever was dismembered
> in me has been dismembered
> all that ever was mutilated
> in me has been mutilated...[8]

As Gregson Davis points out in his reading of the poem, the lines 'the goddess piece by fragment/put back together her disseevered lover' specifically refer to the reconstitution of Osiris by Isis. Césaire has a special priority in Caribbean writing because of this vision of the re-membered body.

In his vision of verbal carnality, Césaire breaks free from an alternative tendency to concentrate on the self-certain subject in Caribbean writing. For instance, what distinguishes Césaire from St. John Perse is the latter's tendency to confine himself to the knowable and ignore or deny that which in elusive or incomplete. As Glissant observes,

> We see that in Perse's writing the more intense the feeling of drifting, the more stable the language becomes.... As if the pure architecture of language was the first response, the only one, to the loss created by wandering.... The threshold of this impossible construction, suddenly emerging from the realm of fragile disharmonies, is the word and the word is also the roof. The flesh transfigured into word.[9]

The imposition of a verbal architecture on the evanescent, the sovereign subject's capacity to voice all meanings, is seen as a deep reflex in Perse's sensibility. This longing for the virtues of clarity, a patrician syntax, an elegant diction, is shared by many early writers who insisted on imposing a disincarnate aesthetic on the mystery and shapelessness of reality. Césaire's work, in its de-centring of the sovereign subject, provides a sustained and radical critique of the structuring ego. His most dramatic deflation of the reconstructive demiurge is in the character of King Christophe, who attempts to reshape the natural contour, rhythm and smell of the bodies in his kingdom through costume, posture and perfume. The revolt of his own body precedes the mutiny of the collective body. Christophe's failed oppression of the body has its verbal parallel, as he attempts to impose his high-minded rhetoric on the polyphony of voices and sounds of the lower strata. He goes to his death with the mocking voice of Hugonin and the voodoo drums ringing in his ears.

Césaire's writing never ceases to insist on the unstable nature of the world. His horror of stasis (*durcir le beau*), his belief that stability is a mirage, has created the possibility of isolating the ideal of unencumbered physical movement or the refusal of corporeal determinism in Caribbean literature. The ideal of revolutionary self-assertiveness is expressed through corporeal imagery. For instance, Frantz Fanon attempts to rewrite the body of colonised man, creating a new subject from the dismemberment and castration inflicted by the coloniser's destructive gaze. In *The Wretched of Earth*, Fanon equates a reanimated body with the liberated voice of the revolutionary intellectual:

> It is a vigorous style, alive with rhythms, struck through and through with bursting life....[13] The new movement gives rise to a new rhythm of life and to forgotten muscular tensions, and develops the imagination.[10]

Fanon's images of verbal muscularity have a resonance in Caribbean writing in which revolutionary potential is evoked through the resurrected flesh. The reanimated body of the land in Jacques Roumain's *Masters of the Dew* and the erotic carnality of René Depestre's *Rainbow for the Christian West* are clear examples of spiritual awakening expressed in images of revitalised physicality.

The rewriting or reinventing of the subject does not always take the form of virile images of sexual hubris. Corporeal metamorphosis can take a totally different direction if the subject is defined in terms of an exemplary reticence or evasiveness. In Simone Schwarz-Bart's novel *The Bridge of Beyond*, the corporeal ideal is one of resilience, slipperiness and manoeuvrability. Bodies are repeatable, can be dissolved or can defy the force of gravity. For instance, Télumée deals with personal tragedy by imagining herself as floating free of the world and its destructive force:

> Then I would lie on the ground and try to dissolve my flesh: I would fill myself with bubbles and suddenly go light – a leg would be no longer there, then an arm, my head and whole body faded into the air, and I was floating.[11]

Her fantasy of an unencumbered body is an imaginative strategy designed to resist the desecrating force of her oppressive world. Schwarz-Bart's novel is a tribute to the survival of a particular group of women because of their imaginative powers. Her narrative is built around the tensions that separate the transcendental from the existential. Her main character yearns for a world divested of fixed, determining matter. The *morne* or hill which offers refuge exerts a vertical pull on the protagonist to counteract the downward pull of the plains with which fiery destruction and physical entrapment are associated.

In Schwarz-Bart's tale of female endurance, the subject is not aggressively impulsive but values suppleness and taciturn stoicism. In the face of the insults of her *béké* mistress Mme. Desaragne, she is 'ready to dodge, to slip between the meshes of the trap she was weaving with her breath'. She clings to this image of elusiveness until Mme. Desaragne disappears like starch dissolved in water. Schwarz-Bart's novel demonstrates the corrective power of the folk imagination. We have insight into a process of psychic *marronnage* that allows the individual to survive even in the most vulnerable circumstances.

This image of an ever-changing body emerges as an even more suggestive symbol in the work of Alejo Carpentier. In it an aesthetic of incompleteness offers an insight into a world where forms are unstable, where an intricate branching, adaptation and accretion governs the existence of all things. Carpentier's imagery is best explained in the symbolism of the grotesque as described by the Russian critic Bakhtin, in which the body 'is not something completed and finished, but open, uncompleted'.[12] In Carpentier's novel *Explosion in a Cathedral*, we are presented with a teeming world inhabited by fluid, evanescent form. Nothing has a fixed contour in this submarine world in which matter cannot be discriminated from non-matter. Esteban, Carpentier's protagonist, realises that this world resists being named or structured. In its unspeakable nature it defies the efforts of the comprehending subject:

> Carried into a world of symbiosis, standing up to his neck in pools whose water was kept perpetually foaming by cascading waves, and was broken, torn, shattered, by the hungry bite of jagged rocks, Esteban marvelled to realise how the language of these islands had made use of agglutinations, verbal amalgams and metaphors to convey the formal ambiguity of things which participated in several essences at once.[13]

The ambiguous space imagined by Carpentier is akin to Harris's zone of 'inarticulacy' or Bahtin's 'unpublicized spheres of speech' in which 'the dividing lines between objects and phenomena are drawn quite differently than in the prevailing picture of the world' (p. 421). Esteban's field of vision does not focus on the concrete and the static but on a world of infinite metamorphosis that seems to defy language itself. It illustrates Harris's conception of Caribbean consciousness caught between sea and forest.

Post-modernism concentrates on the inadequacy of interpretation and the disorienting reality of the unexplainable. Caribbean writing exploits precisely this terrain of the unspeakable. In the radical questioning of the need to totalise, systematise and control, the Caribbean writer is a natural deconstructionist who praises latency, formlessness and plurality. In order to survive, the Caribbean sensibility must spontaneously decipher and interpret the sign systems of those who wish to dominate and control. The writing of the region goes beyond simply creating alternative systems to reflect the futility of all attempts to construct total systems, to assert the powers of the structuring subject. It is not simply a matter of deploying Caliban's militant idiom against Prospero's signifying authority. It is, perhaps, a matter of demonstrating the opacity and inexhaustibility of a world that resists systematic construction or transcendent meaning.

NOTES

1. Wilson Harris, *Explorations* (Aarhus: Dangaroo Press, 1981), p. 7.
2. Edouard Glissant, *The Ripening*, trans. Michael Dash (1958; London: Heinemann, 1985), pp. 40-41.
3. _____, *Le discours antillais* (Paris: du Seuill, 1981), pp. 257-58.
4. Octavio Paz, *Conjunctions and Disjunctions* (New York: Seaver Books, 1982), p. 45.
5. Wilson Harris, *Tradition, the Writer and Society* (London: New Beacon, 1973), p. 51. Harris's treatment of limbo also suggests its capacity to unleash new physical and imaginative possibilities. See his *History, Fable and Myth in the Caribbean and Guianas* (Georgetown: National History and Arts Council, 1970); *Caribbean Quarterly*, 15,2 (1970), pp. 1-32.
6. V.S. Naipaul, *The Overcrowded Barracoon* (Harmondsworth: Penguin, 1976), p. 224.
7. There is a revealing misinterpretation of the Césairean persona by Eldridge Cleaver in *Soul on Ice* (London: Cape, 1968), in which Aimé Césaire epitomises black virility, 'the big gun from Martinique' as opposed to the epicene figure of James Baldwin.
8. Gregson Davis, ed. *Twenty Poems of Aimé Césaire* (Stanford: Stanford University Press, 1984), p. 102.
9. Edouard Glissant, 'St. John Perse et les Antillais', *La Nouvelle Revue Francaise*, 178, (Feb. 1976), p. 68. A useful comparison might be made between Césaire's *Cahier* and Perse's *Anabase*, since the former is a voyage of return and in the latter the nomadic traveller is never released from wandering.
10. Frantz Fanon, *The Wretched of the Earth*, trans. Constance Farrington (1961; Harmondsworth: Penguin, 1969), p. 177.
11. Simone Schwarz-Bart, *The Bridge of Beyond*, trans. Barbara Bray (London: Heinemann, 1982), p. 104.
12. Mikhail Bakhtin, *Rabelais and his World* (Bloomington: Indiana University Press, 1984), p. 364.
13. Alejo Carpentier, *Explosion in a Cathedral*, trans. John Sturrock (Harmondsworth: Penguin, 1972), p. 185.

Opting out of the (Critical) Common Market: Creolization and the Post-Colonial Text

1. 'EUROPEAN FORM, NON-EUROPEAN CONTENT' : POST-COLONIALISM AND THE MODERNIST LEGACY

When, in 1938, Raja Rao wrote in his preface to *Kanthapura* of the difficulty faced by Anglo-Indian writers in 'conveying in a language that is not one's own the spirit that is one's own',[1] he not only outlined the wider dilemma facing all those writers who, in many different social and historical circumstances and from many different parts of the world, have attempted or are attempting to give voice to a distinctively post-colonial culture in a language which has been repeatedly used throughout its history for the purposes of imperial/colonial cultural assimilation; he also anticipated the dilemma currently facing critics of the post-colonial literatures whose attempts to develop theories of and about post-colonialism are vitiated by a critical vocabulary which relies heavily on Eurocentric concepts of literary classification and textual analysis. The now outdated formula that post-colonial writing involves the adaptation of 'European forms' to a 'non-European content' has thankfully lost credence due to a recognition both of its tacit reinforcement of European assumptions of cultural leadership and of its theoretically untenable bifurcation between the formal and thematic properties of the literary text. Yet if the steady development of and, above all, wider academic exposure to critical theory in recent years has resulted in a welcome, if belated, inquiry into the assumptions on which critical reading practices are based, its Euro-American bias has ironically provided the impetus for a different kind of assimilation, this time involving the reincorporation of the various post-colonial heterodoxies within the admittedly pluralist and decentred, but now increasingly institutionalized, domain of European/American 'post-modernism'.[2]

Unfortunately, attempts on the part of post-colonial critics to dissociate or at least differentiate post-colonialism from post-modernism have as yet proved unconvincing, not merely because of the intrinsically problematic nature of both terms but because of the continuing failure to account for their complex relation to the literary/cultural 'movements' which preceded them. One cannot begin to formulate theories of post-colonialism, for example, without first setting up one's parameters of colonialism: the same can be said of post-modernism which, if it remains an elusive, or merely a muddled, concept to some, may well be so because it is founded upon false assumptions about, or an insufficiently informed understanding of, modernism.[3] This paper cannot claim to make up for these insufficiencies but seeks instead to address itself initially to an issue which, in the current lively debate on the relation between and relative merits of post-colonialism and post-modernism, risks being overlooked: namely the interrogation in/by many post-colonial texts of their European modernist predecessors. The critique of modernism will then be seen as an example of the way in which post-colonial writers seek not only to question the Great Tradition of European literature but also to challenge continuing Eurocentric critical and metacritical biases.

The influence of European modernist literature on post-colonial writing is vast; examples which spring readily to mind in the English writing are the many post-colonial revisions of Conrad's *Heart of Darkness* and the frequent references in post-colonial texts to such classic modernist works as Eliot's *The Wasteland* and Joyce's *Ulysses*. But let me make it clear from the outset here that I am not speaking of 'modernism' generally (whatever that amorphous category might mean) but of a particular variant usually referred to as High Modernism. High Modernism, like any other form of modernism, or, for that matter, any other literary category, is fraught with contradiction; for the purposes of this argument, however, I shall outline two aspects generally accepted as salient features: first, the tendency to look upon, portray, and in many cases celebrate the artist as an isolated, unadjusted but somehow salutary figure in an increasingly fragmented and disoriented cultural environment; and, second, the prevalence of cumulative, syncretistic patterns within the literary text which reflect the reparation and/or regeneration of that fragmented culture. Thus, from a post-colonial perspective, a discrepancy immediately emerges in the ideological project of High Modernist art between the supposed break with tradition implied by the notion of modernity and the exercise of cultural retrieval implemented by the High Modernist text which ultimately guarantees the continuity of, rather than portrays the disintegration of or crisis within, Western (European) culture. This retrieval, moreover, involves the critical appropriation of 'non-European' cultural symbols and their subsequent reincorporation within the dominant discursive systems of Europe.

Now, this – admittedly over-simplified – reading of the assimilative practices of High Modernist aesthetics allows us to infer the irony behind many post-colonial writers' usage of the symbolic frameworks of European modernism to inform their own works. Thus, in revisions of *Heart of Darkness* such as Achebe's *Things Fall Apart* or Harris's *Palace of the Peacock*, the post-colonial writer should not be seen as attempting to adapt 'European forms' (or, in this case, European cultural paradigms) to a 'non-European content', but rather as demonstrating the self-empowering process by which such critical distinctions can be made in the first place (in Achebe's case, the 'authoritative' writing of 'primitive' African culture; in Harris's, the 'confirmatory' replay of a catastrophic journey into a 'primeval heart of darkness'). Achebe's and Harris's implied dissociation from the recon-firmatory project of European High Modernism is further enhanced by the former's celebration of the wisdoms contained within and disseminated by an ancient, and predominantly oral, culture, and by the latter's hybridization of European and Caribbean cultural myths is such a way as to stress the mutual benefits brought by alternative perceptions of a colonial past otherwise assumed to take its place within the self-authorizing annals of European history.[4]

Harris's celebration of the hybridity of Caribbean culture in *Palace of the Peacock* and other works supports his belief in the possibilities afforded by a new cross-cultural poetics which participates actively in the transformation not just of post-colonial, but of all, cultures. An interesting comparison can be made here between Harris's theories of the cross-cultural imagination and the historical studies of his Caribbean colleague Edward Brathwaite, particularly the latter's adumbration of the 'interculturative' process of creolization. Brathwaite takes care to distinguish between the prismatic perception of culture afforded by an appreciation of the interculturative nature of the creolization process and the monolithic perception afforded by those negative forms of creolization which either subscribe to the values of, and therefore reinforce the social hierarchy presided over by, the dominant (white) culture or, alternatively, which claim to have effected the total recuperation of the marginalized (indigenous) culture in terms which now exclude external influences of any kind.[5] Brathwaite's specific analysis of the creolization process focuses on the slave revolt in early nineteenth-century Jamaica, a high colonial period in which 'interculturation was being made to take place ... in a predetermined manner, with the inferior/superior ranking of the inherited system maintained and extended' (Rubin and Tuden p. 42). In this situation, claims Brathwaite, the various people and communities involved in the creolization process were faced with a restricted number of choices:

> There could be an acceptance of the colonial system: as was done of course by nearly all, if not all, the whites of the culture, and by the non-whites who had been bribed or coerced into it, or who had come into it through some accident or design of birth. There was also, arising from this acceptance situation, the ambiguous product: the freedom faced with the possibility of privileges and 'perks', the coloured or cultural mulatto, somatically defined as one thing; often socially promoted as something else; but never 'pure', since he was without ancestors (Rubin and Tuden pp. 42-43).

To illustrate his point, Brathwaite uses a symbolic framework familiar to Caribbean and other post-colonial writers, that of Shakespeare's *The Tempest*, but provides it with a cast of 'ambiguous products' which conform to 'the personality types of creole cultures'. In the context of early nineteenth-century Jamaica, claims Brathwaite, 'Prospero, Ariel and Caliban were all creoles: that is, they had a life-style that was tropical, slave/colonial and dependent on independent of the metropole' (Rubin and Tuden p. 44). Brathwaite emphasizes, however, that

> 'to be 'creole' didn't completely mean or imply satisfaction, stabilization or completion of a process; quite the opposite, in fact. To be creole in the changing world of the early nineteenth century was to be in a state of constant bias (from/towards) ancestral cultures' (Ruben and Tuden p. 44).

This state of flux or irresolution, suggests Brathwaite, is most clearly demonstrated in the 'personality type' of Ariel, who acts as a catalyst for and transmitter of the tensions involved both in Prospero and Caliban's increasingly uncertain allegiance with their ancestral past and in their indeterminate or fragmented vision of their immediate (and more distant) future.

Although historically and geographically specific, Brathwaite's analysis, I would argue, is of wider relevance to the state of post-colonial cultures in the late twentieth century, both in 'Third World' nations such as Africa where a Calibanic reversal of Prosperan authority has gradually given way to a more sophisticated analysis of the complex, often indirect or covert, power-relations informing post-colonial societies, and in former 'settler colonies' such as Australia where the ongoing attempt to define a national culture in relation to or reaction against its colonial past has been increasingly problematized by the (re)discovery of alternative ('non-European') cultural affiliations. The critique of ethnocentrism in a great deal of contemporary post-colonial writing can be seen in this context not just as a continuing interrogation of European colonial practices but as a more up-to-date attempt to account for the ethnic diversity of post-colonial societies, a diversity which implicitly questions such notions as the recuperation of a 'common ancestry' or the search for 'cultural unity' and which implicates the transferred ethnocentric biases of post-colonial nationalist discourses.[6] Hence the relevance of Brathwaite's revisionist term creolization, which ultimately implies neither a perpetuation of 'white' (ex-colonial) values or a recuperation of 'black' (indigenous) values within the post-colonial society but an interculturative process within which a series of intermediary postures are struck up that elude or actively work against the binary structures (white/black, master/slave) which inform colonial discourse but which have also survived in modified or transposed forms in the aftermath of the colonial era. Creolization, I would further suggest, provides a theoretical model not only for the contemporary analysis of post-colonial cultures but for the contemporary criticism of post-colonial literatures. Thus, for example, the common post-colonial practice of 'writing back' against a European cultural/literary tradition is not reabsorbed within the contestatory, but paradoxically integrative, terms of contemporary European critical theories and methodologies but is perceived as part of a dialectical process involving the interrogation, displacement and ironic refiguration of the hegemonic practices of European culture.[7]

I suggested before that Brathwaite forges a link between the interculturative process of creolization and the ambivalent concept of 'Arielism' in which the elusive go-between of Shakespeare's play is made to feature as a kind of cultural androgyne, a 'free spirit' ironically in thrall both to a white and, less directly, to a black master, and consequently operating as a catalytic agent for the struggle both between and within nominally opposing, but implicitly interdependent, cultural representatives. This link, I would argue, also informs a recent post-colonial rewriting of *The Tempest* which powerfully dramatizes the forces at work within a post-colonial culture struggling to disabuse itself of its colonial past and to signal its own 'disidentification'[8] from the assimilative designs of the European literary tradition: Keri Hulme's novel *the bone people* (1983).[9]

2. ARIEL MANOEUVRES: *THE BONE PEOPLE* AS A POST-COLONIAL TEXT

Overriding critical concerns with the assertion or refutation of *the bone people* as a 'Maori' novel, a (or even 'the') 'New Zealand' novel, or some combination of both, have resulted in a curious reluctance to consider its wider implications as a post-colonial text. And unfortunately, in the few essays which do consider these implications, the argument is weakened by a failure to understand the ironic treatment of High Modernism in the novel as an implied continuation of the tradition of European cultural supremacy (Simon During's otherwise instructive article in *Landfall*),[10] or by an insistence on the need for post-colonial literatures/cultures to develop their own nationalist discourse, a discourse which has always seemed to me to risk espousing precisely the same essentialist notions as imperial/colonial self-proclamation (Anne Maxwell's implied response to During in *Antithesis*).[11] Both of these essays discuss Hulme's treatment of modernism in the novel, but neither links it to a cultural tradition which traces back through such classic texts of the colonial encounter as *Robinson Crusoe* and *The Tempest*. Yet, although the circular framework of texts such as Eliot's *The Wasteland*, Conrad's *Heart of Darkness* and Joyce's *Finnegans Wake* is there for all to see in *the bone people*, underlying it is the more obviously *binary* framework of Defoe's and, particularly, Shakespeare's texts. This section of the paper therefore addresses itself to the link between Hulme's idiosyncratic 'creolized' reading of *The Tempest* and her ironic reading of European High Modernism in which the regenerative patterns outlined in a series of 'exemplary' texts are discovered to advocate notions of assimilation and recuperation which actually serve to reinforce the values of the dominant culture.

In *the bone people*'s brilliant opening, a child appears as if out of nowhere on the premises of a tower presided over by a reclusive bibliophile. 'Rescued' by her and taken in in what is later to become an ambivalent (dare I say a tempestuous?) alliance, the child awaits the entrance of the third player in the triangle, a physically powerful but emotionally troubled Maori, 'dispossessed' of his family, unsure of his place in society, and susceptible to fearful acts of retributive violence towards the child, whom he considers his own but who consistently deceives, defies or eludes him.

This network of displaced references to *The Tempest* sets the pattern for the narrative which follows. But Hulme's most telling displacement/ refiguration of Shakespeare's text resides, I would argue, neither in her feminization of Prospero[12] nor in her identification of a Maori Caliban but in her creolization of both Prospero and Caliban, a move which gives centre stage to the intermediary, ambivalent figure of *Ariel*. In Kerewin's case, the status of a 'creole' Prospero is not merely a question of her mixed ancestry (Scots/Lancastrian/Maori) but of her eclectic artistic and intellectual preoccupations. An enthusiastic if quickly disillusioned dilettante, she approaches painting, writing, sculpture and music with the same voracious exuberance as she displays towards her reading (Oriental mysticism, medieval lore, fantasy etc.). Moreover, Kerewin's very speech is a kind of 'creole', an unusual but identifiable combination of Elizabethan archaisms and contemporary vernacular interspersed with arcane allusions, colourful regional idioms and Maori proverbs. Joe's status as a 'creole' Caliban is less evident, though we are told near the beginning of the novel that he is not one hundred percent 'pure' Maori and informed later that his topheavy physique is due to a childhood attack of polio which has left him 'imperfectly formed', ironic indications not only that his mixed ancestry precludes any single racial/cultural affiliation but that such unilateral affiliations may support erroneous notions of 'purity' and/or 'perfection' historically associated with imperial/colonial proclamations of cultural supremacy.

But it is above all through the character of the rebellious 'mute' child, Simon, that these apparent stylistic, physical and temperamental 'eccentricities' are transmitted and ironically intensified. Thus, as the relationship between Kerewin, Joe and Simon develops, it becomes more and more apparent that the so-called 'delinquence' of the child is in effect a transposition of the anti-social behaviour of his two self-appointed 'guardians'; for Simon is not only instrumental in bringing Kerewin and Joe together but in galvanizing and, as his abbreviated name, Sim, suggests, simulating their own 'delinquent' activities. Simon's sneak-thievery, for example, ironically reflects Kerewin's magpie intellectual acquisitiveness, while his frequent flashes of temper and petty vandalism mirror the more sinister physical abuse of his unstable foster-father. Simon's ability to mimic the faults of others, along with his elusiveness, his uncooperativeness and his concerted resistance to social norms indicate the disruptive nature of his mediating role: a mischievous but also, it would seem, a malevolent Ariel. But while Simon's persistent deviance leads to the brutal retributive battering which lands him in hospital and plunges his two 'guardians' into suicidal despair, the event also triggers the journeys which are to reveal knowledge of their linked ancestral past. Thus, while Joe and Kerewin recover lost contact with their Maori cultural heritage, they also discover the previously missing links in Simon's past which enable them to connect, and apparently 'integrate', their own multiple ancestries. Simon's disinherited father (Timon) provides one of these links; the discovery of the boat and its illegal 'treasure' (heroin) another: the origin of the 'tempest' jointly played out in the minds of Joe, Kerewin and Simon is revealed in a rancorous colonial past of dispossession, destruction and false (Mephisthophelean) promise.

The recuperative structure of the novel, and in particular its 'happy ending', interpreted by many of Hulme's critics as an optimistic vision of a more integrated Maori/Pakeha future, appear in a less rosy light when seen in this context, as an allegorical playing-out of a repressed colonial past which 'brings to the surface' the grim knowledge of deceit and (self)destruction. Moreover, Simon's silence throughout the novel suggests that a gap, or rather a series of gaps, remain at the heart of the text which controvert its integrative thematics and its neat, apparently all-encompassing structure. I would further suggest that these gaps undermine the synthesizing aesthetic project of the novel, identifying it with Kerewin's individualistic version of, but ultimately collusive relation to, High Modernist artistic practice. In the article to which I previously referred, Simon During rightly points out that the syncretistic tendencies of High Modernism have the effect of assimilating, and therefore of minimizing or even annulling, cultural differences.[13] But whereas During sees this disguised expression of European hegemony as defeating Hulme's apparent purpose in proclaiming the values of Maori culture, I read it as an ironic comment on Kerewin's continued dependence on a cultural tradition which links her back through Joyce, Yeats and Eliot to that archetypal cultural 'gatekeeper', Prospero. For although Kerewin burns down her Tower and destroys the cultural 'treasure' it contains, we find her at the end of the novel enlisting the help of a certain Finnegan to retrieve the wreckage of Timon's boat, a salvage operation which yields an altogether different kind of 'treasure'. It could of course be argued here that the reinforcement of Kerewin's Gaelic ancestry through this latest Joycean reference signals her resistance to the cultural imperialism of the 'European tradition', a resistance implied by her allegiance to a post-colonial culture (Ireland) with a history of militancy that her adopted country (New Zealand) lacks. But the ironic counterpoint between Kerewin's discarded possessions and Timon's re-emergent booty suggests that her previous cultural affiliations have, as it were, merely undergone a 'sea-change': the salvage of Timon's 'treasure' thus reconfirms her residual allegiance to a dominant culture which has absorbed wayward or recalcitrant elements within its own all-enveloping discursive system. In this sense, despite her cultivated eccentricity, Kerewin can paradoxically be seen as embodying the reactionary process of negative creolization: mainly European, part Maori, she appears to disclaim the former in order to recuperate the latter but actually assimilates the latter within the former.

A different aspect of the same process is exemplified in Joe's apparent reinheritance of the land of his Maori forefathers. For Joe's recovery of the greenstone from a remote corner of the North Island, a prerequisite for his and Kerewin's foundation of a revitalized Maori community in the South, is not a unique event which definitively realigns him with his lost Maori ancestry but rather part of a double retrieval also involving the salvage of Timon's boat and the unwanted reclamation of another displaced element of his cultural ancestry. The one, suggests Hulme, cannot exist without the other; the attempt to locate the current position of or to predict the future movements of a creolized post-colonial culture depends on the interaction between the enlightening myths of an indigenous tradition (or traditions) and the benighted history of the colonial encounter, an interaction which at once debunks the falsely homogenizing myths of cultural 'purity' and national 'unity' and implicitly dispels (or at least counteracts) the colonial stigmas of 'mixed blood' and 'cultural schizophrenia'.

An alternative is suggested, however, to the overt antagonism of the colonial encounter or to the implied essentialism of projects of cultural recuperation through the agency of the go-between Ariel, whose ambivalent status, dexterity, defiantly maintained (rather than) silence and persistent frustration of the expectations that others place upon him can all be seen as strategies of resistance which signal his challenge to the standards imposed upon him by the various (legal, medical, etc.) 'authorities' he encounters, but also as his attempted dissociation from the wider discursive system which informs those institutions. And this system, it is implied, owes its predominantly binary structuration to a European rationalist heritage whose Manichean rhetorical divisions have clearly defined historical links with the colonial enterprise. But Simon's own family background unfortunately relates him, at least indirectly, to the very hierarchical structures and institutions he seems intent on resisting; thus, although he is cut off from a father who had himself been disinherited by his aristocratic family, and is therefore twice removed from the country and culture of his forebears, Simon still carries within him and is recurrently haunted by the nightmares of a destructive colonial past.

Yet if, through Simon, Hulme indicates the impossibility of a total disinheritance from the self-destructive ties of the colonial bloodknot, suggesting by analogy that post-colonial societies/cultures cannot dissociate themselves wholly from the implications of their colonial past, she hints at the potential emergence of an emancipated post-colonial voice containing within it the contradictions of and hybrid elements in post-colonial cultures which perceive their creolized status in terms other than those of self-deprecatory assimilation or self-glorifying recuperation. But as I suggested, this is not the voice of the indigenous Maori Caliban; it is paradoxically that of the Pakeha Ariel who, liberated from his erstwhile 'master(s)', becomes an agent of cross-cultural exchange rather than a facilitator/simulator of cultural antagonism. I stress himself/herself, because the gender of Hulme's Ariel, like that of Shakespeare's, is nominally male but otherwise ambiguous (significantly, Kerewin refers to the child in the early stages of the novel as 'it'). Simon/Ariel can be seen in this context as a principle of mobility or ambivalence oscillating between the more defined but, as it turns out, equally unstable presences of Prospero and Caliban. The introduction of an androgynous, or sexually ambiguous, presence into the novel disrupts the socially constructed opposition between male and female (also questioned in Hulme's presentation of a 'macho' female Prospero and an ostensibly virile but latently homosexual Caliban).[14] The powerful intermediary presence of Simon/Ariel also indicates a desire to dismantle other oppositional hierarchies involved in the construction of race and class or caste which trace back beyond their immediate colonial context to a history of Western culture and, more specifically, to a history of European writing, in which the construction of a series of anthithetical 'others' has consistently been employed as a self-empowering strategy designed to promote the values of cultural unity and to justify actions taken against outsiders to, or non-conformist elements within, that culture.[15]

If the emergence of an emancipated post-colonial voice in *the bone people* remains deferred, this is not just because Simon/Ariel remains trapped within the system which nurtures and supposedly 'protects' him; it is also because an articulation of the silences or spaces between prescribed discourses or discursive formations itself constitutes a kind of freedom, a tacit assertion of elusiveness as the condition for post-coloniality.[16]

3. AFTER EUROPE : TOWARDS A POST-COLONIAL POETICS OF DISTURBANCE

The attribution of a positive value to elusiveness in *the bone people* lends weight to Brathwaite's analysis of the creolization of post-colonial societies, a process whose ongoing dialectics preclude any permanent resolution and therefore rule out the possibility of a definitively 'achieved' or fully 'unified' culture. Elusiveness also becomes the watchword for a widespread post-colonial scepticism towards homogeneous or homogenizing categories of critical discourse. This may well sound like a subscription to the destabilizing procedures of European post-structuralist methodologies or to the decentred discourse of Euro-American post-modernism; but there is a crucial difference, for the scepticism shown by many post-colonial writers and critics towards self-contained theoretical systems and explicatory critical terminology is not so much founded on the 'global' concept of linguistic or epistemological crisis or on a perceived loss of faith in the historical continuity provided by the so-called 'master narratives' of the Western (European) literary tradition as on the desire to interrogate that tradition, and the criticism which has so often either explicitly or implicitly reinforced it, in ways which uncover its continuing cultural biases.[17]

I have suggested that one of the ways in which *the bone people* does this is through its ironization of the assimilative procedures of High Modernist art; thus, in a strategy characteristic of post-colonial writing, the text provides its own deconstructive reading of its literary/cultural precursors. The retrospective reading of European High Modernism through the imperial allegory of *The Tempest* provides a further strategy consisting in the ironic reconfirmation of a prescribed cultural pattern or paradigm: ironic again, because the palimpsestic overlay of texts belonging to a shared cultural tradition (*Heart of Darkness/Robinson Crusoe/The Tempest*) creates an effect of hyperbole further intensified by the novel's deliberately overwrought language and overexposed scenes of physical violence.

The combined effect of these textual strategies, I would argue, is to produce an exacerbated allegory of the colonial encounter which also lays bare colonizing practices inherent in the European literary and critical tradition. Ariel, I have suggested, is the medium through which this saga of cultural dispossession/appropriation comes to be told, but is also a vehicle for the articulation of a poetics of disturbance characterized not so much by the realistic expression of psychological complex as by the allegorical exposition of a relativism which problematizes 'normative' prescriptions of both social behaviour and literary/cultural value.

By shifting emphasis in the novel from the antagonistic relationship between Prospero and Caliban to the ambiguous character of Ariel who, despite his 'capture' and 'enslavement' (colonial paradigms ironically alluded to through recurrent images of appropriation and retention[18]), continues to evade comprehension and resist domestication by his two 'guardians', Hulme sets up the possibility for a dissociative critical stance which recognizes the involvement of post-colonial literatures/cultures in but resists their circumscription by the naturalized patterns and paradigms of European literary/cultural history.

If the notion of a poetics of disturbance primarily suggests the implementation of a series of interventionary strategies which problematize 'normative' categories including those of literary criticism (allowing us, for example, to consider Simon's mimicry, silence and androgyny in *the bone people* as metatextual strategies of resistance), the process of creolization investigates ways in which different cultural paradigms may be adapted, displaced and realigned in accordance with a 'prismatic' perception of cultural pluralism (i.e. one which acknowledges the interaction between various elements within the society rather than the fragmentation of that society into a series of discrete, hierarchically structured units: viz. Simon's intermediary role in the (re)connection of his own, Kerewin's and Joe's multiple ancestries). The capacity to 'disturb' established critical perspectives (by which I mean the institutionalized ways in which we read and evaluate literatures, societies, cultures), combined with the ability to formulate critical opinions which draw on different, cross-related cultural sources, suggest in turn that the qualities associated with Ariel – mobility, elusiveness, indeterminacy – are also those of the ideal post-colonial reader, a reader familiar with and resistant to the (re)appropriative tactics of European critical practice. The inscription of a reader (ideal or not) within the literary text is a common ploy in post-colonial writing, suggesting that more work needs to be done in the future on the applicability of reader-oriented theories to the study of post-colonial literatures. I have shown in this paper that the crucial role of Ariel in the post-colonial context implies the benefits of a deconstructive reading which adapts post-structuralist methodology to the critique of European cultural imperatives. But as *the bone people* exemplifies, this kind of reading is anticipated by the post-colonial text; the role of the reader seems therefore to consist in the recognition of alternative reading strategies already implemented within the text. Clearly an inherited Eurocentric vocabulary is not only inadequate to the task of elucidating these strategies, but is in direct contradiction with the interrogative practices of the text; I have suggested as one possible alternative Brathwaite's concept of creolization, which provides a critical framework for an analysis of deconstructive reading strategies internalized within the post-colonial text without resorting to the often mystificatory vocabulary of and paradoxically authoritarian assumptions underlying European post-structuralism. I have also outlined the potential function of the lexical pairings disturbance/creolization, elusiveness/mobility in a post-colonial criticism which seeks to avoid circumscription within the critical/theoretical 'mainstreams' of Europe and America. The avoidance of a fixed critical position or perspective need not be interpreted as obfuscatory or irresponsible; on the contrary, it suggests the manoeuvrability necessary, on the one hand, for a transformational conception of cultural (ex)change involving the dialectical interaction between different cultures or cultural groups not considered as discrete units or diametric opposites but as components within a wider interculturative process; and, on the other, for a distinctively post-colonial critical discourse which neither dispenses with nor subscribes to, but problematizes and adapts, European models of literary/cultural analysis and classification. In this context, I would conclude, the insufficiencies of existing theories and methodologies can no longer by considered as symptoms of a general (Western) 'post-modern condition' but rather as specific examples of a critical 'common market' saturated with protected European goods for an inward-looking public.

NOTES

1. Raja Rao, *Kanthapura* (London: Oxford University Press, 1947).
2. See, for example, Helen Tiffin's critique of post-modernism in 'Post-Colonialism, Post-Modernism and the Rehabilitation of Post-Colonial History', *The Journal of Commonwealth Literature*, 23, 1, 1989, pp. 169-181).
3. See Frank Kermode's argument for a discrimination of modernisms in his essay 'The Modern', in *Modern Essay* (London: Collins, 1971), esp. pp. 39-70.
4. Chinua Achebe, *Things Fall Apart* (London: Heinemann Educ. Books, 1962); Wilson Harris, *Palace of the Peacock* (London: Faber and Faber, 1968). See also Achebe's attack on 'colonialist criticism' in the eponymous essay in *Morning Yet in Creation Day* (New York: Doubleday, 1975) pp. 3-28; and Harris's advocation of a 'new dialogue' in his essay 'The Complexity of Freedom', in *Explorations: A Selection of Talks and Articles 1966-1981* (Mundelstrup, Denmark: Dangaroo Press), esp. p. 116.
5. Edward K. Brathwaite, 'Caliban, Ariel, and Unprospero in the conflict of Creolization: A Study of the Slave Revolt in Jamaica in 1831-32', in Vera Rubin and Arthur Tuden, eds., *Comparative Perspectives on Slavery in New World Plantation Societies* (New York: New York Academy of Sciences, 1977), pp. 41-62. Other references are cited in the text.
6. On the drawbacks of post-colonial nationalist discourse, see Helen Tiffin's essay 'Post-Colonial Literatures and Counter-Discourse', in *Kunapipi*, 9, 3, 1987, pp. 17-38.
7. Tiffin, op.cit.
8. The term is Michel Pecheux'; for a discussion of its relevance within the post-colonial context, see Stephen Slemon, 'Monuments of Empire: Allegory / Counter-Discourse Post-Colonial Writing', *Kunapipi*, 9, 3, 1987, pp. 1-16.
9. Keri Hulme, *the bone people* (Wellington: Spiral, 1983).
10. Simon During, 'Postmodernism or Postcolonialism?', *Landfall*, 39, 3, 1985, pp. 366-380.
11. Anne Maxwell, 'Reading *the bone people*: Towards a Literary Postcolonial Nationalist Discourse', *Antithesis*, 1, 1, 1987, pp. 63-86.
12. See Maxwell's discussion in the aforementioned essay, in which she refers the reader to Gayatri Spivak's 'charting of the complicity between the rise of first-world feminist literature and that of European imperialism' (e.g. in 'Three Women's Texts and a Critique of Imperialism', *Critical Inquiry*, 8, 2, 1981, pp. 243-261). Although Maxwell reads *the bone people* as taking its place 'in the line of descent from the narrative trajectory of the modernist woman artists engendered by Woolf's *To the Lighthouse*', she acknowledges that 'the woman artist's challenge ... is not without its own blindnesses, centred as it is within ideological practices which maintain its class-bound, first-world privileges': Maxwell, op.cit., esp. pp. 80-82.
13. During, op.cit., pp. 373-374.
14. See Judith Dale's discussion of gender in '*the bone people: (Not) Having it Both Ways*', *Landfall*, 39, 4, 1985, pp. 413-428.

15. See, for example, the essays collected in Francis Barker *et al.*, eds., *Europe and its Others: Essex Conference on the Sociology of Literature 1984* (Colchester: University of Essex, 1985).
16. See Sherrill Grace's discussion of Margaret Atwood's 'articulation of the space(s) between' as an alternative to the 'violent dualities' of Canadian social/cultural experience, in 'Articulating the "Space Between": Atwood's Untold Stories and Fresh Beginnings', in S. Grace and L. Weir, eds., *Margaret Atwood: Language, Text and System* (Vancouver: University of British Columbia, 1983), pp. 1-16. The argument is of wider relevance to post-colonial societies/cultures seeking counter-discursive alternatives to the *dualist* discourse of the colonial encounter.
17. Tiffin, op.cit.
18. E.g. the multivalent image of the hook, which at once connotes appropriation, retention and the infliction of pain/suffering. Note also that Simon simulates these, as other, colonial practices; he is first discovered with a splinter in his foot, and later in a fishing accident sinks a hook into his own finger.

The Centre Cannot Hold: Two Views of the Periphery

In George Eliot's *The Mill on the Floss*, Maggie Tulliver, who cannot find a definite agenda to give a direction to her life, laments to her brother, '...you are a man Tom, and have power, and can do something in this world'. Tom's retort, 'then, if you can do nothing, submit to those who can', sums up very simply the lack of option for those outside the power structure.[1] In cultural discourse as well, a certain centrality is appropriated by those who have power, and the rest are left in peripheral positions with no choice other than submission. The relationship between the centre and the periphery need not however be fixed for all time, and theoretically speaking there is scope for synchronic and diachronic variations. In this paper I would like to discuss in very broad terms the relation between the centre and two peripheries – European critical traditions in relation to India and Africa at different points of history.

A generation ago when I began to study literature as an academic discipline, like many others in my situation in India, I submitted to the central ideologies of power in the literary and intellectual domain which at that time in our universities were Anglo-American in origin and male in outlook. One's competence in the field was measured by the extent to which one could emulate the dominant critical tone, assuming a voice that was not intrinsically one's own. If one felt uncomfortable in this double-bind, both as a woman and as a post-colonial subject, it was not an uneasiness that could be articulated in the accepted rhetoric of academic discourse. Hence in India students of literature learnt to operate within the restrictive frameworks of mime and ventriloquism, attempting desperately to convince themselves of the universality of all literary values, the need to safeguard the purity of literature from the contamination of all 'extrinsic' approaches in order to uphold a neutral, systematic and safe methodology.

Since then the position of the central academy has altered – and although changes move from the centre to the periphery somewhat slowly, the shifts taking place in the metropolis are beginning to touch our institutions as well. The Anglo-American traditions of formalism and empiricism have been overtaken by European critical traditions based on dialectical thought; philosophy, history, psychoanalysis and political ideas are now seen as inextricably interwoven in the literary text; ideology, instead of being an impure and embarrassing baggage, has become one of the central concerns of critical discourse. The resultant inclusive and more open ethos offers a greater possibility of voicing the kind of uneasiness I referred to at the outset. The new rhetoric even provides a well worked-out vocabulary of dissent. Journals in English from the centre, like *Poetics Today, Critical Inquiry* or *New Literary History*, not only allocate space for discussing gender and race differences in the reading and writing of literary texts, but also offer special issues on the impact of imperialism on subsequent literature. Most of these discourses, however, have been initiated at the centre. Whatever exciting new ideas have entered this domain in the last ten years – from Edward Said's *Orientalism* to the recent writings of Abdul JanMohamad and Homi Bhabha – have had to pass through the centre; that is, they have had to be validated by Columbia or Cambridge or Sussex in order to return to the periphery. It seems worth speculating whether such radical and rigorously worked-out discourses are at all possible within the limited parameters of the academic institutions in the third world countries (in India at least there is a general obliviousness of the political complexities and cultural contradiction inherent in the situation of an English teacher in a post-colonial classroom), or, worse still, whether even if they are possible they would get a hearing at home unless they are routed through a channel that touches the centre.

One of the difficulties of initiating new theoretical premises at the peripheries, and thereby obliterating the distinction between the centre and the periphery, is that some of the most crucial terms of the discourse, its categories, genres and concepts, are historically linked with certain phases of literary development in Europe. The problem is further compounded in India by the fact that the major literary figures in India from the nineteenth century onwards, even when they wrote in the Indian languages, wrote within the discursive limits set by the study of English literature and in some cases deliberately set out to emulate the examples and sequences that constitute literary history in Europe. For instance, a number of major novelists in nineteenth century India consciously adopted the models of Scott's historical fiction or the formal realism of the nineteenth-century European variety in their attempt to incorporate the new genre called the novel into the existing pre-novel narrative modes.[2] Critics in India for over a century have taken these attempts at their face value, judging these works in terms of how well they correspond to the western paradigm. Only very recently does one perceive a murmuring of dissent, a recognition of the fact that the true importance of these narratives lies in the nature of the mutation that took place, and an assertion that the cultural significance of the altered form need not necessarily be judged by the parameters of the western realistic novel. Another kind of example from the nineteenth century is provided by Michael Madhusudan Dutt (1824-73). After a few undistinguished attempts at writing poetry in English he turned his creative energies to Bengali and emerged as a major poet who extended the syntactical and rhythmic possibilities of the language by drawing simultaneously upon English and Sanskrit models. Tracing this process of interpenetration, not only of style, diction and generic model but also of literary and ideological assumptions, could well have been a step towards a new aesthetic. But instead of entering into this complex endeavour, most discussions of Dutt's work have stopped at highlighting his simpler achievements, like his introduction of the sonnet form and blank verse in Bengali and his writing of a memorable epic poem in supposedly Miltonic style. There is often a gap between a writer's conscious intent and the created artefact, allowing a space for theoretical speculations to enter. The literary texts of nineteenth-century India are rich in such possibilities. Bankimchandra Chatterjee, another seminal intellectual and literary figure of the nineteenth century, was once relegated to a fate similar to Dutt, reduced to merely being 'The Scott of Bengal'. But of late, a body of sophisticated critical writing has been growing around his prolific output (fourteen novels, extensive writings on religion, history, culture and society) – a criticism which focuses on him as the hub of a complex network of historical tensions and cultural pressures and uses his case as a take-off point for a new theoretical discourse on colonial India. It is interesting that much of this recent and interesting writing on Chatterjee has emerged from the academic disciplines of history and other social sciences, rather than from literary studies.[3]

In fact, this cross-fertilization of disciplines that is necessary for critical theory has not been very evident in India until recently, although the situation of the historian in India and the literary critic has some parallels. The basic conceptual frames in both disciplines have been drawn from the centre. The historians, for example, have for some time been engaged in a debate about the nature of the Bengali Renaissance that is supposed to have taken place in the nineteenth century. Originally the term Renaissance was applied to this particular period in India in view of the many parallels between this cultural and intellectual movement and the historical phenomenon that heralded the end of the medieval period in Europe. The idea of the Bengali Renaissance was generally accepted in India until the historians of the seventies challenged it and offered a serious critique of this concept by attempting to show that if modern Europe is taken as 'the classic demonstration of the progressive significance of an intellectual revolution in the history of capitalist economy and the modern state, then the intellectual history of nineteenth century India did not have this significance. As the harbinger of a bourgeois and a national revolution the Indian Renaissance was partial, fragmented; indeed it was a failure'.[4]

It is worth noticing that the historians who evolved the idea of an Indian Renaissance *and* those who challenged it are none of them willing to relinquish the analogy with European history as the basic frame of reference. For the earlier historians it is the similarities, and for the latter the dissimilarities, with European history that constitute the crucial factor. Similarly in literature, the literary histories of different Indian languages – published by the Sahitya Akademi (Academy of Letters) – invariably divide their material into medieval and modern periods, presumably because the same periodisation is generally applied to European literature and because their writers feel uneasy if the material in an Indian language does not fit this pattern. For example, they relegate the Bhaki movement, which was fairly wide-spread in time and place in India, safely to the medieval period, because medieval literature in Europe too is marked by religious modes of perception. Unable to liberate themselves from analogous thinking, they mentally translate the Chhayavad movement in Hindi poetry into Romanticism, and alienation of the existential variety is imposed on post-war writing in India when the actual political situation and philosophical presuppositions were quite dissimilar.[5] Using invisible grids generated in another context to analyse and evaluate texts and events is a practice that seems common both to history and literature in India. Yet the situations of the historian and of the literary critic are basically not the same, because unlike the developments of history which are caused by their internal logic and by larger forces beyond individual control, the texts of literature are often created as conscious artefacts with individual signatures, although the form they actually assume is the product of an interplay between deliberate design and unconscious modification through subterranean cultural pulls. However, in both cases, instead of first adopting an analytical framework in which the specific material is to be then somehow fitted, we should be required to construct independent categories or concepts and other theoretical relations in order to understand the particular literary or historical situation in India.

On the face of it, this may seem an obvious enough requirement. But the actual practice implies many difficulties. Involved in it is the complex problem of opening our theoretical constructs of the perpetual interaction between generalisations formulated at the level of universal theories and particularities perceived at the level of the specific time, place and culture. It is the continuing tension itself that sustains the dynamism of literary theory. In India, so long as the parameters of theoretical discourse are set by the available texts in English, nothing important will ever be achieved, because English texts, regardless of their literary and other values, have always been isolated phenomena in India unconnected with the network of pressures that determine the basic cultural design. These texts do not become points of intersection of larger social, political or historical forces. It is the Indian language texts that throw up theoretical possibilities. An emerging tendency – as yet not fully formed – is to turn to the nineteenth-century texts in the Indian languages and treat them as hinterland that would sustain the trade and the development of theoretical discourse. This enterprise, if it is to be fruitful, needs the collaboration of disciplines other than literature.

The case of literary theory for India is complicated by various factors – its long colonial history; its infinitely longer pre-colonial heritage; its plurality of languages and culture; and its limited literacy rate, which makes any experience with the printed text a special preserve of the privileged. In many ways the experience in Anglophone Africa is similar, and in many ways it is radically different.

In most countries of Africa the colonial history has been much shorter in duration than in India, but the suppression and denial of pre-colonial African culture has been much more ruthless. Perhaps as a reaction to this one finds that the creative writers in Africa take very definite aesthetic stands. All the major writers in Africa today who write in English – including Chinua Achebe, Wole Soyinka, and Ngugi wa Thiong'o – have powerfully articulated their critical norms and defined their positions regarding life and literature, assuming the centrality of Africa to their experience. This is very different from the situation in India, where there is generally much more cultural acquiescence, a greater acceptance of literary and critical fiats issued from the western metropolis and a wider separation between political engagement and literary or critical pursuits. As an illustration of this I would like to examine not a text in discursive writing, but a novel – Ngugi's *Devil on The Cross* (1982) – as a statement in which several theoretical concepts converge. After writing four very successful and much-discussed novels in English –

Weep Not Child (1964), *The River Between* (1966), *A Grain of Wheat* (1967) and *Petals of Blood* (1977) – in all of which Conrad, Greene and Kafka are part of the shared background of the reader and the writer, Ngugi turned to a different kind of narrative in *Devil on The Cross*, which was first written in Gikuyu (*Caitaani Mutharabaini*). This was more than a mere linguistic switch. All texts, it is commonly agreed today, are reinscriptions upon already existing pre-texts. Since Gikuyu does not have a tradition of novel writing (though it has a long tradition of oral narrative), Ngugi did not have to operate within the unspoken framework on any novelistic conventions. The orality of culture in Gikuyu does not put the emphasis on the text as much as a culture based on the printed word does. Ngugi has elsewhere said that in his community 'the spoken word had a power well beyond the immediate and lexical meaning. Our appreciation of the suggesting magical power of language was reinforced by the games we played with words through riddles, proverbs, transposition of syllables, or through nonsensical but musically arranged words'[6] and through parables and stories that were exchanged on every social occasion and meeting. Ngugi tries to capture the quality not only in the texture of the narrative but also in the structure of the novel, which gradually unfolds in a freewheeling manner. Anecdotes are linked with episodes either in a chain or in backward loops, some introduced as fables that link traditional wisdom with contemporary situations, others as part of the realistic fabric of the narrative – all done in very broad strokes and not in the subtle and muted techniques of his earlier work.

From Ngugi's viewpoint the response to a novel is also an important aspect of its total value. 'The reception of a given work of art is part of the work itself; or rather the reception (or consumption) of the work completes the whole creative process involving that particular artistic object'. *Devil on The Cross* sold 15,000 copies in Gikuyu alone in one year, before being translated into Kiswahili and English. It was read out in homes, in buses, in offices during lunch breaks and in public bars, and was reintegrated back into the oral tradition. This appropriation of the novel into the tradition of group reception is an experience quite different from what happens to a printed text, where solitary enjoyment is the norm, reconfirming the one-to-one relationship between the author and the reader. Ngugi consciously attempts to de-isolate the phenomenon of literature and liquidate the distance between the educated few and the people, an important fact that all Third World writers have to come to terms with.

Between the publication of his last English novel (*Petals of Blood*) and the writing of *Devil on The Cross*, his first Gikuyu novel, several important things had happened to Ngugi, and one of them was his involvement with the community theatre in a village called Kamiriithu. The total participation of the community pointed out to him, more sharply than any theoretical argument could, the marginal nature of his earlier novels in English, where his material and his audience were 'geographically' separated. The unprecedented popularity of these plays, scripted and performed by the whole community, was seen as a threat to the government of independent Kenya, and Ngugi was imprisoned for a year without trial. *Devil on The Cross* was written when he was in prison; in Gikuyu, because with the English language one takes on certain conventions and expectations which he wanted to relinquish, and also because the language distanced him from those he wanted most to communicate with; and in the form of a novel, because the isolation of the prison cell precluded the possibility of any community activity like drama. The choric composition that he tried in drama was impossible in a novel, but he attempted a certain transparency in the narrative voice so that the individual point of view of the author would not obtrude.

Choice of the right narrative form was not enough for him unless he could forge a content that would engage the attention of his new audience by touching upon the weight and complexity of their daily struggle. For this purpose he chose a theme which was as much about the situation of a pathetic and exploited girl – a typist without a job, ousted by a landlord and jilted by her boy friend – as about the moral and spiritual chaos of present-day Kenya. Not only emotionally, but physically too the girl was a wreck; in her attempt to fit other models of beauty she painfully bleached her skin and straightened her hair. 'She could never appreciate the sheer splendour of her body. She yearned to change herself in covetous pursuit of the beauty of other selves'. The metaphoric intent is fairly overt. At the ending of the novel, two years later, the transformation of this once-exploited girl has taken place on several levels. She is a more confident and powerful individual now, in control of her life and destiny. Her choice of profession (she is now a skilful garage mechanic, with a degree from a polytechnic) itself is a declaration of her independence from both sexual and racial stereotyping. The battered and passive woman of the opening chapter emerges victorious at the end – and the ritual killing of the rich old man, her seducer and the symbolic figure of corruption and decadence, becomes a necessary act of exorcism. The gun shot at the end throws up melodramatic reverberations – it is certainly tendentious and also marked with a vague sentimentality. Ngugi, schooled in contemporary English fiction and its norms of obliqueness and understatement, could not have been unaware of the dangers of this ending. But he deliberately eschewed neutrality and opted for a mode and style that fitted with his ideology a newly emergent theory of literature which this novel seems to embody.

Several questions arise out of this experiment. Does changing the language itself guarantee a reversal of a process or is it merely a symbolic repudiation of an epistemic model which is indeed too deeply internalised? Ngugi of course does not change the language alone, but attempts to recast his entire narrative mode and change the writer-audience relationship – the production-consumption pattern in literature. Is this then to be seen as Ngugi's resistance to the centre's attempt to appropriate him, as it was about to do: a declaration of his independence from the western literary tradition in which he was schooled? It is significant that in the English translation of the novel, published by Heinemann, the jacket blurb tries to link the book with Bunyan's *Pilgrim's Progress* rather than with Gikuyu oral tradition, certainly indicating a continued effort at appropriation. Ngugi writing *Devil on The Cross* in Gikuyu is a crucial event both as an actual happening and as a gesture, highlighting not only the need to decolonise the mind but also the complex range of difficulties inherent in the attempt, because whether we want it or not, the irreversible process in the world today seems to be more towards homogenisation and standardisation, supported by market economy and political forces, than towards the maintainance of diversity and the autonomy of regional culture. Ngugi's action may be seen as more than an individual and isolated act; it may be seen as part of a strategy of resistance which the sensitive points at the periphery are bound to put up against the manipulation by the centre, and against the possibility of eventual absorption by it.

NOTES

1. George Eliot, *The Mill on the Floss* (1962), Book V, Ch.5.
2. This issue has been discussed in detail in my book *Realism and Reality: Novel and Society in India* (New Delhi: Oxford University Press, 1985).
3. Much of these writings are very recent, and some still unpublished. Some of those who have contributed to the new discourse on Bankimchandra Chatterjee are Partha Chatterjee, Sabyasachi Bhattacharya, Sudipto Kaviraj and Gayatri Spivak.
4. This faith in the sequence of English literary history as the universal sequence has sometimes gone to absurd lengths. Terms like Renaissance, Romantic Movement, Modernism, and Post-modernism have not only been used out of context but have been applied indiscriminately to what is supposed to be a similar historical progression in India. One dissenting voice comments: 'By planting a "Romantic Movement" in the virgin soil of our literary historiography, we hopefully tried to ensure the sprouting of a healthy crop of modern literature in all our languages'. See Sujit Mukherjee, *Towards a Literary History of India* (Simla, 1975), p. 18.
5. Ngugi wa Thiong'o, *Decolonising the Mind: The Politics of Language in African Literature* (London: James Currey, 1986), p. 11.
6. Ibid, p. 82.

Writing Oral History: SISTREN Theatre Collective's *Lionheart Gal*

Lionheart Gal: Life Stories of Jamaican Women is an experiment in narrative form that exemplifies the dialogic nature of oral/scribal and Creole/English discourse in Jamaican literature. For *Lionheart Gal* is dialogic in the old-fashioned, literal sense of that word: the text, with three notable exceptions, is the product of a dialogue in Creole and English between each woman of Sistren and Honor Ford Smith, the sister confessor, who herself confesses all in solitary script, immaculate in English.

In the fashionably modern, Bakhtinian sense of the word dialogic, *Lionheart Gal* is impeccably subversive. For it engenders an oral, Creole subversion of the authority of the English literary canon. Further, its autobiographical form – the lucid verbal flash – articulates a feminist subversion of the authority of the literary text as fiction – as transformative rewriting of the self in the *persona* of distanced, divine omniscience. *Lionheart Gal*, like much contemporary feminist discourse, does not pretend to be authoritative. Indeed, the preferred narrative mode of many feminist writers is the guise of intimate, understated domestic writing by women: letters, diaries or what Sistren, in an oral/Creole context, simply calls testimony. The simultaneously secular and religious resonances of 'testimony' intimate the potential for ideological development from the purely personal to the political that is the usual consequence of this process of communal disclosure.

It is important to distinguish between actual letters and diaries written by women, and the literary use of this sub-genre as fictional frame. For the artifice of these feminist narrative forms is that they are artless, the author having receded in Joycean detachment to pare, and perhaps paint her fingernails, leaving the tape-recorder or word-processor on automatic. For example, Alice Walker in *The Color Purple* describes herself as 'A.W., author and medium', and courteously 'thank[s] everybody in this book for coming'.[1] She presumably ghost writes the text.

With *Lionheart Gal* this feminist illusion of narrative artlessness is complicated by the mediating consciousness of Honor Ford Smith, the editorial persona who performs a dual function in the making of the text.

As testifier, Honor records her own story in 'Grandma's Estate'. As amanuensis, she transcribes the testimonies of the other Sistren (except for 'Ava's Diary' and 'Red Ibo'), shaping the women's responses to her three leading questions: 'How did you first become aware of the fact that you were oppressed as a woman? How did that experience affect your life? How have you tried to change it?'[2]

The full weight of that unprepossessing 'with' on the title page – 'SISTREN with Honor Ford Smith, editor' – is revealed in the polemical 'Introduction', particularly in the section 'How This Book Was Made'. The editorial explanation of the collaborative process is an illuminating sub-text, as interesting as the stories themselves. For the 'Introduction' offers an ideological frame for the stories that defines the boundaries of their meaning: the stories assume a sociological authority that the improvisational authorial process cannot readily support. The sociologist, Herman McKenzie, in his review of the text, issues an instructive caveat:

> There are methodological doubts, however, which make me feel that perhaps it is wiser to view these stories as illustrative of generalizations previously arrived at by other means, rather than as providing an independent basis for such generalizations about women in Jamaica.[3]

Editorial intervention in the making of the text is clearly an important issue in *Lionheart Gal*. Evelyn O'Callaghan argues that 'the life stories related in *Lionheart Gal* stand somewhere *between* fiction and research data. These stories have been so shaped by selection, editing, rewriting and publication that they have become to a large extent ... "fictionalized".'[4] As editor, Honor seems to doctor the text – less in the pejorative sense of that word and more in the sense of obstetrician. This metaphor signifies both the active creativity of the labouring woman telling her story, and the somewhat more passive efficiency of the enabling mid-wife dilating the passage of the text. This distinction between text and story, between ideological necessity and narrative autonomy, is central to the problem of authorship and authority in *Lionheart Gal*.

In her 'Introduction' Honor acknowledges a methodological uncertainty in the making of *Lionheart Gal*: a tension between illustration and testimony – what I call text and story:

> This book started life as a documentation of the work of the theatre collective. The first section was to put the work in the context of Jamaican society and focus on the conditions of life of Jamaican women. It was to include testimonies from Sistren as illustrations of pre-determined themes and then discuss how we work on our plays. Soon it was clear that the testimonies would not sit neatly into an introductory section.

They refused to become supporting evidence of predetermined factors. They threatened to take over the entire project and they would not behave.

So, in the end we gave up trying to trim them and silence them and we decided to change the nature of the entire project. (pp. xxvi-xxvii)

Lionheart Gal does not entirely transcend its ambiguous origins in social history; but perhaps it oughtn't to. For as Herman McKenzie concedes in his lively critique, the hybrid nature of the text is a major source of its appeal:

The collection, therefore, while its mode of presentation (and appeal) places it firmly within the arts, suggests conclusions that challenge social scientists to consider both the problems as well as potential contributions, not to say advantages, of this approach.[5]

Indeed, the ideological frame does not totally circumscribe the range of meanings of the stories. For *Lionheart Gal* is literary less by intent than intuition. Somewhat like *Jane and Louisa Will Soon Come Home* (whose author Erna Brodber once artlessly described herself as 'innocent of literature'),[6] *Lionheart Gal* subverts the conventional generic boundaries between literature and social document, between autobiography and fiction, between the oral and the scribal traditions.

As story, *Lionheart Gal* is for the most part clearly oral. The language of narration is Creole, employing proverb, earthy metaphors and folk tale structures, particularly repetition and apparent digression. In addition, the rural setting of many of the stories reinforces the sense of a 'folk' perspective. The life stories illustrate what Derek Walcott calls the 'symmetry' of the folk tale: 'The true folk tale concealed a structure as universal as the skeleton, the one armature from Br'er Anancy to King Lear. It kept the same digital rhythm of three movements, three acts, three moral revelations'.[7] In the case of *Lionheart Gal*, narrative structure is shaped by Honor's three informing questions which compress female experience into riddle. Decoding the riddle is the key to identity and the moral of the fable.

As text, *Lionheart Gal* somewhat ironically affirms the authority of the written word. Documenting the ideological development of the women of the Sistren Theatre Collective cannot, apparently, be fully accomplished in the medium of theatre. The plays do not adequately speak for themselves: thus the scribal intention of the original project. Further, the search for what Honor calls a 'throughline for each story' (p. xxviii) superimposes on these misbehaving oral accounts a decidedly scribal narrative necessity. The circular line of oral narration becomes diametrically opposed to the ideological, scribal throughline.

This oral/scribal contradiction is quintessentially Creole/English. For, as Honor observes somewhat evangelically in her 'Introduction':

> Those who speak standard English easily are usually middle class. They usually write in English, but a few also write in Patwah (usually poetry or drama only). Those who are working- class and speak Patwah, write English too – or at least very few write Patwah (usually poetry or drama). This means that Patwah is written for performance, which is excellent, but what is not excellent is that it is not written for silent reflection or for purposes other than entertainment. Yet we all know that Jamaican people reflect all the time in their heads or in conversations in Patwah, and we also know that reflection is part of the process of gaining control over one's own life. So, why are certain kinds of written language still dominated totally by English? (pp. xxviii- ix)

This is the seminal/ovular question. But Honor's own written performance, both in 'Grandma's Estate'[8] and the elaborate 'Introduction' serves to confirm not the appropriateness of the Creole mother tongue, but the imperial authority of the English father tongue – more often phallic pen – as the instrument of serious, written reflection. But perhaps it is indelicate to notice: the subversive subverted.

In an unpublished 1986 conference paper, entitled 'Creole and the Jamaican Novelist: Redcam, DeLisser and V.S. Reid', Victor Chang, more sceptical than Honor, poses a series of challenging questions to our writers, which *Lionheart Gal* as story, if not as text, eloquently answers:

> We have been increasingly told that the resources for expression in Creole are no more limited than in Standard English. If this is so, why then is it not used for internal musing and reflection? Could it be that there is still a persistent belief that Creole just will not serve in certain situations, that certain registers require Standard English, or that our writers still have yet to learn to manipulate the Creole with total freedom? Perhaps it could be argued that the very spoken nature of the Creole, its very physicality, militates against its use for inner reflection and introspection.[9]

Recognising the dialogic nature of oral/scribal and Creole/English discourse in the story/text *Lionheart Gal* and seeking to narrow the social distance between the language of the stories and the language of textual analysis, I wish to engage in an experimental Creole subversion of the authority of English as our exclusive voice of scholarship. My analysis of the testimonies of the women of Sistren – their verbal acts of introspective self-disclosure – will now proceed in Creole.

'We come together and talk our life story and put it in a lickle scene'. (p. 72) A so Ava seh Sistren start off: a tell one anodder story. So yu tell, me tell, so tell di whole a we find out seh a di one story we a tell. Oman story. Di same ting over an over. But it no easy fi get up tell people yu business ma! It tek plenty heart. So Foxy seh eena fi her story. She seh:

> Plenty women used to talk bout di children dat we have and di baby-faada problem. At first me was shy to talk about myself. Di impression women always give me is dat dem is a set of people who always lap dem tail, tek yuh name spread table cloth. Me did feel sort a funny at di time, having children fi two different man, especially since me never like Archie. Me never discuss it wid nobody. When me come meet Didi and hear she talk bout her baby faada and how she hate him after she get pregnant, me say, 'Well if yuh can say your own me can say mine, for we actually deh pon di same ting.' Me and she start talk bout it. (p. 253)

An a di same Foxy she come find out seh dat di tings dem dat happen to we jus because we a oman, dem deh tings supposin fi call 'politics', jus like any a di odder big tings deh, weh a gwan eena 'politricks' as di one Tosh him seh. Den wat a way dem kill him off ee! Me no know if a big Politics dat, or a lickle politics, but someting mus eena someting. But dat is anodder story. An di ile dat fry sprat cyaan fry jack, so small fry all like me no suppose fi business eena dem deh tings.

So hear how Foxy seh she start fi find out bout dis oman politics:

> Tings develop so-till we start meet more people and talk bout woman and work and woman and politics. We discuss what is politics and how it affect woman. After we done talk ah get to feel dat di little day-to-day tings dat happen to we as women, is politics too. For instance, if yuh tek yuh pickney to hospital and it die in yuh hand – dat is politics. If yuh do someting to yuh own child dat damage him or her fi di future, dat is politics. If yuh man box yuh down, dat is politics. But plenty politicians don't tink dose tings have anything to do wid politics. (p. 253)

A true. For yu cyaan understan 'di little day-to-day tings dat happen to we as women' if yu no understan seh dat di whole ting set up gainst plenty oman from di day dem born. Tek for instance how so much a di oman dem weh a tell dem story eena *Lionheart Gal* jus find out seh dem pregnant. Yes! It come een like a big surprise. Grab bag. A no nuttin dem plan for. A no like how yu hear dem people pon radio and t.v. a tell yu seh 'Two is better than too many' – like seh pickney is sums: add an multiply an divide an subtract! Wear yu down to nuttin. Nought. Dat a weh pregnant do plenty oman. Not even oman good. Young gal. Force ripe an blighted.

But even though life hard, di oman dem still a try. Hear how Barbara put it:

> Di pregnancy a never someting me plan or choose. It just happen. Nadine born '71. After she born, me did just love her. Me always feel a tenderness inside me dat me no waan do notten fi hurt her. At di same time me no pet her till she spoil. (p. 138)

But oman an pickney cyaan live pon so-so love. An a when di oman dem start fi try fi find lickle work dat story come to bump. For a den di politics beat dem down. Ongle certain kind a people fi do certain kind a work. An dawg nyam yu supper if *yu* no one a dem. All yu fi do a fi look after odder people business. Yu no have no business fi look after. Dat a weh happen to Doreen. Never even get a chance fi go a day school. Pure evening school, an nah learn nuttin:

> Me did waan learn, for me did waan be nurse, or a teacher, but me couldn't grasp notten. Me know definitely seh if me no pass di exam, me nah go get di job me did want. As di months pass by and me see seh me couldn't manage di work in di evening school, me know dere and den seh me nah go noweh in life. After school, ah used to walk past di residential areas and wish it was in deh me live. Sometime me used to pretend seh me live deh and dat me get fi go a school like dem pickney. (p. 92)

So now when pickney problem jine aan pon no-get-fi-go-a-no-good-school, cyaan get no work, haffi a siddown wait pon man fi set yu up, dat a when de politics get hot. Dat a Didi story. Hear her:

> Sometime when yuh no have notten and yuh have di pickney dem and dem a look to yuh fi food and fi shelter, yuh haffi do sometings weh yuh no really waan fi do, just fi survive. Sometimes a better yuh cyaan do, mek yuh tek certain man. Sometime yuh really in need. A man might use dat fi ketch yuh. Yuh might know a so it go, but yuh in need. Yuh want it, so yuh haffi tek it. (p. 201)

But a no all di time yu cyan tek it. For might-as-well turn eena livin hell. For now man all waan beat yu if yu no mek up yu mind fi do weh *him* seh. An if yu married to him, dat no mek no difference. It could a all worse, for now him directly feel dat him own yu. Dat a di prekkeh Yvonne get herself een. She seh:

> Ah say ah have me three pickney now and ah married. Dem time deh when yuh married, dem say yuh married fi life. Ah never expect fi me and him separate. Me depress and unhappy. Everyting just get confuse inna me brain. Me feel seh me life mash up tru me never understand bout sex and man. Me never know what me could a do bout di problem. Me say is everyday problem. It cyaan change. Me grow in it. A so life hard. Me no chat to nobody more dan so. Me no know no odder woman fi talk to. Me never have no consideration. Me, like me unconscious. (p. 151)

Dem deh blow good fi kill yu. Lick yu down flat. Di ongle ting fi bring yu back from grave-side a fi find out seh a no yu one. Odder oman eena di ring wid yu a go help yu pen up di bull. So yu talk, act out yu lickle scene, an nex ting – yu eena book.

So how dem mek di book? Accorden to di ring-leader, Honor, di whole ting start off wid she a ask di Sistren dem question bout how dem grow up, an di different different tings dat happen to dem fi mek dem find out seh life hard. An dem go roun and roun, an talk an talk, like dem a play 'Show me yu Motion'. All dis time dem a tape everyting dem seh. Den Honor she listen back to di tape an fix-up fix-up wat she tink di Sistren dem a seh, an dem gwan talk an talk so tell dem en up wid las version. An den dem write it down.

Plenty a di story dem soun like a so di oman dem talk. But some a dem mek me wonder. Dem no soun so caseer. Tek for instance 'Ava's Diary'. It kind a mix-up mix-up. It come een like seh how she talk a her yard eena war wid how dem did want her fi talk an write a school; an di school nah win! See't ya now:

> Since me and the children are alone, if a man come to me other than him, I would have to leave them and go out with him. Therefore I have decided not to have any relationship with another man for the time being.
>
> Bertie know seh me no have no man friend, so him come if him want to come, till me and him start to talk good and him start come intensively. (p. 271)

Den now, 'Grandma's Estate' an 'Red Ibo'. Me never like how di two a dem jus prims up demself eena so-so English. An dem no inna no talkin business me dear; a pure write dem a write. School definitely win out yasso. An it look like seh Honor did know seh people a go ask her bout it, for she try fi clear up herself. She seh:

> With the two middle-strata members of the group, the oral interviews did not work well. Accustomed to standard English and the conventions of academic expression, their stories sounded stilted when spoken, full of jargon, and hollow. Both 'Red Ibo' and 'Grandma's Estate' were written responses to the interview questions. (p. xxviii)

An yu know, me think me understan: Parson christen dem pickney first. But me still seh, supposin dem did gi we di chance fi hear wat dem did *seh*? Maybe notten never did wrong wid it. Den nex ting: It no soun like seh dem a seh seh dem cyaan *talk* good, dem cyan ongle *write* good? Me no know; me just a wonder.

Den again, yu no see seh fi dem story no personally deal wid no man an oman business to dat; no lickle rudeness. But me nah seh dem faint-a-heart because dem nah tell people di whole a fi dem personal an private business – like di odder lionheart gal dem! Is jus dat fi dem story come een like seh yu a try fi explain yu self, yu know seh people a listen, so yu haffi fix it up. 'Red Ibo' story all soun like seh she a preach. But no testimony meeting! Everybody a testify inna dem owna way. But me dear mek me lef it. For puss an dawg no have di same luck, an me no waan nobody seh a bad mind me bad mind mek me a ask dem ya lickle question.

An still for all, yu haffi gi it to dem. A true seh Ella an Red Ibo story soun like book. But wat is fi yu cyaan be un fi yu. An more time dem still ketch a nice lickle roots vibe inna di English. Hear how Red Ibo she start off fi her story cultural: 'When I think of childhood, I think of a village squatting on hillslopes with a river running through it and a bridge and a fording midway along the road which ran by the river'. (p. 221) An a Ella granny nearly spoil up di poor lickle pickney. No want her fi ask no question bout her people dem. She fi go read book. Not even play di lickle pickney cyaan play. Poor ting. She seh:

> I packed leaves of croton and pimento into a basket I found in the kitchen. I twisted a piece of cloth into a cotta and put it on my head. I placed the basket on top of it and practised walking while balancing it on my head. Then I stepped off down the pathway arriving with my produce under Grandma's window. 'Lady, Lady, yuh want anyting to buy, maam?' I readjusted the basket, which proved difficult to control.
>   At first there was no answer, so I repeated 'Lady, Lady, yuh want anyting to buy, maam?'
>   My grandmother pushed her head through the window.
>   'Ella! Come inside at once and put down that basket!'
>   I obeyed.
>   'What do you think you are doing, Miss?'
>   'Playing market woman, Grandma,' I said, not sure what I had done wrong.
>   'Never let me see you doing that again.'
>   'Why grandma?' I asked. 'What is wrong with market ladies?'
>   'Ladies? They are not ladies. They are women. Go and take a seat in your room.'
> [pp. 180-81]

A so it go. *Lionheart Gal* is a serious book. An oonu better read it. It might a lickle hard fi ketch di spellin fi di first, but after yu gwan gwan, it not so bad. Den one ting sweet me: Yu know how some a fi we people simple; from dem see sinting set down eena book dem tink it important. So now plenty a dem who never go a none a Sistren play, dem same one a go read Sistren book, because book high. Dem a go get ketch. For a six a one, half a dozen a di odder: oman problem, man problem, pickney problem. Plenty politics. An whole heap a joke! For yu know how we know how fi tek bad tings mek joke. Stop yu from mad go off yu head. Doreen know how it go. Hear her nuh:

> All my life, me did haffi act in order to survive. Di fantasies and ginnalship were ways of coping wid di frustration. Now me can put dat pain on stage and mek fun a di people who cause it.

Go deh, Sistren! Last lick sweet.

NOTES

1. Alice Walker, *The Color Purple* (1982; New York: Washington Square Press, 1983), p. 253.

2. SISTREN with Honor Ford Smith, editor, *Lionheart Gal: Life Stories of Jamaican Women* (London: The Women's Press, 1986), p. xxvii. Subsequent references cited parenthetically in text.

3. Herman McKenzie, Review of *Lionheart Gal, Jamaica Journal*, 20, 4 (Nov. 1987-Jan.1988), p. 64.

4. Evelyn O'Callaghan, Review of *Lionheart Gal, Journal of West Indian Literature*, 2, 1 (Dec. 1987), p. 93.

5. McKenzie, op. cit., p. 63.

6. In an unpublished talk to students in the West Indian Literature class, Department of English, U.W.I., Mona, 1984.

7. Derek Walcott, 'What the Twilight Says: An Overture' in *Dream on Monkey Mountain and Other Plays* (New York: Farrar, Straus and Giroux, 1970), p. 24.

8. Ella *does* use Creole when she role plays as the market lady: ' "Lady, Lady, yuh want anything to buy, maam?" I readjusted the basket, which proved difficult to control.' (p. 180). A Freudian slip?

9. Victor Chang, 'Creole and the Jamaican Novelist: Redcam, Delisser and V.S. Reid', Sixth Annual Conference on West Indian Literature, U.W.I., St. Augustine, 1986, p. 5.

Constitutive Graphonomy: A Post-Colonial Theory of Literary Writing

The written text is a social situation. That is to say, it has its existence in something more than the marks on the page, namely the participations of social beings whom we call writers and readers, and who constitute the writing as communication of a particular kind, as 'saying' a certain thing. Just as the sociologist attempts to uncover structures and regularities in social situations, so it is assumed that the meaning of writing is an *a priori* to be uncovered existing either as a function of the language, or the inscription of something in the mind of the writer, or the reconstruction of the reader's experience. Constitutive Graphonomy, the constitutive ethnography of writing systems, is concerned to examine the objective meanings of writing as social accomplishments of these participants. This is because meaning is a social fact which comes to being within the discourse of a culture, and social facts as well as social structures are themselves social accomplishments.

Constitutive Graphonomy is a post-colonial literary theory. It can be described as such for several reasons: it affirms the fact that a literary theory is a cultural formation; it resists the reification of the art form out of its social and cultural provenance; it confirms the text as originating in material practice at a dual site of production and consumption; it contributes to a dismantling of our nominal and largely unexamined assumptions of literary definition, reassessing what kinds of writing 'fit' or could be considered to fit into the category 'literature'; it questions the assumptions of the process of ascribing merit through critical practice. But above all it focuses the meaning event within the usage of social actors who present themselves to each other as functions in the text, and by its privileging of cultural distance at the site of this usage it resolves the conflict between language, reader and writer over the 'ownership' of meaning. These characteristics do not represent an 'essential' feature of post-colonial theory, nor are they necessarily exclusive to it. Rather they are individual and overlapping features of this particular discursive formation.

Clearly the notion of the text as dialectical accomplishment requires some clarification, since our assumption of the givenness of texts is supported at the very least by the evidence of their physical tangibility. To the question, 'How do you mean?', we could say that the *meaning* of a word is *meant* by the person who utters it and is *taken to mean* something by the person who hears it. As a radical over-simplification of the history of European literary theory we could say that such history has been an arena in which all of these participants – the language, the utterer or writer, and the hearer or reader – have been locked in a gladitorial contest over the ownership of meaning. But on closer examination it can be seen that all three 'functions' of this exchange participate in the 'social' situation of the written text. The constant insistence of that discourse which operates through hybridity and marginality is that writing is a social practice. There is simply no room in post-colonial literature for a reified art that 'exists for its own sake'. Admittedly, the political impetus of post-colonial theory has been to focus meaning at the site of production. But such theory is in a unique position to resolve some of the lingering questions of European theory because it exists in a permanent and creative tension with the metropolitan centre and its privileging of standard code, intrinsic value and veridical truth.

Meaning is a social accomplishment characterised by the participation of the writer and reader 'functions' within the 'event' of the particular discourse. Meaning may thus be called a 'situated accomplishment' – a term which takes into account the necessary presence of these functions and the situation in which the meaning occurs. It is easy to see the understanding reached in conversation as a 'situated accomplishment', for the face-to-face interaction enables a virtually limitless adjustment to the flow of talk. The central feature of such activity is *presence*, the presence of the speaker and the hearer to each other constituting language as communication. Yet even in the most empathetic exchange the speaker and hearer are never fully present to one another. The experience of one conversant can never *become* the experience of the other: the 'mind' is a retrospective and largely hypothetical concomitant to what is 'revealed' in language. Meaning and understanding of meaning can occur because the language encodes the reciprocity of the experiences of each conversant. It is the situation, the *'event'* of this reciprocal happening which 'tells', which 'refers', which 'informs'.

The example of conversation alerts us to the extent and the limitation of the structuring activities of individuals in any social situation. No person is a totally free agent, for that would be to deny the effects of society, culture, and history upon the individual and the situation in which s/he is acting. But neither is s/he purely a cypher for broader social forces. The situation, with all its attendant antecedents operates in conjunction with rather than *upon* the participating individuals. And though these individuals can direct or unleash the potentialities of the antecedents, affecting the situation, they cannot change them. The apparently simple example of a casual conversation clearly demonstrates the complex array of structuring participations in the social event. But it is the 'event', the *situation* of its structure and structuring participations rather than the contingent intentions or psychological sates of speakers, which imparts a direction and a meaning to the conversation.

The discursive 'event', the site of the 'communication', therefore becomes of paramount importance in post-colonial literatures because the 'participants' are potentially so very 'absent'. Indeed, unlike spoken discourse, the central problematic of studies of writing is *absence*. It is not so easy to see the written meaning as the 'situated accomplishment' of participants because the message 'event' occupies the apparent social fissure between the acts of writing and reading, the discursive space in which writer and reader as social actors never meet. Whether the writing is a newspaper article, instructions for the assembly of a model aeroplane, or a philosophical treatise, the writer and reader have access to each other only through the mutual construction of the text within certain linguistic and generic parameters. That distance between minds, which seems to be compensated for in the spoken conversation by the situation of the dialogue, would appear to elude writing. The written text stands apart in its own material integrity, apparently unrelated to persons, to language or to social systems in any purely mechanical or isomorphic way, but grounded in the semiotic systems by which such persons and systems are imputed. How meaning is constructed in the writing by its absentee users becomes a central question in writing studies and is made much more salient by post-colonial writing systems in which writer and reader might have ranges of experience and presuppositions which may not be expected to overlap greatly, if at all. The additional perspective which the consideration of post-colonial literatures brings to this discussion is obviously their accentuation of this phenomenon of *distance*: they present us with writers and readers far more 'absent' from each other than they would be if located in the same culture; they present a situation which in some cases (because the genre of written prose is so removed from some cultures) provides a totally ambivalent site for communication. One qualification to this may be that the sharing of an imperial system of education and cultural patronage, issuing forth in the widespread uniformity of curriculae, readers, and other cultural 'guides' used throughout Britain's empire, considerably ameliorates this distancing within the post-colonial world. But even in the monoglossic settler cultures the sub-cultural distancing which generates the evolution of variant language shows that the linguistic cultures encompassed by the term 'English' are vastly heterogeneous. Most importantly, post-colonial literatures provide, through the metonymic function of language variance, a writing which actually *installs* distance and absence in the interstices of the text.

The face-to-face situation of spoken discourse is replaced by the distanciation of the writing system, a distance which frees the meaning from the constraints of speech and creates a vehicle which at once confirms and bridges the absence of writers and readers. As writing, the message event is not merely a different physical mode, but a different ontological event. Derrida claims that:

> Inscription alone ... has the power to arouse speech from its slumber as sign. By enregistering speech, inscription has as its essential objective ... the emancipation of meaning ... from the natural predicament in which everything refers to the disposition of a contingent situation. This is why writing will never be simple 'voice painting' (Voltaire). It creates meaning by enregistering it, by entrusting it to an engraving, a groove, a relief, to a surface whose essential characteristic is to be infinitely transmissible.[1]

By freeing language from the contingent situation, writing, paradoxically, gives language its greatest permanence, whilst, at the same time, giving meaning its greatest volatility, because it opens up horizons within which many more sets of relations then those pertaining to the contingent situation can be established. Writing does not merely inscribe the spoken message or represent the message event, it *becomes* the new event. Nor is it merely the inscription of thought without the medium of speech, for such thought is only accessible as a putative associate of the event. Post-colonial literature reveals this most clearly when its appropriation of English, far from inscribing either vernacular or 'standard' forms, creates a new discourse at their interface. Post-colonial writing *represents* neither speech nor local reality but constructs a discourse which may intimate them. This distinction ought to be made as clearly as possible. While writing is a new ontological event it does not cut itself off from the voice. The inscription of the vernacular modality of local speech is one of the strategies by which a 'marginal' linguistic culture appropriates the imported language to its own conceptions of society and place. This discourse also questions the Derridian conclusion that writing is infinitely transmissable and hence infinitely interpretable. Infinite transmissability assumes a totally homogeneous world. It elides the political and cultural limits of interpretation and subsumes all writing into a universalist paradigm which is essentially that of the metropolitan centre.

The danger exists that within this universalist paradigm writing may become reified. In fact, this problem begins with structuralist linguistics, which tends to reify the linguistic code. In Saussure's distinction between *langue* and *parole, langue* is the code or set of codes on the basis of which a speaker produces *parole*, a particular message.[2] While *langue*, the description of the synchronic systems of language, is the object of linguistics, the *parole*, the language in use, the intentional message, focuses a study of language on its actual operation. Now *parole* is precisely what Saussure's *Course in General Linguistics* (1916) is *not* about, and ever since its publication, linguistics, the handmaiden of structuralism, has bracketed the message in order to concentrate on the code, in which it is primarily interested.

A post-colonial approach to linguistics, however, redresses this imbalance by focusing on the message, reinstating the *parole* as the realisation of the code in social life. This has the consequence of re-establishing the 'margins' of language as the substance of theory. This reassertion of the margins of language use over the dominance of a standard code, a centre, is the most exciting conclusion of the theory of the 'creole continuum'.[3] But it is also instrumental in conceiving the discourse of the post-colonial as rooted in conflict and struggle, as 'counter-discourse',[4] since the perpetual confrontation with a 'standard code' is that which constructs the language. This does not mean the replacement of one canon for another, or the reconstruction of the centre which is being subverted. Such a re-orientation emphasises the fact that the code is abstracted from the activity, and re-installs the priority of the practical or constitutive semiology of the message. This observation reveals that language has its only practical existence in the *parole* within which the usage of members, rather than a supervenient system or *a priori* referentiallity, determines meanings. This becomes particularly true of english in which the notion of a standard 'code' is dismantled by the continuum of practices by which the language is constituted.

This constitutive semiology radically modifies the most fundamental tenets of Saussurian theory, namely;

> (a) That in semiotic system there are *differences* but no substantial existence. No entity belonging to the structure of the system has a meaning of its own; the meaning of a word, for example, results from the opposition to the other lexical units of the same system.

> (b) That all systems are closed, without relation to external, non-semiotic reality.[5]

While it is certainly true that meaning is not necessarily determined by the external relation of a sign and a thing, meaning *is* determined within the relations actualised within the *message* rather than those purely abstracted in the system. In short, language is a social medium for individuals rather than a self sufficient system of inner relationships. Though it does not determine meaning ostensively, it is a social act within which reality is determined. Consequently, the message event marks the terrain of meaning for the written work, for only the message event gives currency to language within the relations of social beings. Neither the mental lives of speakers and writers nor the objects of their talk can usurp this fundamental concern.

Constitutive Graphonomy reassesses traditional approaches to meaning such as those in speech act theory.[6] While we can inscribe the propositional content of a speech act we cannot, for instance, inscribe its illocutionary force. Such force is carried in the situation of the message. Both the illocutionary and perlocutionary force of the sign THIS WAY are embodied entirely in its character as sign and the social conventions surrounding its role. Similar conventions surround and determine the forms of different kinds of writing, particularly those given the designation 'literary'. The illocutionary force of these texts similarly cannot be *conveyed* by means of grammar, italics, and punctuation, but rather is actualised constitutively in the conventional practice – the situation – of the reading. The writing 'event' thus becomes the centre of the accomplishment of meaning, for it is here that the system, the social world of its users, and the absent 'participants' themselves, intersect.

The post-colonial affirms the orientation of writing to the message event. The immense 'distance' between author and reader in the cross-cultural or sub-cultural text undermines the privilege of both subject and object and opens meaning to a relational dialectic which 'emancipates' it.[7] This emancipation, however, is limited by the 'absence' which is inscribed in the cross-cultural text, the gulf of silence installed by strategies of language variance which signify its difference. Inscription therefore does not 'create meaning' by enregistering it; it initiates meaning to a horizon of relationships cirsumscribed by that silence which ultimately cannot be traversed by an interpretation. It is this silence, the active assertion of the post-colonial text, rather than any culture-specific concept of meaning, which questions metropolitan notions of polysemy and resists the absorption of post-colonial literature into the universalist paradigm. We can thus see how important is the cross-cultural literary text in questions of meaning. Nothing better describes to us the distance traversed in the social engagement which occurs when authors write and readers read. But it is clear that the distances *are* traversed. Writing comes into being at the intersection of the sites of production and consumption. Although the 'social relationship' of the two absent subjects is actually a function of their access to the 'situation' of the writing, it is in this threefold interaction of situation, author function, and reader function that meaning is accomplished.

LANGUAGE

We may now examine more closely the contending claims in the struggle for the dominance of meaning. The first of these is language, which is commonly held to embody or contain meaning either by direct representation or, in a more subtle way, by determining the perception of the world. Constitutive Graphonomy raises the question of language to prominence because language that exists in complexity, hybridity and constant change inevitably rejects the assumption of a linguistic structure or code which can be characterised by the colonial distinction of 'standard' and 'variant'. All language is 'marginal'; all language emerges out of conflict and struggle. The post-colonial text brings language and meaning to a discursive site in which they are mutually constituted, and at this site the importance of usage is inescapable.

Although the view is rarely expressed by anyone conversant with languages in different cultures that language 'represents' or 'reflects' an autonomous reality, it is probably the most ubiquitous Western assumption about the operation of language because our sense of how words mean operates within a discourse in which the world (the object) is irremediably separated from the speaker (the subject). The Lockian separation of subject and object, the separation of the consciousness from the world of which it is conscious, is the schema which still underlies the modern Western episteme with its passion for 'scientific' objectivity and its tendency to see the world as a continuum of technological data. Such a view is possibly the most crucial factor separating Western society from those societies in which much (though not all) post-colonial literature is generated. The view of language which this schema installs is best represented by the theories of 'reference' which dominated Anglo-empiricism in the earlier part of this century, but which still hold sway in most empirical philosophies. According to this view words have referents in the real world, and what a word refers to is, for all intents and purposes, what it means.

But words are never so simply referential in the actual dynamic habits of a speaking community. Even the most simple words like 'hot', 'big', 'man',

64

'got', 'ball', and 'bat', have a number of meanings, depending on how they are used. Indeed, these uses are the ways (and therefore what) the word means in certain circumstances. A word such as 'bat' can operate as a noun with several referents or as a verb describing several kinds of action. Many other words, such as 'bush' (which has found hundreds of uses in post-colonial societies), reveal that the meaning of words is also inextricably tied to the discourse of place. Post-colonial literature has continually shown both the importance of this discourse and the inescapable linking of meaning to the usage within the event. In his novel *The Voice* Gabriel Okara demonstrates the almost limitless prolixity of the words 'inside' and 'insides' to describe the whole range of human volition, experience, emotion and thought.[7] Brought to the site of meaning which stands at the intersection between two separate cultures, the word demonstrates the total dependence of that meaning upon its 'situated-ness'.

Language cannot, therefore, be said to perform its hermeneutic function by reflecting or referring to the world in a purely contingent way, and thus meanings cannot remain exclusively accessible to those speakers who 'experience their referents', so to speak. The central feature of the ways in which words mean things in spoken or written discourse is the situation of the word. In general, one may see how the word is meant by the way it functions in the sentence, but the meaning of a word may require considerably more than a sentence for it to be adequately situated. The question remains whether it is the responsibility of the author in the cross-cultural text to employ techniques which more promptly 'situate' the word or phrase for the reader. While post-colonial writing has led to a profusion of technical innovation which exists to span the purported gap between writer and prospective reader, the process of reading itself is a continual process of contextualisation and adjustment directly linked to the constitutive relations within the discursive event.

An alternative, determinist view which proposes that language actually constructs that which is perceived and experienced by speakers is less problematic for post-colonial literature. Edward Sapir proposed the exciting and revolutionary view that what we call the 'real' world is built up by the language habits of a group, and that the worlds in which different societies live are quite distinct, not merely the same world with different labels attached.[9] The central idea of Whorf and Sapir's thesis is well known. It proposes that language functions not simply as a device for reporting experience, but also, and more significantly, as a way of defining experience of its speakers:

... the linguistic system (in other words, the grammar) of each language is not merely a reproducing instrument for voicing ideas but rather is itself the shaper of ideas, the program and guide for the individual's mental activity, for his analysis of impressions, for his synthesis of his mental stock in trade ... We dissect nature along the line laid down for us by our native languages. The categories and types that we isolate from the world of phenomena we do not find there because they stare every observer in the face; on the contrary, the world is presented in a kaleidoscopic flux of impressions which has to be organised in our minds – and this means by the linguistic system in our minds. [10]

But even this more attractive view of the link between language and the world may give rise to a number of objections from constitutive theory. Clearly, language offers one set of categories and not another for speakers to organise and describe experience, but to assume that language *creates* meanings in the minds of speakers misconceives the way in which meaning is constituted in discourse. While it is quite clear that language is more than a 'reproducing instrument for voicing ideas' (for what do thoughts or ideas look like apart from their expression in language?), the same objections can be applied to the idea of language as the 'shaper' or 'programmer' of ideas. Such ideas are still inaccessible apart from language. To possess a language is to possess a technique, not necessarily a quantum of knowledge about the world; and therefore it is tautological to say that one speaker 'sees' the world in the same way as another because they share a technique for putting certain rules into practice – the 'seeing' is embedded in the practice. To speak of language as 'shaping' ideas also logically leads to the identification of one particular 'shaping' with a particular language, or more commonly, with the use of language in a particular place. This sort of identification leaves itself no conceptual room to cope with the phenomenon of second language use or vernacular linguistic variance, for it is only in the most metaphorical sense that we can talk about a speaker 'seeing' a different world when s/he speaks in a second language.

But it is the situation of discourse rather than the linguistic system in the speaker's mind in which the 'obligatory terms' of language are structured. For instance, Whorf's discovery that Inuit languages have a variety of words for 'snow', thus suggesting they see the world differently from non-Inuits, overlooks the fact that skiers of all languages have a similar variety of words for snow, but could hardly be said to see the world differently in the way Whorf means. The meaning and nature of perceived reality are not determined within the minds of the users, nor even within the language itself, but within the use, within the multiplicity of relationships which operate in the system. Margaret Atwood makes an interesting reference to a North American Indian language which has no noun-forms, only verb-forms. In such a linguistic culture the experience of the world remains in continual process. Such a language cannot exist if language is either anterior or posterior to the world but reinforces the notion that language inhabits the world, *in practice*. The semantic component of the sentence is contained in the syntax: the meaning of a word or phrase is its use in the language, a use which has nothing to do with the kind of world a user 'has in his or her head'.

What the speaker 'has in mind', like a linguistic system or culture, or intentions or meanings, is only accessible in the 'retrospective' performance of speaking. The categories which language offers to describe the world are easily mistaken to shape something in the mind because we naturally assume that, like the rules of chess, we hold the linguistic system 'in our minds', in advance of the world. But language is co-extensive with social reality, not because it causes a certain perception of the world, but because it is inextricable from that perception.

Languages exist, therefore, neither before the fact nor after the fact but *in the fact*. Languages constitute reality in an obvious way: they provide some terms and not others with which to talk about the world. Because they provide a limited lexicon they may also be said (metaphorically) to 'use' the speaker, rather than vice versa. But the worlds constituted in this way do not become fixed composites in the speaker's mind, a set of images which differs, by definition, from the set in the mind of the speaker of a different language. Worlds exist by means of languages, their horizons extending as far as the processes of neologism, innovation, tropes and imagination will allow the horizons of the language itself to be extended.

THE READER FUNCTION IN THE WRITING

If the written text is a social situation, the post-colonial text emphasises the central problem of this situation, the 'absence' of those 'functions' in the text which operate to constitute the discursive event as communication: the 'writer' and 'reader'. The author function, with its vision and intentions, its 'gifted creative insight', has historically exerted the strongest claim upon the meaning of writing. But the concept of the author is quite alien to many post-colonial cultures and, as Foucault has pointed out, is really a quite recent phenomenon in European culture. The need to ground discourse in an originating subject was the reason to accord it the status of a possession. Speeches and books were assigned real authors only when someone had to be made responsible for them as possessions and therefore subject to punishment, first for transgressing religious rules and later for transgressing or affirming the rules of property ownership.[11] To attain this social and legal status the *meaning* had to be a product attributable to a subject. Consequently, the immense and complex forces of which the text was a product could be conveniently located in an originating mind.

This should assist us to find some balance in assessing the author's place in the 'production' of the text. We have made an important start by rejecting the notion that meaning is a mental act, a sort of picture which the author translates into words or vice versa. But how *does* the non-English speaker, for instance, mean anything in English? Firstly, the writer, like the language, is subject to the *situation*, in that s/he must say something *meanable*. This does not mean s/he cannot alter the language, and use it neologistically and creatively; it does mean, however, that the writer becomes limited, *as any speaker is limited*, to a situation in which words have meaning. In literature the 'situation' refers to something of extremely wide range. It is, at its simplest, the place of the word within a meanable context, the grammar or rules which make the context meanable, but it is also a continuously unfolding horizon which ever more finely articulates the meaning. (From the reader's point of view it is important to realise that the 'situation' extends beyond the text.) Literature, and particularly narrative, has the capacity to domesticate even the most alien experience. It does not need to *reproduce* the experience to construct the meaning. Thus although there is no word in English which has the associations of *mana* (oneness with the world) in Polynesian or *Tjukurrpa* (the 'Dreaming') in Pintjantjatjara, there is no insurmountable conceptual difficulty in articulating their associations.

One could go further than this to say that the author is subject not only to the situation of discourse but to the reader as well. The reader is present, as a *function*, in the writing of the text. Thus the relationship between these social forces and the text is the same as that between the linguistic system and the 'text' of a particular world view: neither causal nor representative, but co-extensive. The crucial assertion of Constitutive Graphonomy is that within the framework of these social antecedents, the writer and reader functions are as 'present' to each other in the acts of writing and reading as conversants are in conversation. The reader may be present in the writing at a conscious level, in the author's sense of an audience, of a purpose for writing, but it is not necessarily so specific. To detect the presence of the reader function in the writing let us first think clearly whether the act of writing can ever exclude the simultaneous act of reading. That moment of writing in which the self is objectivated is also the moment of a reading in which the other is constituted. It is the other, even when the other is oneself which confers objectivity on the writing, constitutes it as written. In this sense, as Sartre says, the others 'were already present in the heart of the word, hearers and speakers awaiting their turn'.[12] The requirement of meanability itself implicates the reader function. The space within which the writer meets the reading other is neither one culture nor another, neither one language nor another, but the *parole*, the situation of discourse

THE WRITER FUNCTION IN THE READING

Just as the reader 'writes' the text because s/he takes it to mean something, and just as the reader function is present in the writing as the focus of its meanability, so the author is present in the reading. Again, this is firstly true at a conscious level, where the reader accepts the convention that the author is telling him or her something in the text. S/he responds to the text as 'telling' him or her something because such ways of using language as this literary text represents come within the rules for the activity of 'telling'. But one cannot 'tell' others anything that they do not incorporate or 'tell' themselves. The mind is active in knowing. Whether in a child learning a language or in a scientist 'observing' an 'objective' universe, knowing is conducted within the *situation* of horizons of expectations and other knowledge. In reading, a horizon of expectations is partly established by the unfolding text, while a *relevant* horizon of other knowledge (actually other texts) is established by exploration.

The reader constructs the other dialogic pole of discourse because speaking is a social act. But the reader does not simply respond to the convention of the authoring other; s/he responds to the 'intentionality' of the work itself, quite apart from any imputation of an author. The work is a way of seeing and responding, a way of directing attention to that which is 'given to consciousness'. It is more accurate to say that the reader sees 'according to' or 'with' the text rather than sees 'it'. This orientation to the intentionality of the text occurs whether there is an actual author or not.[13] We can deduce from this that the intentionality of the text can be *put for* the direction of the author's consciousness. Thus interpretation is never univocal, but the reader is subject to the situation, to the rules of discourse, and to the directing other, as the author is subject to them.

As with language, our natural assumption about understanding is that it must be a discrete experience, that when we 'understand' there must be characteristic experiences of understanding which have corresponding identifiable mental correlates. Otherwise how could we 'understand' a writer (even one writing in a common language) who has a profoundly different experience of the world? But we can test this assumption that understanding is an identifiable experience. Take the example of a bricklayer who uses the term 'Brick!' as an elliptical form of the phrase 'Pass me a brick'. Neither the bricklayer nor the person to whom s/he is talking needs to translate the word 'Brick!' into the phrase every time it is used in order to understand it. The word operates perfectly well as a communication within the exchange and it is its use and the continuation of the job which locates the understanding of the word 'Brick' as an order. The same process applies when English variants, neologisms and borrowings are situated in the written English text. As with most words there may be many possible uses but it is the use in this situation which locates the meaning. Gabriel Okara's use of 'inside' and 'insides' is an obvious case in point.

The processes of understanding are therefore not limited to the minds of speakers of one mother tongue and denied the speakers of another. Meaning and the understanding of meaning exist outside the mind, within the engagement of speakers using the language. Understanding, then, is not a function of what goes on in the 'mind' at all, but a location of the hermeneutic object in its linguistic situation. When I understand a language, I can go on to continue the discourse. When I understand what other people say, I am not required to have their mental images; and when they communicate meaning they are not obliged to transfer to the listener the 'contents' of their mind, nor any of the mental images and associations which may be aroused by that language.

THE METONYMIC FUNCTION OF POST-COLONIAL LANGUAGE

Given the multiaccentuality of meaning which a Constitutive Graphonomy uncovers, the question remains as to how the post-colonial text itself resists the reincorporation of its discursive practice into an amorphous universal textuality. As I have suggested, it does this by actually *installing* alterity and absence in the interstices of the text. Whether written from monoglossic, diglossic or polyglossic cultures, such writing uses language to signify difference while employing a 'sameness' which allows it to be understood. Such difference is signified by language 'variance', the part of the wider cultural whole which appropriates the language of the centre while setting itself apart.

One of the most interesting features of post-colonial literature is that kind of writing which is informed by the linguistic principles of a first language, or by the idiomatic variations of a language adapting to a new place and new culture. This is an 'overlap' of language which occurs when texture, sound, rhythm and words are carried over from the mother tongue or idiom to the adopted literary form. And it is this intersection of language which many writers propose as *the* distinguishing feature of post-colonial literature. This use of language is something for which the writer usually takes as evidence (of both his or her ingenuity and ethnographic function) an insertion of the 'truth' of culture into the text by a process of metaphoric embodiment. But quite simply, language variance is *metonymic*, a synechdocic index of cultural difference which affirms the distance of cultures at the very moment in which it proposes to bring them together.

The use of english inserts itself into a political discourse in post-colonial writing, and the transcription of english variants of all kinds captures that moment between the culture affirmed on the one hand as 'indigenous', or 'national', and that on the other as 'imperialist', colonialist, or 'metropolitan'. In the play *The Cord* by the Malaysian writer K.S. Maniam the english variant establishes itself in clear contradistinction to the 'standard' within the dialogue itself.

Muthiah:	What are you saying? Speaking English?
Ratnam:	The language you still think is full of pride. The language that makes you a stiff white corpse like this!
Muthiah:	But you're nothing. I'm still the boss here.
Ratnam:	Everything happens naturally. Now the language is spoke like I can speak it ... I can speak real life English now.
Muthiah:	You can do that all day to avoid work!
Ratnam:	You nothing but stick. You nothing but stink. Look all clean, inside all thing dirty. Outside everything. Inside nothing. Taking-making. Walking-talking. Why you insulting all time? Why you sit on me like monkey with wet backside?[14]

There are two principles operating in this passage which are central to the writing of all cross-cultural literature. On the one hand there is a repetition of the general idea of the interdependence of language and identity – you are the way you speak. This general idea includes the more specific Malaysian and Singaporean debate about whether 'standard' English or local variants should be spoken in the region. The language of power, the language of the metropolitan centre is that of Muthiah, while the 'real life English', the language variant of cultural fidelity, is the one spoken by Ratnam.

But the other, more distinctive act of the cross-cultural text is to inscribe *difference* and *absence* as a corollary of that identity. The articulation of two quite opposed possibilities of speaking and therefore of political and cultural identification outlines a cultural space between them which is left unfilled, and which, indeed, locates the core of the cross-cultural text. This unbridged and redolent gulf of silence remains the energising centre of post-colonial

71

writing. It is undiluted and perfect because it exists beyond language, the ultimate signifier of difference. This gap becomes itself the sign of a fracture between different worlds, worlds which may be sharable in language, but whose apartness – the difference of lifetimes of associations, traditions, simple experiences, learned responses and conventional allusions – is explicitly confirmed. In this way the integrity of the traditional interpretation of the world is articulated by difference and located firmly within its own 'world' of experience.

But the location of this aphasic cultural gulf in the text is made most often and most strikingly by uses of language which we could call the 'devices of otherness', the devices which appear specifically utilised to establish the difference and uniqueness of the post-colonial text. Apart from direct glossing in the text, either by explanation or parenthetic insertions, such devices include syntactic fusion, in which the english prose is structured according to the syntactic principles of a first language; neologisms (new lexical forms in English which are informed by the semantic and morphological exigencies of a mother tongue); the direct inclusion of untranslated lexical items in the text; ethno-rhythmic prose which constructs an english discourse according to the rhythm and texture of a first language; and the transcription of dialect and language variants of many different kinds, whether they come from diglossic, polydialectical or monolingual communities.

At its extreme, as in the insertion of unglossed foreign language in the text, such language use is a direct confrontation with the requirement of meanability. Signifiers of alterity are not necessarily inaccessible; rather they explicitly establish a distance between the writer and reader functions in the text as a cultural gap. The gap of silence reaffirms the parameters of meanability as cultural parameters, and the language use offers its own hybridity as the sign of an absence which cannot be simply traversed by an interpretation. It directly intercepts notions of 'infinite transmissability' to protect its difference from the incorporating universalism of the centre.

In conclusion we can say that post-colonial theory offers a particular insight into questions of literary ontology and hermeneutics. The post-colonial writing, by stressing the distance between the participants, re-emphasises the constitutive nature of the meaning event and the complex nature of the usage in which meaning is accomplished. But the most interesting possibilities of this theory are provided by the way in which it distances itself from the tendency of European theory to establish universal laws and principles. Post-colonial writing questions assumptions about meaning and its transmissability, and privileges the conception of writing as a social act conceived within the fusion of culture and consciousness.

NOTES

1. Jacques Derrida, *Writing and Difference*, trans. Alan Bass (London: Routledge, 1978), p. 12

2. Ferdinand Saussure, *Course in General Linguistics*, trans. W. Baskin (Glasgow: Collins, 1974)

3. Derek Bickerton, 'On the Nature of a Creole Continuum', *Language*, 49, 3 (1973), pp. 640-69.

4. Richard Terdiman, *Discourse/Counter-Discourse: The Theory and Practice of Symbolic Resistance in Nineteenth-Century France* (Ithaca and London: Cornell University Press, 1986).

5. Saussure, pp. 71-140.

6. J.L. Austin, *How to do Things with Words* (Oxford: Clarendon, 1962).

7. Derrida, p. 12.

8. Gabriel Okara, *The Voice* (London: Heinemann, 1970).

9. D. Mandelbaum, *Selected Writings of Edward Sapir* (Berkeley and Los Angeles: University of California Press, 1949), p. 162. See also Edward Sapir, 'Conceptual Categories in Primitive Languages', *Science*, 74 (1931).

10. Benjamin Lee Whorf, *Collected Papers on Metalinguistics* (Washington: Foreign Service Institute, Dept. of State, 1952), p. 5.

11. Michel Foucault, 'What is an Author?', *Language, Counter-Memory, Practice* (Oxford: Blackwell, 1977), pp. 124-125.

12. Jean Paul Sartre, *Saint Genet: Actor and Martyr* (New York: Mentor, 1964), p. 494.

13. I discovered this in an experiment conducted at the Australian National University in 1978. Participants were offered progressive lines of separate poems selected randomly in the belief that they were progressively reading a single poem. Respondents of high professional competence revealed great ingenuity in interpreting the 'poem' and in all cases directed their response to a constructed intentionality generally identified as 'the poet'.

14. Ooi Boo Eng, 'Malasia and Singapore', *Journal of Commonwealth Literature*, 19, 2 (1984), pp. 93-99.

Of Marx and Missionaries: Soyinka and The Survival of Universalism in Post-Colonial Literary Theory

One of the most enduring projects in the criticism of African literature has been the attempt to define the exact relationship between the local product and the so-called 'universal' tradition. The early criticism was dominated by the Eurocentric tendency to assume a simple continuity between Western forms and artistic aims and those of African writing, a tendency echoed by many of the writers themselves. Christopher Okigbo, for example, claimed the right to 'belong, integrally'[1] to European societies as well as his own. He argued that 'the time has come to question some of our prejudices, to ask ourselves ... whether there is such a thing as African literature'.[2] This tendency exercised not only European but also African critics – for example, in the search for quasi-historical parallels such as those drawn by Emmanuel Obiechina between Africa and the mediaeval situation in which European vernacular literatures developed from the presumed universal originating Latin source.[3] Chinua Achebe's early and decisive intervention in this dispute was crucial, and no one has stated the case against universals in post-colonial criticism with more forcefulness and accuracy since:

> In the nature of things the work of the western writer is automatically informed by universality. It is only some others who must strive to achieve it. As though universality were some distant bend in the road you must take if you travel far enough in the direction of America or Europe.[4]

Homi K. Bhabha provides us with a perceptive gloss on Achebe's comments:

> What Achebe's criticism shows quite clearly is that within a Universalist problematic, criticism exists only to resolve the material significations of historical and cultural difference into a deeply ethnocentric transcendence.[5]

The debate on universals, though, in all its implications, really came out into the open with the exchange of articles between Wole Soyinka and the so-called 'troika' of Chinweizu, Jemie, and Madubuike, published in the early seventies. Despite the extreme tone of the troika's attack, the debate, at that time, was little more than a formalist dispute over what did or did not constitute the 'essential' nature of African writing (more especially, poetry). It was as if the quarrel were about which features could be interposed as the authenticating sign of Africaness between the terms 'good' and 'literature' – as if these surrounding terms were not, in themselves, problematic. There was little attempt by either side in the dispute to question the role played by sociological and ideological *practices* in the constitution of post-colonial literature, and by the institutions which reflexively sustained them, such as publishing networks, patronage systems, educational curriculae and the like.[6] In other words, there was little attempt to make an analysis of ideology in the continuing power relations preserved by neo-colonialism within post-independent African societies. What little analysis of this that did exist was present only at a fairly simple level – for example, the splenetic identification of the iniquities of the so-called 'Leeds School',[7] an identification which did little more than generalise the theory of false values and corrupt influence from the level of the individual to that of a supposed group or cabal. In other words, a kind of melodramatic conspiracy theory replaced genuine analysis in the Soyinka-troika exchange. No theories encompassing the ideological influences on the construction of the various discursive practices emerged, nor was there any attempt to dismantle the underlying and stifling ideological assumption that criticism and indeed creative writing were supported (or even created) by a system of 'values' subject to no hegemony beyond that of the individual or group 'sensibility'.

It must be admitted that at this stage in the debate even Soyinka's contribution was largely formalist and essentialist. However, there was less than justice in the troika's attack on Soyinka as being concerned with a conservative, mythic view inherently opposed to the more radical perspectives beginning to exercise the minds of his younger colleagues. The simplistic politics of such a division, which cast Soyinka as the conservative patriarch and the troika as the radical *enfants terribles*, ignored the fact that both their critical practices were informed by the same inadequate level of theoretical analysis, an analysis which took no account of the determining forces of social and cultural practice, nor of the need to relate this practice very specifically to the distinct articulations of the ruling class ideology (to use Althusser's term) within which each specific historical response ('text') came into being.

Nevertheless, the view that Soyinka's position was inherently conservative took hold. Andrew Gurr, for example, was led to suggest that Soyinka's 'mythopoetic' vision inevitably undercut his assertions of a radical and modern programme for Nigerian culture.[8] Such a view, of course, ignored the fact that content or even 'metaphysic' (to use Biodun Jeyifo's paraphrase) is not locked inescapably into a specific function. No less a critic than Trotsky understood this clearly enough, and said so forcibly:

> The quarrels about 'pure art' and about art with a tendency took place between the liberals and the 'populists'. They do not become us. Materialist dialectics are above this; from the point of view of an objective historical process, art is always a social servant and historically utilitarian. It finds the necessary rhythm of words for dark and vague moods. It brings thought and feeling closer or contrasts them with one another, it enriches the spiritual experience of the individual or of the community, it refines feeling, makes it more flexible, more responsive, it enlarges the volume of thought in advance and not through the personal method of accumulated experience, it educates the individual, the social group, the class, and the nation. And this it does quite independently of whether it appears in a given case under the flag of a 'pure' or of a frankly tendentious art.[9]

As a recent commentator on Trotsky's commentaries on literature and art has said,

> Trotsky ... far from minimising the role of tradition in literature, insists upon it as much as does T.S. Eliot. He adds, however, that the continuity of literary history is dialectical, proceeding by a series of reactions, each of which is united to the tradition from which it is seeking to break ('artistic creation is always a complicated turning inside out of old forms'). Nor are these reactions merely mechanical, the eternal swing of the pendulum from 'classical' to 'romantic'. They take place under the stimuli of new artistic needs as the result of changes in the psychology of social classes attendant upon changes in the economic structure.[10]

As this suggests, a more complex model is needed to assess the political consequences of Soyinka's stand, or indeed to assess the function of 'traditional' versus 'modern' or 'reactionary' versus 'radical' elements in the work of all those engaged in the seventies debate on appropriate form and content.

This need can be diagnosed with even greater clarity by turning to the second stage of the debate over Soyinka's work, which stretched from the mid-seventies to the early eighties. The most recent crop of writers and critics, many of them deeply influenced by Soyinka,[11] also failed to analyse fully the complex and contradictory features of Soyinka's position. What was missing from the alternative programme that these younger critics outlined was a genuine historical or chronological assessment both of the work of the earlier writers and critics in terms of the specific political and social forces acting upon them at the time of their production, and of the forces acting upon the critics at the time when they assessed those texts. In other words, what was missing from these accounts was a genuine sense, first, of the text as the product of an endless and changing dialectic involving writer, reader and critic, and secondly of the larger mechanisms of production both of the text *per se* and of the social text with which it engages. Instead, what emerges is the importation of a relatively vulgar form of Lukacian determinism, in which the social realist misapprehension that a text can 'lay bare' its social conditioning is imported into the African debate at a time when it was already long discredited in Marxist critiques in much of the rest of the world. Once again, the essential features of what has come to be called 'neo-colonialism' can be detected, only in a 'radicalised' form and operating now in the sphere of culture. The ex-colony becomes the dumping ground for the discarded versions of Eurocentric 'truth', forced to accept that its liberation from its marginalised position can only be achieved by its breaking out of its local limitation into some wider perspective from which a modern, civilised (or in the case of this particular version of the discourse, radically 'liberated') perspective can be attained. The process involves the rejection of the traditional society except as a subject for contrastive techniques with a new, 'liberated' model in which the signs of consciousness and modernity are equivalent with those of the new authenticating centre. It is as if we must add Moscow and, in the case of post-structuralism, Paris to Achebe's list of destinations to which the road labelled 'universalism' must travel.

In fact, as this paper implies,what may have been needed in Africa in the late seventies and early eighties was neither a new 'allegiance' of this type nor a reflex rejection of traditional cultural and creative models, but rather the development of a more conscious means of articulating the social and cultural implications of literature – one requiring a more sophisticated model of ideology and so a more effective appropriation of current Marxist and post-structuralist theory to the African context in particular, and to post-colonial societies in general.

This wider perspective necessarily raises the question of how far, and to what effect, these issues reach out to the larger relationship between post-colonial criticism and modern European theory. Blind partisanship and sloganeering is of little use here. Contemporary post-colonial critical practice increasingly suggests the importance and meaningfulness of appropriations from European critical discourse. European theory does not (or ought not to) supercede or replace the local and the particular. To suggest this, as Soyinka asserts in *Myth, Literature and The African World*, is to engage in a new form of cultural missionary activity, replacing the adherents of the Christian bishops with another generation of self-negating 'converts', this time to the post-structuralist or Marxist faith.[12] It is continually necessary, therefore, to avoid the facile assumption that such theories are self-evidently superior to the local and particular varieties.

However, it is also necessary to avoid the pretence that theory in post-colonial literature in the 1980s is somehow conceived independently, free from all coincidents, or even that these theories have functioned merely as 'context' for the recent developments in post-colonial criticism (whose origins, it is implied, lie elsewhere in some prior and timeless dimension raised above history and its determinants). No simple theory of 'origins' is of much use here. If anything emerges clearly from the debate between Soyinka and the troika it is that the contemporary African intellectual inhabits a world of profound and inescapable hybridity. Soyinka, as he himself has said, does not inhabit a world in which African ontology, the mask, or the Ogun cult is hermetically sealed from the discursive practices which inform such modern African phenomena as engineering (oil rigs and trains, not 'iron snakes'), aviation, macro-economics, or critical theory. To use Edward Said's term, we may need to distinguish a large number of distinct and important 'beginnings',[13] each with its own discursive practice and political consequence.

One such indigenous 'beginning' is identified by Dennis Duerden, whose early work on the relationship between African iconography and the institutional practices of 'traditional' society provides us with a way of situating the junction of ideology and textuality in the work of Soyinka.[14] In its own local form, post-colonial criticism must appropriate the discourses of post-structuralist language theories and the recent theories of ideology and textuality while avoiding the tendency implicit in much recent usage to allow these theories to reincorporate the post-colonial difference into a new universalist and internationalist ('multi-national') paradigm. Powerful as such criticism is, it must be careful not to act in such a way that it becomes a coloniser (or rather neo-coloniser) in its turn.

Critics have begun to operate in these terms, exploring the texts of African writing in terms of the full complex of its definitive discursive practices. African writers such as Soyinka and Ola Rotimi exhibit, to use Northrop Frye's term, a 'displacement'[15] of all these ideological discourses: a colourful, paradoxical and radical production of Yoruba and Greek heroes, Christian messiahs and modern existentialists. Rather than perceiving such displacements as the sign of a cultural betrayal or of a suspect pragmatism resulting from a liberal pluralism (both positions which lead to a monist view), such hybridities are read as the characteristic marks of the possibilities inherent in post-colonial discourse to escape the simplicity of binary opposition and to generate a new, powerful and creative synthesis of disparate and contradictory elements – a synthesis which embraces difference as a sign of possibility, not as a marker of closure. The presence

78

of these hybridities suggests what Wilson Harris calls the 'complexity of freedom':[16] of how a writer limited, constrained and shaped by the historical conditions of his or her literary production manages within these limits to go some way towards expanding the borders.

In practice, unfortunately, most African criticism which adapts or exploits the possibilities of the European discourses – whether those of post-structuralism or those which seek to radicalise the analysis of texts from a Marxist or neo-Marxist perspective – shares a limitation in that it fails to recognise the continuing importance of Soyinka's cry for the preservation of a sense of self-identity. Despite recent advances in Marxist anthropology, the discourse remains profoundly Eurocentric, still locked into universalist assumptions in which terms as complex in their application to African conditions as 'masses', 'urban proletariat', and even 'class' are simply renewed without question in the new culture. Such a process, as Soyinka himself has argued, in effect replicates in an unconsciously ironic manner the transposition of cultural absolutes in the 'missionary' stage of colonialism. The development within the analysis of capitalist Europe and America of more sophisticated models for handling the complexities of late-capitalist societies (for example, Althusser's theory of varying articulations of the dominant mode of production within specific regional or subclass situations[17]) has proven useful in articulating the practice of capitalism in the neo-colonial phase of Europe's expansion. But in Africa, the possibilities this has offered to date for a profound critique of the limitations of European theory have not been extensively developed.

In fact, with few exceptions, a fairly vulgar form of critique still dominates, one which lays stress on the notion of the 'real' forces of a given epoch, or which replaces the analysis of the complex interaction of ideology, institutional practice and individual 'aesthetic' in any textual situation with a dismissal of texts as flawed or inadequate because of their 'theme' or form. Even the most sophisticated and valuable of such recent accounts, for example that of Biodun Jeyifo, occasionally falls into this trap. For example, in discussing the limitations of Soyinka's play *Death and The King's Horseman* (which he finds wanting in comparison with the earlier Soyinka works, or with a work such as Ebrahim Hussein's *Kinjeketile*), Jeyifo stresses the choice of social group and class origin of the play's protagonist, Elesin, as a limiting factor in the text:

> It is illustrative of the gaps and dents in Soyinka's present ideological armour that he selected this particular metaphysical and philosophical order to symbolise pre-colonial African civilisation and NOT other more egalitarian African cosmogonic and metaphysical systems, the erosion of which ideological and political progressives

79

can, with greater reason, regret. A metaphysic which idealises and effaces the conflicts and contradictions in African societies, which rationalizes the rule of the dazzling FEW (such as Elesin) over the deceived MANY (the women, the retinue, Amusa etc...) is an extension, in the ideological sphere and in the realm of thought, of class rule in the economic and political spheres.[18]

Despite the argument elsewhere in Jeyifo's essays – especially the very convincing account of *The Road*, which rightly recovers the theme of the marginalised and dispossessed figures from what Jeyifo calls 'pretentious metaphysical non-meaning' (p. 21) – the underlying critical practice here is suspect since it is rooted in an equation of theme and subject with the political project of the text. In itself this is to ignore the need stressed by contemporary Marxist criticism to focus on the very complex relationship between what a society thinks about itself – its own views of its choices and practices – and the powerful influence of 'ideologies' and ideological institutions on the shaping of this practice. To suggest that this problem can be resolved by writers making the 'right choices' between approved or disapproved themes and subjects (call them 'metaphysics' if you will) is to resurrect the simplest form of textual reification. Significantly even the persuasive Jeyifo must bend the material in a very overt way in order to achieve his simplified readings of Soyinka's work.

For example, in the case of *Death and The King's Horseman*, Jeyifo ignores the powerful satiric element in the text, notably in the presentation of the young girls and their imitation of the white colonial society. Jeyifo also ignores the fact that in the play Elesin is never rendered as a Hegelian 'tragic hero', whose death can be simply attributed to the colonial intervention of the evil 'white' Pilkings. Ignoring the prefatory note, which he quotes seemingly without registering its ambivalence, Jeyifo argues that the dramaturgy of the text itself insists on the self-contradictory function of Elesin's role as 'hero'. Indeed, even when we adopt Jeyifo's own mimetic method of analysis, it is just as possible to see the work's concentration on the role of 'the horseman' as embodying a powerful critique of the failure of the 'traditional' elite at a vital point in Nigeria's colonial history. We would argue that by broadening our analysis considerably, and by seeing the work as being 'inter-textual' with Soyinka's other productions, the play can be seen as a radical and ironic 'de-construction' of the writer's own aesthetic mythology of Ogun. In its turn, this casts the stress onto Olunde's ironic and unwilling acceptance of Elesin's 'heroic' traditional role, a role which the text clearly shows Olunde regarding as necessary and yet open to change – indeed, as *having* to be changed if the society is to survive the challenge of colonialism. The role is necessary in that it helps to maintain the society's sense of 'self-identity', and yet it is false in so far as it contradicts Olunde's own clear commitment to the need for a radical change in the structure of Nigerian society and in the underlying ideological forces which operate to maintain the power both of the colonial society and of the indigenous elite which, in political practice, supports it. Olunde, the potential radical who has seen the white man's 'civilisation' for himself, is prevented from making a radical change or from responding to the changes which are already manifesting themselves in his generation (the young girls for example) by the equal if apparently opposed imperative to maintain a sense of the difference of his society from the European society which seeks to 'other' it.

The issue here is less the correctness of Soyinka's choice of subject or of the revolutionary character of the 'class' of his protagonists than the project which the choice of subject and protagonist serve. It seems to us that Soyinka's is a profoundly de-colonising project, and that Jeyifo has lost sight of this in his demand that an alternative (although not actually opposed) project be undertaken by African writers: that is, the need to celebrate and dramatise those figures and groups dispossessed in post-colonial society though the material practices of neo-colonialism. However, the route forward in Nigeria, as in all post-colonial societies, is in part through a preservation of what Soyinka has called 'self-apprehension'[19] in relation to imported ideology: the recognition that the class struggle or the formation of ideology is part of a continual process of the production of texts in a mutual and inherently dialectical enterprise. In this dialectic, the reader, the writer and the critic are all engaged in the task of unravelling how the meanings they produce come about, not in affirming that one or other 'inherent' meaning is or is not acceptable to some universal, determining theory. This process, difficult enough, and requiring the most scrupulous and detailed attention to the particulars of any moment of production and consumption and to the social and professional practices which traverse the site of the text at such moments, is even more complex than usual in the case of the post-colonial text.

With post-colonial texts there is a need for the theorist to take into account the specific material and ideological realities of the colonised society, including the unique 'self-apprehension' of the indigenous 'masses' themselves. To blandly apply the same Marxist theoretical discourse to a materialist discussion of Nigerian literature is to repeat the 'Eurocentric' crimes of the metropolitan critics themselves. These latter critics speak of the 'growth' of African literature a if it were a branch of the colonial tree; they talk of its 'emergence' as if it were from a lower evolutionary stage; and they analyse its 'development' as if it were a child of the British Mother.

Similarly, to describe Nigerian literature simplistically in terms of 'masses', of the 'proletariat', of the 'bourgeoisie', and even of 'mystification' is to assume that Nigeria is merely a branch of metropolitan capitalist operations, without its own alternative roots of ideological nourishment. This is itself only another expression of the ideology of colonialism itself, which sees the colonised culture as an appendage, region, mine or plantation. Colonialism, however, works its own peculiar damage: a damage that must be analysed locally, within each colonised situation. It is 'colonialism', therefore, and not the more general notion of 'capitalism' at this stage of African history, which must provide our primary, definitive, historical and critical discourse. The story of post-colonial literature is the history of the struggle for de-colonisation.

We would argue that this is what Soyinka means when he insists on the need to preserve 'self-apprehension' within any critical model. This is the larger, important insight in Soyinka's criticism – a criticism which in other registers can be seen to be profoundly tainted with essentialism. And because of this insight, we cannot therefore dismiss Soyinka's critical work as representing merely the falsified and falsifying product of a liberal, pluralist and anti-radical position.

The crucial difference between Soyinka's position and that of the younger Marxist writers lies in the former's perception of the need for a radical transformation of society to remain rooted in a specifically Africa practice. This, despite the stress on mythic and ontological imperatives in Soyinka's work (not least in the essays in *Myth, Literature and The African World*), is not, finally, 'mystifying' in its effect. In practice it expresses a very direct and pragmatic philosophy, one which recognises that the real threat to post-colonial societies at large resides in a broad-scale internationalist incorporation which erases differences in the name of some new universalist imperative. For Soyinka it is of little consequence or comfort that this new imperative wears the garments of recent Marxist theory when in practice its effect is to deny Nigerians their dignity and self-identity yet again.

Of course, it is not only Marxist criticism which is open to these charges. If this paper concentrates on some Marxist examples of this practice, it is because they have dominated the scene in Africa in recent times. Nevertheless, the contemporary critical practice of critics such as Bhabha, Gayatri Spivak, and Abdul JanMahomed, which lays stress on the need to dismantle colonialist discourse and expose the subversive possibilities it contains, is itself open to strong criticism from the perspective of the politics of its practice.[20] Benita Parry's recent critique of these anti-colonialist theorists draws attention with some force to the limitations of their critical discourse and to the effects it may unconsciously produce in denying the tradition of national liberationist narrative.[21] Parry notes especially the neglect in recent years of the perceptive analysis of Fanon, whose stress on the stages by which a post-colonial society de-colonises itself is at least as crucial to any real understanding of Nigerian literary texts as are the theories of Marx or Hegel. The latter pair's concerns are articulated in terms which are sometimes inimical to an effective analysis of societies in pre-capitalist or neo-colonial, multi-national, capitalist modes.

Fanon's long-neglected analysis forces us to ask the central question, 'What is decolonisation?' This is not the place to engage in a complex economic discussion; however, if we are not to use the term merely as a slogan, we must at least try to give it some substance. Generally, colonialism is the complete domination of one people by another for material profit. The power of the coloniser, its 'hegemony', extends over all aspects of the exploited people's life: the latter are 'colonised' economically, culturally and psychologically. Economically, the colony supplies raw materials, cheap labour and a new market for the metropole's manufacturing industries; culturally, the colony is seen as primitive and peripheral to the mainstream of 'tradition'. Because of this, a psychological dependency can emerge within colonised space – a denial of one's own identity. Political independence does not substantially alter this relationship; colonialism is merely supplanted by 'neo-colonialism', where the coloniser rules through local deputies. Real nationhood must be struggled for on several accounts. Bhabha's reminder that the simplistic 'coloniser/colonised' antithesis is a misleading one[22] does not alter the central, quite material reality which no amount of theoretical gymnastics can avoid: that is, if the 'coloniser' is in practice a complex of fragmented economic, cultural and institutional practices, and the 'colonised' is compromised in its own servitude, it is nevertheless true to say that it is the people of the post-colonial state who quite materially suffer in the final analysis.

It need hardly be said that the 'underdeveloped', completely dominated nature of neo-colonial society, a society which nevertheless still possesses its own internal ideologies and institutions of cultural and political authority, complicates the task for the materialist critic. For example, where does a writer belong in the radically mobile, fragmented and dependent Nigerian 'comprador' middle-class? How does the powerful remnant of traditional, pre-colonial social authority influence the ideological conditions under which a text is produced?

It is at this point that Marx may need to be strongly supplemented, if not supplanted, by Fanon as our principal theorist in this regard, at least in the 'present phase', for Fanon's 'phases' of de-colonisation[23] provide us with an hypothesis with which we can test the case of each post-colonial society's specific and particular struggle for liberation. In the first phase of colonial culture, Fanon argues, all criteria for legitimacy are based on the standards, both overt and covert, of the metropolitan culture. The educated African adopts the habits of the master, even though the 'hybrid' manner of the product of that adoption itself radically 'interrogates' the universalist pretensions of the colonialist sign.[24] In the second phase of the dialectic, the nationalist culture protests against its subordination by celebrating its own distinct identity; therefore, theories of indigenous aesthetics, even personality, are promulgated. While this vocal self-promotion restores a sense of pride, it nevertheless reinforces the colonial lie itself – which is that the colonial culture is 'other', incapable of being one of the 'us' of the metropolis. In the third, more truly liberated, phase, the ex-colony 'appropriates', or annexes, those parts of its former master's culture it finds useful, having less need of the rhetoric of nationalism, and being more immediately concerned with the material welfare of its citizens.

Many contemporary critics working in the field may believe that the task facing the post-colonial world today is less that of dismantling colonialist criticism than of addressing the more complex, insidious and hidden controls which characterise contemporary neo-colonial practice and the operation of multi-national capital which it sustains. It is in the light of this task that we can sympathise with the desire of critics, such as Jeyifo, who forcibly direct our attention to the task of dismantling those assumptions which in barely modified form have survived through the transition from a colonial to an indigenous ruling elite. Nevertheless, the task will not be helped by exchanging one set of crude and vulgar assumptions for another, nor by assuming that in seeking to discover the prevalent 'modes of articulation' of societies such as Nigeria, a continuing sensitivity will not be needed towards the specific cultural and social continuities which inform and 'overdetermine' the expression of their material basis. In this context the re-evaluation of Soyinka continues to be an important site for the struggle to articulate the critical issues for contemporary post-colonial criticism.

NOTES

1. Christopher Okigbo, interviewed in 1965 by Robert Serumaga in *African Writers Talking*, eds. Dennis Duerden and Cosmo Pieterse (London: Heinemann, 1972), p. 144.
2. Okigbo, interviewed by Dennis Duerden in 1963, *ibid.* p. 142.
3. Emmanuel Obiechina, *Culture, Tradition and the West African Novel* (London: Cambridge University Press, 1975).

4. Chinua Achebe, 'Colonialist Criticism', in *Morning Yet on Creation Day* (London: Heinemann, 1975), p. 9.

5. Homi K. Bhabha, 'Representation and the Colonial Text: A Critical Exploration of Some Forms of Mimeticism', in *The Theory of Reading*, ed. Frank Gloversmith (Brighton: The Harvester Press, 1984), p. 104.

6. cf. Louis Althusser and Etienne Balibar, *Reading Capital* (London: New Left Books, 1975).

7. The theories of Chinweizu *et al.* are developed most fully in *Toward the Decolonisation of African Literature*, Volume 1 (New York: Fourth Dimension, 1981).

8. Andrew Gurr, 'Third World Drama: Soyinka and Tragedy', in *Critical Perspectives on Wole Soyinka*, ed. James Gibbs (London: Heinemann, 1981).

9 Leon Trotsky, *Literature and Revolution*, tr. R. Strunsky (Moscow: 1925).

10. Paul N. Siegal, *Leon Trotsky on Literature and Art* (New York: Pathfinder Press, 1970), p. 11.

11. Cf. Kole Omotoso, 'Form and Content in Ideologically Committed Societies', *Afriscope*, Vol. 5, No. 12, 1975, pp. 40- 43; Femi Osofisan, 'Ritual and the Revolutionary Ethos', *Okike*, Vol. 22, 1982, pp. 72-85.

12. As Soyinka puts it in *Myth, Literature and the African World* (Cambridge: Cambridge University Press, 1976), p. xi, 'The man who because of ideological kinship tries to sever my being from its self-apprehension is not merely culturally but politically hostile. ... When ideological relations being to deny ... the reality of a cultural entity which we define as the African world while asserting theirs even to the extent of inviting the African world to sublimate its existence in theirs, we must begin to look seriously into their political motives'.

13. Edward Said, *Beginnings* (Baltimore: John Hopkins University Press, 1978), pp. 76-77.

14. Dennis Duerden, *African Art and Literature: The Invisible Present* (London: Heinemann, 1975).

15. A concept developed most fully in Northrop Frye's *Anatomy of Criticism: Four Essays* (Princeton: Princeton University Press, 1957).

16. Wilson Harris, 'The Complexity of Freedom', in *Explorations* (Aarhus: Dangaroo Press, 1981).

17. Althusser and Balibar, *op. cit.*

18. Biodun Jeyifo, *The Truthful Lie: Essays in a Sociology of African Drama* (London: New Beacon Books, 1985), p. 35.

19. Soyinka, *op.cit.*

20. See Bhabha, *op.cit.*; Gayatri Chakravorty Spivak, 'Three Women's Texts and a Critique of Imperialism', *Critical Inquiry*, Vol. 12, No. 1 (1985), pp. 243-61; Abdul JanMohamed, *Manichean Aesthetics: The Politics of Literature in Colonial Africa* (Amherst: University of Massachusetts Press, 1983).

21. Benita Parry, 'Problems in Current Theories of Colonial Discourse', *Oxford Literary Review*, Vol. 9, Nos. 1-2, 1987, pp. 27-58.

22. Homi K. Bhabha, 'Signs Taken for Wonders: Questions of Ambivalence and Authority Under a Tree Outside Delhi, May 1817', *Europe and its Others: Proceedings of the Essex Conference on the Sociology of Literature*, July 1984, Vol. I (Colchester: University of Essex, 1985), pp 93-94.

23. For a full elaboration of these theories, see Frantz Fanon, *Black Skin, White Masks*, trans. Charles Lam Markmann (1952; London: Pluto Press, 1986).

23. cf. Bhabha, *op.cit.*, pp. 101, 104.

Oral Cultures and the Empire of Literature

Mudrooroo Narogin's (Colin Johnson's) novel *Doctor Wooreddy's Prescription for Enduring the Ending of the World*[1] is a hybrid cultural artefact, and can be *situated between two discourses* each of which is generally regarded as mutually exclusive. It is a novel – that is, its form is derived from *European traditions of literate discourse* – which nonetheless seeks to articulate the breadth and riches of *non-book, pre-literate oral culture*. It is an Australian novel by an Aboriginal writer, and thus presages the possible shape of Commonwealth writing to come.

How we read this novel, how we contextualise Mudrooroo's *writing* within the frames of Australian literature is not difficult. Nor is it too difficult to position the narrative in the realms of new literatures in English; but this last context opens what is the novel's strangeness for non-Aboriginal readers. In this way, Mudrooroo's novel suggests some of the literary, theoretical, discursive and – to return another repressed to the realms of critical discussion – ethical demands made by similar texts now being published in the white-settled Commonwealth.

Commonwealth literary studies – either in terms of the broad international perspective, or in the more specifically domestic – cannot contain and mediate these new texts which, written by or from native perspectives, demand a thorough-going and more severely self-critical awareness of just what it is we do in the name of literary studies in the academies of this former empire than many Euro-American theorists of late have suggested. I think here, for example, of the pedagogical dilemmas posed by writing such as, from Canada, Anne Cameron's *Daughters of Copper Woman* and *Child of Her People*, Beatrice Culleton's *In Search of April Raintree*, or Jeannette Armstrong's *Slash*, and, from Australia, Sally Morgan's *My Place* or Mudrooroo's *Doctor Wooreddy*.

What is difficult, and obviously alien, about *Doctor Wooreddy's Prescription for Enduring the Ending of the World* is its very status as new writing from the margins of empire. It is a writing which derives from oral culture. As Mudrooroo's chronicle of Aboriginal contact with European prisoners and the administrators of settlement develops, his concern to represent this other, the oral mother-culture, is refracted through the various modes of representation employed within the text, and generates the revisions and figures of history which occupy this new territory in the narrative.

Describing the possibly difficult access non-Aboriginals might feel on beginning to read such work, Bob Hodge writes that 'Aboriginal culture seems intrinsically alien and incomprehensible' to Australians of European descent and then describes the chasms across which literate discourse struggles to perceive oral culture.[2] White culture traditionally appropriates the myths, fables, themes, and images of Aboriginal culture through the coffee table book, he claims. Therein, exotic pictures and distorted text guarantee that whatever mythic power the tales may carry – or for that matter whatever account is being offered of material or social reality – is lost, untranslated, and unperceived because the conventions which govern such cross-cultural translations (appropriations) cannot contextualise the actual performance of the pieces which are oral in their first language. Nor do such misappropriations allow for an individual performer's personal signature through inflection and stress of both syntax and theme. Instead, we – the non-Aboriginal consumer of coffee-table books on Aboriginal culture – read snippets wrenched from all contexts, and are informed textually that this piece or that comes from this tribe or that. We are denied the full insights that a truer translation – crediting both linguistic and speakerly difference and variation – might allow. Of course, the great blindness is our own indifference, personally and institutionally within the English-speaking Commonwealth, to indigenous cultures and the languages which might allow us some perception of the distinct otherness and its richness which exists often on our doorsteps, at the margins of our affluence and studies.

Hodge argues that such cultural blindness is generated by a predetermined and 'tacit assumption that the original would have been so incomprehensible in form as well as content that there is no point in trying to do justice to it' (p. 278). In other words, Aboriginal culture is preconceived by white discourse to be foreign, untranslatable, quaint and otherworldly. And white culture consumes artifacts which prove this, thus justifying the consequent indifference to native voices in the definition of its national cultures. It is a remarkably efficient practice, and one which is directly applicable to social practice in Canada, too.

The model coffee-table book purports to make accessible and to popularise otherwise inaccessible indigenous mythologies. This process is accompanied by its justifying claims for the value of such exotic stories: 'One has only to consider the incalculable influence of the myths of ancient Greece on the literature, drama and art of the civilized world for over 2,000 years, and that of the Nordic myths on the music, drama and literature of Northern Europe, to realize how the living myths of the aborigines, which belong so fully to Australia, could contribute to the cultural life of this country'.[3] In order to popularise these timeless myths, however, the myths must be dislocated from their topology as performance pieces, and forcefully translated into the reflexive, verbal and mimetic modes of representation through which we, the intended alien 'readers', have been taught to access, consume and privilege our own culture and its models of reality. This disjunctive process destroys those traces of non-literate culture which the tales in merely verbal translation might retain:

> Is there beauty, artistic skill or any aesthetic quality in the myths themselves? We would not know ... The myths are attributed to no author, no tribe, no language. If there is a budding Homer here, her name has been erased. All traces of the specific oral form of the texts, the narrative devices and strategies, the situation and purpose, have been effaced. What is left is content without form: or rather, since that is impossible, a ruthless extraction of the content from its original conditions of existence, re-presenting in summary form, in pedantic but childlike prose, without life, energy or the possibility of beauty. Homer treated in this way would not have inspired the civilized world for a minute, much less two millennia.[4]

But, you may well ask, what is required of us before we can grasp the otherness of native cultures that are oral? This question confronts the ways in which we have organised our culture-specific discourses, and begins to suggest how the imperial expansion which begets Commonwealth literature also carries with it the germs of its own refutation.

In order to understand this 'return of the repressed', we must attempt to understand just what it is that oral culture does not share with literate culture. First, and most importantly from the perspective of colonial encounter narratives, oral cultures do not have archival documents. There are no historical records, charts of the land, or narratives that a group of people might transcribe for another group of people: there are, in short, none of those kinds of 'documents' or 'texts' which European culture not only privileges with notions of authority, but through which that same invading culture defines itself, and the concept of civilisation and humanity itself.

This may sound ingenuous but when Aboriginal explanations of unheeded and unrecognised land claims and rights begin with the furious recognition that 'everything must be put in writing. That's a demand that they put and it's one that Aboriginal people, and all other people in fact, have to adhere to',[5] the gap between discursive orders is clear. In the systems of empire – and post-imperial, domestically independent government administration is even yet within that discourse for non-accredited native cultures – there is no authority without documents; and, without authority, there can be no 'truth' or 'meaning', 'purpose' or 'justification'. Groups of humans who do not use script are – by definition – inferior, and often less than human.

Should an inquisitive European intelligence seek to discover other kinds of texts, there is very little in book culture which allows that intelligence to conceive of such cultural practices in the first instance, and less to nurture such a questioning should it perceive the existence of another way of articulating human existence and cumulative experience. To imagine even a part of what non-written histories can and do preserve of that articulation across generations and epochs, without storable records, however, has been beyond the grasp of our discursive practices. Not recognising such oral systems, literacy has historically categorised its agents as ignorant, underdeveloped, uncivilised and savage.

Such categorisation, too, justifies the subordination of non-European peoples wherever literacy has confronted orality: an encounter always already pre-determined by the power which literate culture derives from failing to recognize the full humanity of its antagonist.

Let us hypothetically assume, however, that we can encounter orality from this late twentieth-century post-literate vantage. Having imagined the hitherto unimaginable, a vital and self-authenticating non-book culture, we are still damaged in our attempts to interpret that way of being. As Hodge explains,

> There is the problem of language, for a start. There are very many Aboriginal languages, some with only a few living speakers. No white Australian knows even half of these languages, and most know none. But Homer's Greek, by the same token, is a dead language. Translation may be a necessarily imperfect mediation of an original, but even so, good translations can still be attempted, from carefully established texts.
>
> Equally important is the cultural knowledge required to read a text, the reading regimes which map the processes of production and consumption of meaning on to other social practices. Anthropologists make strong claims about specific modes of insertion of Aboriginal myths into their way of life. 'Mythology, sacred or secular or in-between, is the basis upon which Aboriginal life is constructed,' write the Berndts, in their influential introduction to Aboriginal life. Exactly how the truncated stories (which circulate through white Australian culture via the coffee-table book) ... could be the basis of a way of life is not clear. Stories of motiveless murders, casual liaisons between people and animals, and inexplicable transformations seem hardly an adequate account of material or social reality. Their simple prose, which seems to have no place for any speaker, Aboriginal or white, may seem a carefully neutral literary medium, avoiding irrelevant and misleading associations for white readers. But it isn't possible to write without any relation to generic conventions ... (and there

is) a particular set of conventions for rendering Aboriginal myths in English: conventions which have close affinities to those used on books with a quasi-educational purpose for children, about such topics as dinosaurs, or astronomy. In the process, ... [the translator] leaves no clues in his text about the discursive practices in which the originals were embedded. It does not even seem to be the case that he has tried to translate these aspects in some way but has found it difficult. In the tradition he writes in, there is no recognition of a problem here in the first place. (p. 279)

Our inherited canons and modes of representation, then, do not permit of an aesthetic based on performative values. Even where we might admit some congruence, in the ways in which drama has been incorporated into the textual discipline called literary studies, again we study texts, not performances, and invest integrity and authenticity in the ideal of an uncorrupted, properly typeset script. What happens under the mis-guidance of individual directors, or in the pressure of performance on isolated actors, is at variance with the authority vested in such a figure as Shakespeare.

It is tempting, at this point, to digress into a new historicist recognition that what it is we do in English departments throughout the European-settled Commonwealth is determined by this literary figure, his texts and our practice of them. Plays written and performed at the time of imperial first contact and massive expansion – and thus, part of the systems of empire – now block our own recognition of their very play-ness. Beyond this, our practice and our reification of these plays found and articulate a discourse which cannot figure or represent a non-literate cosmology. Caliban must learn Prospero's language, we decree, even if only to spit. The self-declared magic is always already in the hands of the self-declared magician cum European, who is – after all – merely a subject in the literate discourses of international economy, trade and exploitation.

However, one must leave such digressions behind. Like the studies they generate, Renaissance texts not only demand competence in their terms before we speak, they also carry such a long-established body of practices that our own interests are lost in the shadows of their language-systems. And generating their own arguments, for and against whatever position we may assume to take, these texts block newer words. Similarly, although we must at times, and do at others unacknowledgedly, borrow from Euro-American critical theories, this horizon of textuality must also be suppressed if we are to focus on non-literate narratives and their attendant cosmologies. Our quest, returning to the repressed of oral culture, is to un-block, to learn to hear and see the cultures which exist not – as is currently fashionable – in or on the margins of, but actually outside our documents and archives.

And here, the very old begins to look like the very new. So-called primitive cultures – systems wherein shamans, historians, bards or even ordinary representatives of another generation or time stage and recount communal stories and collectively shared narratives – value what is told, not for its content but rather for its form. Form is always a message, part of the content or narrative. Similarly, in post-modern artifacts, form is frequently *the* most significant message any such cultural product conveys. A performative aesthetic operates: just as it does when we read the most up-to-date postmodern document or text. What we value is not what we're told, but the play through which the artist-creator reveals what we're told.

Look at any postmodern building, if you doubt this – for example, the new Babylonian palace which houses LePage Realty at the corner of Smythe and Hornby Streets in downtown Vancouver. Functionally, it's just another office building (the content is boring); but we are invited to admire, we are assaulted with an aesthetic that demands we admire, the architect-designer's ability to perform in any number of various structural and thematic conventions (form is exciting, the message of the construction). And that's what is missing in the coffee-table version of oral cultures: the dramatic presence of the story-teller's idiosyncratic and social dynamic performance – the 'play' buried in the description of 'dis-play'.

Therefore, as we move to understand the social construction of our own realities with ever-increasing self-consciousness (which is what looking at a postmodern building is about – or watching a film or listening to music or reading a book which is about its own production and our watching/ listening/reading of it), so we have the opportunity to recognise that what begins by looking alien and exotic, or primitive and uncivilised, is actually very close in many ways to our post-industrial existence.

This is what motivates Hodge in his essay to argue for new lenses, new acts of mediation, with which to learn about the hitherto silenced voice of Aboriginal Australia. His essay is very ambitious: initiating such an inquiry, Hodge turns the tables. The last part of the essay 'reads' the most widely popular of contemporary Australian cultural products – the Mad Max films, with focus on the most recent installment, 'Beyond the Thunder Dome' – through the lens of Aboriginal narrative form and mythic content. What should be obvious, the comparative study of two narrative modes, is unfortunately eccentric.

It may sound all very bizarre, to learn what we're about at this late stage of Western technological 'culture' by looking to pre-technological human habits of experience and societal organisation. Our very reticence is the revelation of our continuing imperialism.

And again, an anomaly confounds us within our very academies: comparative literature, its study and departments, is always concerned solely with the family of European languages and literary cultures. It's all well and good to think of studying other cultures, but usually we carry psychic baggage with such intentions. Studied cultures are always chosen for a predetermined ideal dialogue and sharing. We must be equal, first, by popular consensus. We ignore our own to learn from our masters.

Inter-disciplinary study, an empowering concept if ever there were one, is also neutered and made irrelevant by our neglect of the obvious: that in Southern Africa, Canada, New Zealand and Australia, comparative literature is undeniably a domestic concern.

What I mean, using for me what is an obvious example – Canada – is that our own literatures are already comparative, and yet we are already blind to this fact because we constitute our academies on that European 'civilised' norm. In Canada, for example, we in English departments have the audacity to teach so-called 'Canadian' literature (the singular is very operative here) with little attention, if any, to even the second national language. Ethnic studies allows non-English speaking immigrant fictions in the door, but not into the limelight: a tactic which preserves, despite some bureaucratic claims to the contrary, an inalienable Anglo-Saxon complexion to this nation's literature. Native people's narratives stand little chance of inclusion.

But the academy also carries its own repressed. It is while studying the grandeur of truly alien literatures – those from another continent, epoch and dispensation – that we learn how to change our perceptions and discourse itself. In those literatures and in the vast critical commentary which grows even now like some incubus-appendage, we learn that cross-cultural exchange must be a full dialogue, or else be revealed for sham and pretence and unworthy of any degree or similar accreditation.

We can only legitimate what fulfils a pre-given charter of 'humanistic' studies. The exclusion of native cultures from our studies of Commonwealth literatures, and the refusal to alter our disciplinary bounds and modes of knowledge-production which such inclusions would demand, hides what Mudrooroo Narogin has called 'cultural and genocidal imperialism'.[6] And the fact of the matter is that – aside from an inquiry like this, which is so obviously, sadly, modelled on the kinds of information storage and retrieval which literacy mobilises and defines – the presence of oral cultures is only infrequently admitted by our discourse. Anthropologists sometimes attempt to teach students of literature, and contemporary theorists of literature reach towards anthropology for the occasional insight: both avenues assert the need for new, inter-disciplinary modes of inquiry, transcription and analysis.

We perpetuate the oppressions of empire if we admit to our study of Commonwealth literature only those forms of text which metropolitan culture (the invader/colonist/settler – our white, European canons) allows the name 'literature'. We oppress because we do not admit, that is we negate as unworthy to be heard, the voices of oral culture – the myths, narratives, songs and celebrations of the invaded, colonised, usually destroyed, and always non-white original inhabitants of the Commonwealth territories.

Mudrooroo, of course, has another programme. *Doctor Wooreddy's Prescription for Enduring the Ending of the World* is very obviously a novel and, as such, can therefore be inserted into the discourse of English Departments across the world with little formal difficulty. There is always the confrontation with the canon, of course, but that battle is no longer fought by and for solitary texts. What is important to recognise is that this novel does not present forms of discourse, ways of being and achieving meaning, in any way that is different from the kind of dialogue with its reader that every novel initiates. That is to say, as Bakhtin reminds us,

> The study of the novel as a genre is distinguished by peculiar difficulties. This is due to the unique nature of the object itself: the novel is the sole genre that continues to develop, that is as yet uncompleted ... We know other genres, as genres, in their completed aspect, that is, as more or less fixed pre-existing forms into which one may then pour artistic experience.[7]

In other words, each time we pick up a novel and begin to read, we enter into a new contract, a new dialogue with text, which redefines how we think of reading, and of the worlds within and beyond the text.

Mudrooroo is not challenging our notions of book culture but is, rather, offering us a variation on the novel which may suggest the otherness of oral culture – through the discourse of *literature* and a not uncommon set of familiar readerly expectations. In this way, *Doctor Wooreddy's Prescription for Enduring the Ending of the World* might appear to sidestep the issue of Aboriginality, but it actuality foregrounds non-European consciousness in a form learned from Europe. It is, therefore, an example of what Mudrooroo has called the appropriation of the forms of imperialist culture, and the filling of these forms with indigenous, non-European content.[8]

Mudrooroo prefaces that essay, 'White forms, Aboriginal content', with an assertion that links such new directions in Australian literature with an emerging international literature of previously colonised peoples. His argument also reveals a common purpose with other similarly recent revisions of colonial history such as George Bowering's *Burning Water*, Patrick White's *A Fringe of Leaves* or Robert Hughes's *The Fatal Shore*. In these, and in most of what we now read as Commonwealth literature, inherited notions of what passes for history, and inherited models of representation, are examined and modified. Indeed, some scholars claim that such consciously and self-reflexively post-colonial texts are, in fact, the first writing genuinely deserving of the label, postmodern.

In order to create an arena, claim a forum, in which those voices which have been silenced or erased by official histories and canons of literature might articulate their truths and the primacy of their experiences, this revisioning of history and of narrative modes begins with very clear stylistic or aesthetic, political and ethical intentions. White, for example, destroys any complacency we might have preferred, as readers faced with a somewhat conventional narrative of nineteenth-century English life, quite simply by forcing us to realise that how we read determines how we construct our realities and our social values – especially, in *A Fringe of Leaves*, the discourse of class, power, wealth, gender, race, and empire. In *Burning Water*, Bowering is equally concerned to de-naturalise such normative mediations, and moves us to re-consider how we articulate native and white or nature and culture, by foregrounding the games our inherited language plays against our perceptions.

As Mudrooroo proclaims his project, such initiatives are clearly no longer marginal, but crucially central to the study and theory of literature. The silent voices of previous chronicles can now be heard. And the clamour is international:

> ... Aborigines do not occupy a unique position in this world. They are just one of the many peoples that became immersed in the European flood which flowed out from the fifteenth century onwards. The Aboriginal response to this threatened drowning has been and is similar to that of many other peoples. Unfortunately many white settlers in Australia have little or no sense of any history or culture apart from their own, and too often it seems that a lot believe that they were created in Australia sometime in the recent past after Captain James Cook and Governor Arthur Phillip (two Poms) arrived in Australia. Naturally we all know better than this, and how important our roots are.[9]

Mudrooroo clarifies this bond common to the literatures we should be studying from the Commonwealth, and asserts the presence of a unifying discourse to be constructed in the wake of the canon, or 'majority literature' as he terms it in his essay's concluding remarks:

> Australian aboriginal literature is a literature of the Fourth World, that is, of the indigenous minorities submerged in a surrounding majority and governed by them. It must and does deal with the problems inherent in this position and it must be compared to similar literatures, for example the American Indian, for the correspondences and contradictions to be seen. It should not be compared to the

majority literature. Perhaps the most that can be said for modern Australian literature, or rather current literature, is its utter complacency and the fact that it is becoming more and more irrelevant to the society with which it seeks to deal. Aboriginal literature is and can be more vital in that it is seeking to come to grips with and define a people, the roots of whose culture extend in an unbroken line far back into a past in which English is a recent intrusion. (pp. 28-29)

The most evocative concept here (which is to say, useful for my immediate purposes in this paper) is that of 'fourth world' literature. Not only does Mudrooroo thereby offer us a guide into such works, he also historicises and internationalises this writing in frames which transcend that of the British Empire.

To read these new Commonwealth fictions, we must read comparatively through other such strivings for voice and presence: we must learn to read American native works, and learn from them how to read and contextualise Aboriginal Australian writing, or native Canadian. *Doctor Wooreddy's Prescription for Enduring the Ending of the World* cannot be critically examined without the critic situating it within a discourse bounded by texts such as Hugh Brody's *Maps and Dreams*, John Cove's *Shattered Images*, Joan Halifax's *Shamanic Voices*, or Brian Swann and Arnold Krupat's recent collection of theoretical, analytical and interpretive essays, *Recovering the Word*.[10] It's a very big order, self-representation, but the rewards are the ontology of our enterprise as scholars of Commonwealth literatures. Indeed, as Ngugi wa Thiong'o and others involved in the criticism of African literatures have suggested already,[11] such indigenisation of our English departments is the first step towards an apprehension of just what these literatures are. Such study engages dialogue, subverting the monologue of our inherited and imperially-derived disciplinary frontiers.

Thus, we begin to appreciate the significance of just how Mudrooroo, wearing the critic's cap this time, has articulated the course of Aboriginal literature: that new writing from previously oral cultures. Mudrooroo explains the dilemma of a critic looking for models ('I would have liked to have used another minority literature for the comparison, but I have been unable to collate one as yet') and then attempts to explain how Aboriginal literature can be read. It is also a part of his task that such 'theorising' should entail some description of representative works:

The first stage we should note is *the movement away*. This may be represented by biographies showing how the Aborigine is being assimilated into the majority society ... It must be pointed out that until the 1960s, except for a few legends, this was the extent of Aboriginal literature in English, and these life stories were put together by whites. Aborigines everywhere were on the outside looking in. Then in the sixties came the awakening of the Aborigine. He and she became conscious of his or her

95

position in Australia and with it came a profound disillusionment ... but from this hopelessness came a search which resulted in perhaps the best piece of Aboriginal literature written – I refer to Kevin Gilbert's *Because a White Man'll Never Do It*. The search appeared at an end and poetry such as that by Kath Walker and Jack Davis confirmed this. As a result their work began a movement back, the counterpoint in literature to that of the homelands movement, and this movement is still continuing today. It is a homecoming and a re-entry. A return from exile and alienation into Aboriginality. Thus in my novel, *Long Live Sandawara*, I try and show this return through the actions of my main character ... At the end of the book he is shown as returning home, in a sense to rediscover the roots of his culture and his being. He has succeeded in doing this, but at a cost, and others have fallen by the roadside. In my next novel, *Dr. Wooreddy's Prescription for Enduring the Ending of the World*, I re-enter Aboriginal history and culture and give the story of Wooreddy, the husband of Trugernanna. I believe we should recapture our history and culture and a means of doing this is through literature.[12]

NOTES

1. Colin Johnson, *Doctor Wooreddy's Prescription for Enduring the Ending of the World* (New York: Balantine, 1983). In 1988, as an anti-bicentennial gesture, Johnson changed his name to Mudrooroo Narogin – the second term of which indicates a tribal affiliation.
2. Bob Hodge, 'Aboriginal Myths and Australian Culture', *Southern Review*, 19, 3 (November 1986), 277-90.
3. Cited in Hodge, p. 278.
4. Hodge, p. 278.
5. Bruce McGuinness and Denis Walker, 'The politics of Aboriginal literature', in *Aboriginal Writing Today: Papers from the First National Conference of Aboriginal Writers Held in Perth, Western Australia, 1983*, ed. Jack Davis and Bob Hodge (Canberra: Australian Institute of Aboriginal Studies, 1985), p. 47.
6. Colin Johnson, 'Guerilla Poetry: Lionel Fogarty's Response to Language Genocide', *Westerly*, 31, 3 (September 1986), 47.
7. M.M. Bakhtin, *The Dialogic Imagination: Four Essays*, ed. Michael Holquist, trans. Caryl Emerson and Michael Holquist (Austin: University of Texas Press, 1981), p. 3.
8. See Colin Johnson, 'White forms, Aboriginal content', in *Aboriginal Writing Today*, pp. 21-33.
9. Ibid, p. 21.
10. Hugh Brody, *Maps and Dreams: Indians and the British Columbia Frontier* (Harmondsworth: Penguin, 1983); John Cove, *Shattered Images: Dialogues and Meditations on Tsimshian Narratives* (Ottawa: Carleton University Press, 1987); Joan Halifax, *Shamanic Voices: A Survey of Visionary Narratives* (Harmondsworth: Penguin, 1980); *Recovering the Word: Essays from Native American Literature*, ed. Brian Swann and Arnold Krupat (Berkeley and Los Angeles: University of California Press, 1987).
11 See Ngugi wa Thiong'o, *Decolonising the Mind: The Politics of Language in African Literature* (London: James Curry, 1986) and 'On the Abolition of the English Department', in *Homecoming: Essays on African and Caribbean Literature, Culture and Politics* (London, Ibadan and Nairobi: Heineman, 1972), pp. 145-50.
12. Johnson, 'White forms, Aboriginal content', p. 29.

Finding the Centre: 'English' Poetry After Empire

The Australian poet Les Murray has talked about 'the dreadful tyranny where only certain privileged places are regarded as the centre and the rest are provincial and nothing good can be expected to come out of them. I figure the centre is everywhere. It goes with the discovery that the planet is round, not flat. Every point on a sphere is the centre. It seems to be a corollary of the discovery of the roundness of the world that people haven't taken seriously yet'.[1]

The chief problem for anyone attempting to determine where the 'mainstream' of current English language writing is flowing today is the impossibility of finding, after the disintegration of so many linguistic, literary and cultural 'centres', a ground from which canonical judgements can be made. The question now is not where does one find a vantage point sufficiently empyrean to show where the 'mainstream' of poetry in the twentieth century is flowing, but rather what need is there to seek out such a vantage? In whose interests are such judgements maintained?

In the 1960s and '70s the problem looked simpler because of the shift in cultural power from the old originating centre of England to the new one of the United States. It was a period when post-war (and largely postmodern) American poetry was exported globally: its formal openness, its easy rhythms, its irresistible vernacular energies turned up in Sydney, Auckland and Vancouver and a succession of anthologies of 'new' Australian, New Zealand or Canadian poetry appeared, all significantly influenced by Donald Allen's 1960 anthology, *The New American Poetry*. All this was liberating and positive so long as the American influence meant an openness to a new range of poetic possibilities. It was not liberating where an obsession with American postmodern poetics fostered the view that there was only one narrow and rigid channel through which the historically significant poetry of this century has flowed, from Pound and Williams by way of Olson and Creeley down to the L=A=N=G=U=A=G=E poets. As Creeley himself observed in a review of a somewhat messianic New Zealand postmodernist poet, Alan Loney, 'There is certainly no use in importing, wholesale, chunks of

"American" temper and preoccupations into the charming isles of New Zealand.'[2]

Creeley recognizes here that the mere substitution of an American-centred poetry 'mainstream' for an English one would be constricting. A new formal orientation in poetry does not manifest itself throughout the English-speaking world at a single moment in time as the obvious and only way of writing poetry now. The English-speaking world is not (and arguably never was) an hierarchically organized, unified whole through which the great movements in poetic style and formal orientation proceed uniformly. In *Make It New* Pound observed: It is quite obvious that we do not all of us inhabit the same time', and Robert Creeley picked up on this when he observed: 'We literally do not, all of us, inhabit the same time. There are speeds in it, deeper roots'.[3]

Yet that American influence arrived in the 'provinces' not as a break with Tradition as such but as a different tradition, and invariably what bore a twenty or a thirty year date stamp was presented by the *avant gardes* in those places as the new. Here is George Bowering, the Canadian West Coast poet:

> By now it is apparent that the mainstream of today's Canadian poetry (in English) flows in the same river system as the chief American one – that one (to change figures of speech in midstream) nurtured firsthand or secondhand by followers of W.C. Williams and Ezra Pound. The *Contact* people in Toronto of the fifties, and the *Tish* people in Vancouver of the sixties are in the middle of what has been happening in Canadian poetry, mid wars.

One can readily find New Zealand or Australian equivalents to this statement, referring the poetry scene in the distant place to that 'river system'. The trouble with this kind of internationalism is that it tends to distort the local scenes into which it is carried by making them conform to borrowed terms and definitions without allowing for their peculiar currency in those places. The claim to be able to judge accurately where the 'mainstream' of literary history flows, necessarily appeals to the notion of some authoritative Tradition.

What is at stake here is the breadth and historical accuracy of our sense of the word 'Tradition', and whether, in acknowledging the limitations of T.S. Eliot's high-modernist understanding of the term, we merely exchange an intelligibly conservative concept of tradition for a narrowly *avant-garde* one such as Bowering's. Here we may detect the need for a new understanding of literary change and development, one in which a truly international sense of literature leads to an acceptance that there are no longer any secure vantage points – Bloomsbury or Rapallo – from which to look back and form a 'Tradition' sufficiently authoritative and sufficiently encompassing to account for and include the truly adventurous writing (what Eliot himself called 'the really new') of both the present and the past.[5]

In a 1942 essay, 'The Classic and the Man of Letters', Eliot puts very clearly the choice facing English literature with the steady break-up of the European 'Tradition' derived from Greece and Rome, a tradition dependent on the continued prestige and knowledge of the classics among an educated elite:

> For many generations the classics provided the basis of the education of the people from whom the majority of our men of letters have sprung: which is far from saying that the majority of our men of letters have been recruited from any limited social class. This common basis of education has, I believe, had a great part in giving English letters of the past that unity which gives us the right to say that we have not only produced a succession of great writers, but a literature, and a literature which is a distinguished part of a recognizable entity called European Literature. We are then justified in inquiring what is likely to happen to our language and our literature, when the connection between the classics and our own literature is broken, when the classical scholar is as completely specialized as the Egyptologist, and when the poet or the critic whose mind and taste have been exercized on Latin and Greek literature will be more exceptional than the dramatist who has prepared himself for this task in the theatre by a close study of optical, electrical and accustical physics? You have the option of welcoming the change as the dawn of emancipation or of deploring it as the twilight of literature; but at least you must agree that we might expect it to mark some great difference between the literature of the past and that of the future – perhaps so great as to be the transition from an old language to a new one.[6]

Whether the change Eliot describes signals the dawn of emancipation or the twilight of literature is one of those problems that looks different depending on where you stand and on how you read history. In the nineteenth century a few European nations acquired empires and slowly began to discover the relativity of the modes of thought they had considered universally valid. It was (and still is) a painful process. Imperialism, like nationalism, promulgates a unity only by submerging difference. As the old presumptions of the superiority of Anglo-imperial culture broke up with the lapse of empire, a world of difference began to assert itself. In places as disparate as North America, Australasia and Africa, writing began to exert a local provenance.

In *Widening Horizons in English Verse*, John Holloway recounts the response in English verse to the discoveries of the literatures of other cultures. He considers Celtic, Saxon, Norse, Islamic, Indian, Eastern and Egyptian literatures and their effects on English poetry, and concludes:

> We in Western Europe and America have opened up to our literary consciousness, one after another of the major literatures and major cultures of the planet ... We

have reached in our literary culture the point reached by the geographical explorer some time ago ... The process of exploration which began in the Renaissance with our own native past and western classics, and then opened its horizons wider and wider is certainly near the limit of its range.[7]

As Holloway points out, the last person to bring home the prize of a central corpus of work from an exotic culture was Pound in his translations of the Noh drama or later from the Chinese Classic Anthology. These are masterpieces of the histories of Japanese and Chinese literatures. 'Nowadays', Holloway continues, 'the most popular kind of contact is rather with a mere contemporary *avant garde* – in the West Indies, Australia, Africa, wherever it might be. I do not condemn this in any way. It is clearly an image of our time and our preoccupation everywhere with the topical. But it is another kind of thing; and by definition it cannot have the same magnitude'.

Holloway draws our attention to an historical epoch which has ended or is ending. Since his book was published in 1965 there has been nothing to disprove his contentions. A New Zealand critic has recently pointed out that in 1916 in Lawrence's *Women in Love* the whole world which separates the West African from the West Pacific could be passed over easily. By now, however, that blank slate has been 'filled in', even for white, First World intellectuals.[8] The heartlands of English literature are in the process of being charged with the discovery of difference.

If the English-speaking world has suffered a diaspora, then we must begin to look not only to what Allen Curnow called 'the neglected middle distance', that is, to other former colonies, but also to the grounds of a cultural encounter with the richness, the complexity and the otherness that lie immediately to hand.[9] Of course, we will continue to look back to all that we inherit from Europe in general and Britain in particular. Nevertheless, we must question that longstanding and entrenched assumption within English studies that the Renaissance, with its rooting in the classics, remains the torso of English studies while all the subsequent periods constitute the outer limbs.

In our reading of contemporary English-language poets we discover new ways of understanding the relations among the various far-flung parts of the English-speaking world, connected in the first place by the legacy of colonialism. We gain a new sense of the language itself in the face of that long process of the collapse of the imperial 'centres', European or American, and of what the Scottish poet, Hugh MacDiarmid calls 'linguistic imperialism'. ' – All dreams of "imperialism",' he writes in *In Memoriam James Joyce*, 'must be exorcized, / Including linguistic imperialism, which sums up all the rest'.[10] By shifting the focus of English studies away from the *centrality* of the European inheritance we begin to encounter a multiplicity of other traditions.

A literature content to sit on its laurels or even to remain in ignorance of the borders or shores which delimit it, has had it. Equally, a literature or culture fragmented or dissolved by colonial occupation can only reassert itself through a vast act of reconstitution and recuperation. In either case, turning abroad, engaging in world literature, is an act of healthy curiosity as well as being politically necessary. Identity most fully resides in the struggle in which it is engaged, and that struggle is inevitably a political one. For identity is a function of position and position is a function of power.

Such a way of understanding allows us to see the 'new literatures' in English not as the etiolated remains of a dying 'Tradition', but as what Wilson Harris calls 'complex wholeness[es]': that is, as fictive totalities composed of the various inheritances, traditions, cultural memories (including those which 'may once have masqueraded themselves as monolithic absolutes') which make up the post-colonized world.[11] It also allows us to envisage a greater complexity in the cultural scenes of the old 'centres'.

The view that the 'mainstream' of English poetry in this century proceeds from Hardy by way of Auden to Larkin shows the dangers of abandoning Eliot's European 'Tradition' for a merely national one. To do so is to allow that 'English' literature has simply shrivelled to its parochial confines and thereby become of interest only to the people who live within those confines, and to few of them at that. If we see 'English' literature in an international context, however, we can arrive at a more complex and a more accurate picture of a literature that includes not only the Movement and the Martians but also popular culture, Scots and Anglo-Irish writings, the writing of Caribbean and other immigrants (not to mention Gaelic, and other non-English language cultural minorities). Where two or more of those competing traditions are coming together in a particular writer – Wilson Harris, for instance – 'really new' writing is being produced.

Modernism was nothing if not international, but it was a Eurocentric movement, not a global one. One of the most pervasive changes in poetry since around 1945 (when global vulnerability became materially demonstrable) has been precisely this apprehension of being, in the words of a young New Zealand poet, Leigh Davis, 'under the technology of arms'.[12] Simultaneously, there has been a growing recognition of the discrete, the various, the multiplicity of difference and the vicarious problems of identity. This is what underwrites Ian Wedde's special pleading in his introduction to *The Penguin Book of New Zealand Verse*: 'The history of a literature with colonial origins is involuntarily written *by* the language, not just in it: the development of poetry in English in New Zealand is coeval with the developing growth of the language into its location, to the point where English as an international language can be felt to be original *where it is*'.[13] The converse is just as true: that English as an international language cuts itself off from wherever it is used. As the language of domination and exploitation it is the most pervasive symbol of the colonial process. It is everywhere a foreigner. These opposed views of the English language as 'original where it is' or as a 'perpetual foreigner' are the extremes between which all specific uses of that language occur.

Certainly, the decentering of English literature that has characterized the post-war scene presents itself as a source of possibility, a gainful 'lowering of the sights', as Charles Olson put it. Eliot's sense of Tradition with its hierarchy, its blindnesses and its exclusiveness has surely been consigned often enough to the museum of literary history.[14] But once allow that there are no longer any authoritative centres from which to determine what is peripheral, and the classical 'Tradition' defended by Eliot becomes one among many traditions currently available to the writer. As such, it ceases to be 'Tradition' as Eliot understood the term: the memory of the culture of the European peoples informing and holding together the best work of the present. Yet it remains a part of the *bricolage* of the contemporary cultural scene.

In Les Murray's poetry, in spite of his celebrated quarrel with modernism and in spite of his announced determination to write 'against the grain of Literature',[15] the whole continuity of the English literary tradition is as present as it is in a selfconsciously 'Attic' Australian poet like Peter Porter. (Murray, after all, read all of Milton in a single long weekend as a schoolboy.) Yet it never crowds out his lithe grasp of the vernacular energies of that rich idiom, Australian-English, not to mention his debts to Celtic and indeed Aboriginal sources. This does not mean simply that in practice Murray's poetry has been enriched by the language of popular usage as was Eliot's high-cultural Tradition. It means that the European inheritance has been obliged to cohabit in a given body of poetry with an utterly alien sense of tradition. Behind Murray's poetry we sense the presence of English literature as a whole, not just the inheritance of canonized texts. In other words, the writing is vitalized, charged with a sense that the energy of the language proceeds from the differences with which it is riddled. In his own words, he is trying 'to make not so much "high" as rich and flexible art out of traditional and vernacular materials'.[16]

The problems of nationality emerge clearly when we compare current writing in Britain with that in the Caribbean. Let's look at Derek Walcott's poem 'The Schooner *Flight*'. The poem's speaker, Shabine, explains his name as 'the patois for / any red nigger' and claims:

> I had a sound colonial education
> I have Dutch, nigger and English in me,
> and either I'm nobody, or I'm a nation.[17]

A rich complexity of reference is worked into the poetry of those who choose to start out from that sense of displacement, of unhousing, which is part of the general condition which terms like postmodern or post-colonial attempt inadequately to account for. The sustenance of ideas like 'home' and 'heartland' has always been fostered by migratory myths of an original Eden and an ultimate resurrection. These myths need not be dismissed as mere colonial nostalgia. When they are co-opted into a poetry which confronts and reinterprets history, which questions the motives behind linear chronology and which understands meaning to be multifaceted, they figure as vital and necessary fictions.

> Now that peasantry is in vogue,
> Poetry bubbles from peat bogs,
> People strain for the old folk's fatal gobs.
> Coughed up in grates North or North East
> 'Tween bouts o' living dialect,
> It should be time to hymn your own wreck,
> Your home the source of ancient song.[18]

So begins Guyanese poet, David Dabydeen's 'Coolie Odyssey', leading from the dry fireside where coconut shells are cackling, by way of Seamus Heaney's evocation of reclaimed ancestors in Irish peat bogs, to a winter of England's scorn where memories are huddled and hoarded from the opulence of masters. Dabydeen commemorates his narrative in a parodic reflection and rejection of the classic colonial narrative. Instead of adopting the expansive viewpoint of the colonizer setting out from Europe, Dabydeen moves out from the position of the exploited and oppressed:

> We mark your memory in songs
> Fleshed in the emptiness of folk,
> Poems that scrape bowl and bone
> In English basements far from home,
> Or confess the lust of beasts
> In rare conceits
> To congregations of the educated
> Sipping wine, attentive between courses –
> See the applause fluttering from their white hands
> Like so many messy table napkins.

These images reveal that much noted duality that runs through Caribbean literature. But one finds a similar note in unexpected places where the only cultural link is that of a common experience of having been colonized and deprived of language. In many Scottish writers, for instance, we find this two-fold understanding of identity as something that is, whether one likes it or not, constituted by a multiplicity of differences, racial and linguistic. In the post-colonized subject, Caribbean or Scottish, we find the internalized conjunctions of different histories, whose presence necessitates a continual reinterpretation, demands varieties of reading stance, and calls forth contradictory modes of expression. At the same time, however there is the sense that these apparently centripetal tendencies at least potentially exist in a creative relationship with one another, that a peculiar species of coherence is granted them because the pressures of history acting within the individual are forcing them into new, curious and shapely ways of seeing.

In the writing of Wilson Harris we find exemplary confrontations with mythic material. In a sense Harris's Guyana is a methaphor for the English language itself in the world after empire (*malgré* Grenada and the Malvinas). Harris doesn't merely consign the older notions of tradition to some capacious museum of cultural history: he dismantles, reconstitutes and resituates those traditions, makes them part of the current scene, if not privileged, still useful and present. Harris's writing shows an extraordinary openness to the variety of traditions meeting in a post-colonized country.

Here we find a sense of the English language that puts the legacy of colonialism at the centre of its attention without simplifying the ways in which that legacy continues to bear upon writing in the colonizing as well as in the colonized worlds, is present for the descendants of the colonizers as well as for those of the colonized. What Harris calls for is a 'radical aesthetic' which visualizes in broken post-colonial worlds communities tolerant enough to include renovated versions of the codes of imperial power alongside those of the cultures that have been mutilated by imperium. In other words, Harris manages to allow for the conflicting demands of tradition *and* difference. He suggests a view of the new literatures not as mere branches of the host trunk growing at various speeds into mature traditions in their own right but as complex and rich totalities made up out of conflicting elements existing in dialectical tension. This view is the enabling condition of an approach to current English writing because it discovers common features by recognizing the full complexity of culture since colonialism.

Like Harris, Wole Soyinka is aware not simply of the national and racial components of existence, but also of the historical, geographical, psychic and economic conditions which go into their formation. He is as clearly a representative of black Africa as he is of a common humanity when he stands before existence's chthonic forces. In these terms, he is a writer of major significance in the context of world literature. By the range and specificity of his knowledge, he refuses the option of sectarianism and dismisses as cowardly the craving for national exemption. As he says in the introduction to *Six Plays*:

> There's no way at all that I will ever preach the cutting off of *any* source of knowledge: Oriental, European, African, Polynesian, or whatever. There's no way anyone can ever legislate that, once knowledge comes to one, that knowledge should be forever excised as if it never existed.[19]

Soyinka's is an exemplary attack on xenophobia. If his apprehension of the world is shaped by the peculiar stresses and urgencies of Nigeria, it is liable to be explained in terms the relevance of which should not be lost in New Zealand, Canada or Scotland:

> In defence of that earth, that air and sky which formed our vision beyond lines drawn by masters from a colonial past or redrawn by the instinctive rage of the violated we set out, each to a different destiny.[20]

NOTES

1. Les Murray interviewed by Iain Sharp, *Landfall*, Vol. 42 No 2 (June 1988), p. 160.
2. Robert Creeley, rev. by Alan Loney of *Dear Mondrian*, *Islands*, Vol. 4 No. 4 (Summer 1975), p. 467.
3. Letter of Robert Creeley to Charles Olson, 23 October 1951, in *Charles Olson and Robert Creeley: The Complete Correspondence*, Vol. 8, ed. George F. Butterick (Santa Rosa: Black Sparrow, 1987), p. 83.
4. George Bowering, *A Way With Words* (Ottawa: Oberon, 1982), p. 23.
5. T.S. Eliot, 'Tradition and the Individual Talent', *Selected Essays*, by T.S. Eliot (London: Faber and Faber, 1972), p. 15.
6. T.S. Eliot, 'The Classics and the Man of Letters', *T.S. Eliot: Selected Prose of T.S. Eliot*, ed. John Hayward (Harmondsworth: Penguin, 1963), p. 215.
7. John Holloway, *Widening Horizons in English Verse* (London: Routledge and Kegan Paul, 1966), pp. 108-9.
8. Simon During, rev. by Subramani of *South Pacific Literature: From Myth to Fabulation*, (Suva: University of the South Pacific Press, 1985), in *Landfall*, Vol. 41 no 3 (September 1987), p. 359.
9. Allen Curnow, 'Modern Australian Poetry', in *Look Back Harder: Critical Writings, 1935-1984*, ed. Peter Simpson (Auckland: Auckland University Press, 1987), p. 83.
10. *Hugh McDiarmid: Complete Poems, 1920-1976*, ed. Michael Grieve and W.R. Aitken (London: Martin Brian and O'Keefe, 1978), Vol. II, p. 790.

7. John Holloway, *Widening Horizons in English Verse* (London: Routledge and Kegan Paul, 1966), pp. 108-9.

8. Simon During, rev. by Subramani of *South Pacific Literature: From Myth to Fabulation*, (Suva: University of the South Pacific Press, 1985), in *Landfall*, Vol. 41 no 3 (September 1987), p. 359.

9. Allen Curnow, 'Modern Australian Poetry', in *Look Back Harder*: Critical Writings, 1935-1984, ed. Peter Simpson (Auckland: Auckland University Press, 1987), p. 83.

10. *Hugh McDiarmid: Complete Poems, 1920-1976*, ed. Michael Grieve and W.R. Aitken (London: Martin Brian and O'Keefe, 1978), Vol. II, p. 790.

11. Wilson Harris, *Explorations* (Aarhus: Dangaroo Press, 1981), p. 135.

12. Leigh Davis, *Willy's Gazette* (Wellington: Jack Books, 1984), n.p.

13. Ian Wedde, Introduction to *The Penguin Book of New Zealand Verse* (Auckland: Penguin, 1985), p. 23.

14. See, for example, Charles Madge's obituary for Eliot, 'In Memoriam, T.S.E.', in *New Verse*, Nos. 31-2 (Autumn 1938), p. 18.

15. Les Murray quoted in C.K. Stead, 'Standing Up to the City Slickers', rev. by Les Murray of *Selected Poems* and *The Daylight Moon, London Review of Books*, (18 February 1988), p. 11.

16. Ibid., p. 12.

17. Derek Walcott, *The Star-Apple Kingdom* (London: Johathan Cape, 1980), p.4.

18. David Dabydeen, *Coolie Odyssey* (Aarhus: Dangaroo Press, 1988). 'Coolie Odyssey' is the title poem.

19. Wilson Harris, *Explorations* (Aarhus: Dangaroo Press, 1981), p. 135.

20. Wole Soyinka, Six Plays (London: Methuen, 1984), p. 5

On Eurocentric Critical Theory: Some Paradigms from the Texts and Sub-Texts of Post-Colonial Writing.

As quiet as it is kept, the realisation is gaining wide currency in literary circles around the world that the volume of writing now coming from the non-Western, Third World countries far outstrips that emanating from the 'First World'. Moreover, it is also increasingly being recognized that this vast harvest, this cornucopia from the Third World contains some of the most interesting and innovative writing in contemporary literature. Think about it: if, with 'Anglophone', 'Francophone' or 'Lusophone' writing from the non-Western world you include writing in the most prominent literary languages of the Third World say, Arabic, Bengali, Chinese, Urdu, Gujerati, Swahili and Amharic, you can begin to get a grasp of the shifts in the densities and concentrations of the literary map of the world. But parallel to this phenomenal reconfiguration of the global balance of forces in the production of literature is the view also prevalent throughout the world, that the most penetrating, the most seminal criticism, metacriticism or 'theory' is coming from the metropolitan centres in Europe and America. Just how prevalent this view of a new international division of labour in the world of literature and criticism has become is afforded by a recent short but thought-provoking article in no less a publication than *The Chronicle of Higher Education*, written by W.J.T. Mitchell (April 19, 1989). Mr. Mitchell is a professor of English at the University of Chicago and moreover, is editor of *Critical Inquiry*, one of the most influential academic journals of contemporary criticism and literary theory in the English-speaking world. Let me quote some salient observations from the article:

> The most important new literature is emerging from the colonies – regions and peoples that have been economically or militarily dominated in the past – while the most provocative new literary criticism is emanating from the imperial centres that once dominated them – the industrial nations of Europe and America.
>
> Horace noted long ago that the transfer of empire from Greece to Rome (the *translatio imperii*) was accompanied by a transfer of culture and learning (a *translatio studii*). Today the cultural transfer is no longer one-way. But what is the nature of

the transference going on between the declining imperial powers and their former colonies, and between contemporary literature and criticism?

Professor Mitchell's views and positions in this important article come from the liberal critical vanguardism of the American literary establishment, one that is particularly responsive to new currents, new directions from the 'non-canonical' traditions of both literature and criticism. Moreover, Professor Mitchell advances the view in this article that powerful and increasingly desperate and hysterical neo-conservative critics and scholars are up in arms against the 'reconceptualizations' and 'reconfigurations' now emerging in the world of literature and criticism and that an alliance, 'a positive, collaborative relationship between post-imperial criticism and post-colonial literature' might be needed to stave off this projected neo-conservative redoubt. This is an important, weighty observation and I would like to frame my reflections in this short essay around what I perceive to be its many ramifications.

The call of Professor Mitchell in this article for collaboration and solidarity between 'post-colonial literature' and 'post-imperial criticism' no doubt comes from a genuine, enlightened solicitude which relates itself to serious areas of cultural politics, even if the designated terms and entities of the collaboration – 'post-colonial literature' and 'post-imperial criticism' – are not so unproblematic. [But more on this later.] The journal which Mr. Mitchell edits has been an important forum for important interrogations of canonical orthodoxies and exclusionary critical practices which ignore texts and traditions other than the hegemonic literary production and critical discourses of Europe and America. One can only wish that more journals and institutions would, like the one Mr. Mitchell directs, and which are strategically located in the apparatus of theoretical inquiry and critical discourse, be more responsive to, or even be more aware of developments and trends beyond the concerns and obsessions of a self-cocooned Western canonical enclave.

But it must be recognized that the solicitude and enthusiasms of many Western critics and scholars for non-Western, post-colonial literature, have behind them a problematic history which is encapsulated by that troubled, loaded buzz word 'Eurocentrism'. For if Eurocentrism has often expressed itself, in different forms of cultural racism, as a denial of, a supercilious condescension towards non-Western literary traditions, it is also often conversely expressed as a generous solicitude, an authenticating embrace which confers what it deems a badge of authenticity, for the non-Western text, writer or whole literary traditions, only to be accosted with charges of paternalism and subtle forms of prejudice and will-to-domination.

At this late stage of the history of debates over imperialism and its discontents, one states the obvious by pointing out that Eurocentrism is a vast cultural and intellectual phenomenon which subsumes its more local and particular expressions in literary criticism, and now 'theory'. The work of contemporary writers like Aime Cesaire (*Discourse on Colonialism*), Eric R. Wolf (*Europe and the People Without History*), Edward Said (*Orientalism*), Johannes Fabian (*Time and the Other*) and Talal Asad (*Anthropology and the Colonial Encounter*), among others, shows the dispersal of the phenomenon among disparate disciplines and fields of inquiry. All of which goes to demonstrate that without having the models and standards of the exacting scholarship and broad, capacious vision of these scholars in mind, one enters the terrain of discourse and counter-discourse on Eurocentrism at the risk of gross simplifications and unsuspected discursive traps. And need I add that this last observation is intended not only as a general cautionary nudge to literary criticism, which often purposes itself as a substitute for all of critical thought, but also as a reminder to myself about the lurking pitfalls of *this* discursive terrain.

It will thus be readily appreciated that I have chosen to approach the subject in this essay by way of a calculated detour through the discourses on Eurocentrism embedded in some selected literary texts. In such contexts a host of textual strategies and rhetorical mediations absorb and defamiliarize the tensions and sensitivities that discussions of Eurocentrism almost always generate. In particular I have chosen two texts of Derek Walcott, *Dream on Monkey Mountain* and *Pantomime* as paradigmatic deconstructions of the two types of Eurocentrism broadly hinted at above: the Eurocentrism which withholds, which excludes, which disdains; and that which embraces, invites, gives.

The distance covered in contemporary post-colonial writing in the debunking, the demythologization of Eurocentric claims to the embodiment of absolute Truth or Knowledge, especially of non-European peoples and societies, is, I believe, provided by the paradigmatic move in the dramaturgy of Derek Walcott from *Dream of Monkey Mountain* (1967) to *Pantomime* (1978) concerning the respective emblematic explorations in these two plays of the response of the 'native' as the Object of Eurocentric discursive, signifying and explanatory systems. A savage, iconoclastic, mythoclastic assault on the ethical-universal postulates of the Western intellectual traditions, and specifically the objective, positivist human sciences (like jurisprudence) marks what we may identify as the epistemological theme of these plays, where 'theme' is an inaccurate, inadequate conceptual representation of these aspects of both Walcott's dramaturgy and a host of other post-colonial writers, from Achebe to Coetzee, from Soyinka to Rushdie, from Mariama Ba to Ama Ata Aidoo. We see this common iconoclastic impulse particularly in the characters of Corporal Lestrade and Moustique in *Dream on Monkey Mountain* and Jackson Philip in *Pantomime*. What powers this impulse is the thinking that 'white' domination is not only political and socio-economic, it is also, or aspires to total effectivity in the naming of things, in signifying and explanatory systems; in other words, it seeks to be an *epistemic* order of control and manipulation. Corporal Lestrade and Jackson Philip in particular deploy a surfeit of brilliant, witty conceits and tropes to debunk this epistemic, nomenclatural hegemony. But there are important, even decisive departures in the respective overall demythologizing impulse and postures of these two plays, and it is this pattern of differentiation which commends them as suggestive paradigms for the debates on Eurocentrism and critical theory.

Between Corporal Lestrade and Moustique in *Dream on Monkey Mountain* what we encounter is the 'native' who, having rejected both Eurocentric discursive colonization *and* autonomous indigenous epistemologies and ritual beliefs, can only lapse into a desperate cynicism, charlantanism, and in the case of Moustique, a convenient opportunism. The powerful 'healing' dream scene of Act One of the play renders this aspect of Moustique's vocation as an 'explainer', who, despising both the colonizer and the colonized and their respective panoply of signification, appeals to a Transcendent, omniscient Spirit [God] outside, beyond and above the contest, a Spirit in whom Moustique does not believe but only deploys in order to manipulate the colonized 'native' population:

MOUSTIQUE
Ah, ah you see, all you.
Ain't white priest come and nothing happen?
Ain't white doctor come and was agone still?
Ain't you take bush medicine, and no sweat break?
White medicine, bush medicine,
not one of them work!
White prayers, black prayers,
and still no deliverance!
And who heal the man?
Makak, Makak!

All your deliverance lie in this man.
The man is God's messenger
[He opens his haversack and holds it before him]
So, further the cause, brothers and sisters.
Further the cause,
Drop what you have in there...
God's work must be done
and like Saint Peter self,
Moustique, that's me,
is Secretary-Treasurer

The logic of this cynically opportunist, self-cancelling, double assault on both Eurocentric epistemologies and signifying systems *and* the countermanding nativist response reaches its most brilliant, relentless articulation in the famous Apotheosis scene of the play [Scene Three, Part Two]. Walcott indisputably wrote this magnificent cautionary allegorization of the natives' revenge against what Gayatri Spivak has theorized as the totalizing 'epistemic violence' of imperialism with the spirit of Bandung active in his creative consciousness, the heady spirit in the Fifties and Sixties of 'emergent' Africa and Asia coming into their own and settling scores with their former colonial overlords. The allegorical power of the scene derives, I think, from Walcott's frank, unflinching engagement with the violence of Eurocentric signifying practices and explanatory systems, in their imbrication in the objective of imperialistic domination. It is indeed useful to note that Walcott has the following quote from Sartre's famous Introduction to Fanon's *The Wretched of the Earth* as an epigraph to Part Two of *Dream on Monkey Mountain*, the movement of the dramatic action of the play which brings the nihilistic confrontation with Eurocentrism to a head:

> Let us add, for certain other carefully selected unfortunates, that other witchery of which I have already spoken: Western culture. If I were them, you may say, I'd prefer my mumbo-jumbo to their Acropolis. Very good: you've grasped the situation. But not altogether, because you aren't them – or not yet. Otherwise you would know that they can't choose; they must have both. Two worlds; that makes two bewitchings; they dance all night and at dawn they crowd into the churches to hear Mass; each day the split widens. Our enemy betrays his brothers and becomes our accomplice; his brothers do the same thing. The status of 'native' is a nervous condition introduced and maintained by the settler among colonized people with their consent.

Only against the background of this phantasmic but deadly serious agonistic encounter does the arraignment and trial of the whole of 'Western culture' in this scene make 'sense', a 'sense', a logic which in fact was later to be acted out by Idi Amin in his gratuitous antics against some of the most resonant colonialist symbols and tropes of Eurocentrism such as the famous enactment in which he was borne aloft in a litter by four white men, this as a parodistic signification on the 'White man's burden'. It is, I think, necessary to quote from the scene at some length:

[All have assembled. The CORPORAL steps forward, then addresses MAKAK]
CORPORAL
Inventor of history! [Kisses MAKAK's foot]
MAKAK
I am only a shadow
CORPORAL
Shh. Quiet, my prince.
MAKAK
A hollow God. A phantom.
CORPORAL

Wives, warriors, chieftains! The law takes no sides, it changes the complexion of things. History is without pardon, justice hawk-swift, but mercy everlasting. We have prisoners and traitors, and they must be judged swiftly. The law of a country is the law of that country. Roman law, my friends, is not tribal law. Tribal law, in conclusion, is not Roman law. Therefore, wherever we are, let us have justice. We have no time for patient reforms. Mindless as the hawk, impetuous as lions, as dried of compassion as the bowels of a jackal. Elsewhere, the swiftness of justice is barbarously slow, but our progress cannot stop to think. In a short while, the prisoners shall be summoned, so prepare them, Basil and Pamphilion. First, the accused, and after them, the tributes.

[The prisoners are presented]
Read them, Basil!
BASIL

They are Noah, but not the son of Ham, Aristotle, I'm skipping a bit, Abraham Lincoln, Alexander of Macedon, Shakespeare, I can cite relevant texts, Plato, Copernicus, Galileo and perhaps Ptolemy, Christopher Marlowe, Robert E. Lee, Sir John Hawkins, Sir Francis Drake, The Phantom, Mandrake the Magician [The TRIBES are laughing] It's not funny, my Lords, Tarzan, Dante, Sir Cecil Rhodes, William Wilberforce, the unidentified author of The Song of Solomon, Lorenzo de Medici, Florence Nightingale, Al Jolson, Horatio Nelson, and, but why go on? Their crime, whatever their plea, whatever extenuation of circumstances, whether of genius or geography, is that they are indubitably, with the possible exception of Alexandre Dumas, Sr. and Jr., and Alexis, I think it is Pushkin, white. Some are dead and cannot speak for themselves, but a drop of milk is enough to condemn them, to banish them from the archives of the bo-leaf and the papyrus, from the waxen table and the tribal stone. For you, my Lords, are shapers of history. We await your judgement, o tribes.
TRIBES
Hang them!

'Their crime, whatever their plea, whatever extenuation of circumstances, whether of genius or geography, is that they are ... indubitably white'. The utter seriousness, the implacable, crystalline logic of this absurd arraignment – Shakespeare and Al Jolson, Galileo and the KKK – can only be grasped if we pluck from its dispersal in disparate semiotic contexts and significatory locations the coding and re-codings of 'white' as the unmarked marker, 'white' fetishized as ultimate repository of Beauty, Reality, Value: 'Whites Only', 'Honorary Whites' (a term officially accorded the Japanese in South Africa, but not other Asian national groups like the Chinese and Indians), the white-robed and hooded 'Knights of Klu-Klux-Klan', the white anthropomorphic iconography of divinity and sainthood in Christianity, white bleaching creams. All these interfuse with more specifically *epistemological* coordinates: Western 'white' civilization *racialized* (and not only by the Nazis) and encoded as the ultimate marker of Truth, Knowledge, Rationality in the elaborate constructs of 'the great chain of being', as Arthur O. Lovejoy informs us in his famous treatise of that title. Derek Walcott is barely in control of the relentlessly parodistic smashing of icon and fetishes in this play, given the utter negativity of the epistemic revolt, itself a response to the unstinting negation projected by *this* particular paradigm of a Eurocentrism which withholds and excludes absolutely. At the end of it all, Makak has exorcised the demons and phantoms of his bewitched, schizophrenic subjectivity; but he does so away in the mountains to which he now withdraws completely, into a private space of subjectivist autarky. He cannot be the 'King of Africa', the 'Conquering Lion of Judah' of his dreams since he has seen how hollow that turns out to be in a world never quite free of both Eurocentric 'epistemic violence' and the giddy paroxyms of nihilistic revolt and manipulation which it engenders: *aut ceasar, aut nihil*.

Although it has a much smaller cast of characters, *Pantomime* encapsulates a much more engrossing and dialectical frame of referents of epistemic Eurocentrism and its demythologization than *Dream on Monkey Mountain*. The dramaturgic 'trick' employed to achieve this seems derived from the principles of dramatic form and performance styles developed by Athol Fugard and the South African anti-apartheid theatrical movement of Barney Simon, John Kani, Winston Ntshona, the Market Theatre and others; small casts of two or three characters constantly changing roles, constantly constructing and deconstructing, totalizing and detotalizing social wholes, social macrocosms and their fragments and microcosms. A 'perfect' formalistic vehicle for a drama which seeks the epistemic deconstruction of the texts and signs of Eurocentrism.

The figural, metaphoric strategy which establishes *Pantomime* as a decisively different paradigm of epistemic demythologization than *Dream on Monkey Mountain* is that the 'text' deployed in this play has been devised out of Defoe's *Robinson Crusoe*, a classic 'megatext' of Eurocentrism. Moreover, the roles are now reversed, a reversal significantly voluntarily proposed and *demanded* by the white character, Harry Trewe, a retired British actor who has removed himself from personal, domestic and professional disasters and decline in Britain to the island of Tobago in the Caribbean. Here he establishes the 'Castaway Guest House' and hires a retired Trinidadian calypsonian and carnival maestro, Jackson Philip, as his 'factotum'. So as to draw guests to his decrepit establishment Trewe devises an improvisational script reversing the roles, the identities, the figural binarisms of Defoe's classic text: the white Trewe will play Friday; the black Philip will play Crusoe. But Harry Trewe's project comes only partly out of business calculations; he is also a liberal, a progressive who insists on the edifying potentiality of such an entertainment for both the white tourists to the island and the local black creole community:

JACKSON
>   That is white-man fighting. Anyway, Mr. Trewe, I feel the fun finish; I would like, with your permission, to get up now and fix up the sun deck. 'Cause when rain fall...'

HARRY
>   Forget the sun deck. I'd say, Jackson, that we've come closer to a mutual respect, and that things need not get that hostile. Sit, and let me explain what I had in mind.

JACKSON
>   I take it that's an order?

HARRY
>   You want it to be an order? Okay, it's an order.

JACKSON
>   It didn't sound like no order.

HARRY
>   Look, I'm a liberal, Jackson, I've done the whole routine. Aldermaston, Suez, Ban the Bomb, Burn the Bra, Pity the Poor Pakis, et cetera. I've even tried jumping up to the steel band at Notting Hill Gate, and I'd no idea I'd wind up in this ironic position of giving orders, but if the new script I've been given says: HARRY TREWE, HOTEL MANAGER, then I'm going to play Harry Trewe, Hotel Manager, to the hilt, damnit. So sit down! Please. Oh, goddamnit, sit ... down ...
>   (Jackson sits. Nods)
>   Good. Relax. Smoke. Have a cup of tepid coffee. I sat up from about three this morning, working out this whole skit in my head.
>   (Pause)
>   Mind putting that hat on for a second, it will help my point. Come on. It'll make things clearer.
>   (He gives Jackson the goatskin hat. Jackson, after a pause, puts it on)

JACKSON
>   I'll take that cigarette.
>   (Harry hands over a cigarette)

HARRY
>   They've seen that stuff, time after time. Limbo, dancing girls, fire-eating...

114

JACKSON
    Light.
HARRY
    Oh, sorry.
    (He lights Jackson's cigarette)
JACKSON
    I listening.
HARRY
    We could turn this little place right here into a little cabaret, with some very
    witty acts. Build up the right audience. Get an edge on the others. So, I thought.
    Suppose I get this material down to two people. Me and ... well, me and
    somebody else. Robinson Crusoe and Man Friday. We could work up a good
    satire, you know, on the master-servant – no offense – relationship.
    Labour-management, white-black, and so on ... Making some trenchant points
    about topical things, you know. Add that show to the special dinner for the
    price of one ticket ...

Things do not, of course, work out the way Trewe's script envisions a
revision of *Robinson Crusoe*. For one thing, Trewe's revision does not go far
enough for Philip. Philip renames Friday Thursday. He renames all the
props and paraphenalia of survival and 'civilization' that master and servant,
colonizer and colonized have to share. And he disagrees violently with Trewe
over what spiritual qualities sustained Crusoe on the island and allows him
to establish dominion over it, its flora and fauna, and Friday. The twists and
turns, the explosive negative racial and cultural material thrown up by this
encounter are made bearable and commensurable only by the powerfully
enabling and metaphorically suggestive fact that both men have been actors,
performers, entertainers. The performance idioms of the English music hall
and the Trinidadian calypsonian carnival become vehicles of thoroughgoing
textual revisions of Defoe's classic novel and deconstructive assault on a vast
array of cultural systems and codes which have defined the encounter of the
colonizer and the colonized. At the end of it all, Trewe finds that the
'pantomime' cannot be played innocently; there is too much at stake:

HARRY
    Look, I'm sorry to interrupt you again, Jackson, but as I – you know – was
    watching you, I realized it's much more profound than that; that it could get
    offensive. We're trying to do something light, just a little pantomime, a little
    satire, a little picong. But if you take this thing seriously, we might commit
    Art, which is a kind of crime in this society .. I mean, there'd be a lot of things
    there that people .. well, it would make them think too much, and well, we
    don't want that ... we just want a little ... entertainment.
JACKSON
    How do you mean, Mr. Trewe?
HARRY
    Well, I mean if you ... well, I mean. If you did the whole thing in reverse ... I
    mean, okay, well, all right ... you've got this black man .. no, no ... all right.

115

You've got this man who is black, Robinson Crusoe, and he discovers this island on which there is this white cannibal, all right?

JACKSON

Yes. That is, after he has killed the goat ...

HARRY

Yes, I know, I know. After he has killed the goat and made a ... the hat, the parasol, and all of that ... and, anyway, he comes across this man called Friday.

JACKSON

How do you know I mightn't choose to call him Thursday? Do I have to copy every .. I mean, are we improvising?

HARRY

All right, so it's Thursday. He comes across this naked white cannibal called Thursday, you know. And then look at what would happen. He would have to start to ... well, he'd have to, sorry ... This cannibal, who is a Christian, would have to start unlearning his Christianity. He would have to be taught ... I mean ... he'd have to be taught by this – African ... that everything was wrong, that what he was doing ... I mean, for nearly two thousand years ... was wrong. That his civilization, his culture, his whatever, was ... horrible. Was all ... wrong. Barbarous, I mean, you know. And Crusoe would then have to teach him things like, you know, about Africa, his gods, patamba, and so on ... and it would get very, very complicated, and I suppose ultimately it would be very boring, and what we'd have on our hands would be ... would be a play, and not a little pantomime ...

JACKSON

I'm too ambitious?

HARRY

No, no, the whole thing would have to be reversed; white would become black, you know ...

JACKSON

(Smiling)

You see, Mr. Trewe, I don't see anything wrong with that, up to now.

HARRY

Well, I do. It's not the sort of thing I want, and I think you'd better clean up, and I'm going inside, and when I come back I'd like this whole place just as it was, I mean, just before everything started.

JACKSON

You mean you'd like it returned to its primal state? Natural? Before Crusoe finds Thursday? But, you see, that is not history. That is not the world.

HARRY

No, no. I don't give an Eskimo's fart about the world, Jackson. I just want this little place here *cleaned up*, and I'd like you to get back to fixing the sun deck. Let's forget the whole matter. Righto. Excuse me.

The play however does not end on this note of a return to a 'colonial' *status quo ante*, at least on the individual, person-to-person, existential level. Indeed, Trewe and Philip both ultimately abandon completely the distance, formality and protocols of employer and employee, 'white' and 'black', English and Creole that had prevented them from playing the revised text of *Robinson Crusoe* to the bitter end. And that is precisely the 'point' of this play (is it?): There is a history of Eurocentrism; Eurocentrism is also *in* history, including significantly, present history; we can neither innocently re-enact the text(s) of the 'old' history, nor shake the texts of the 'new' history completely free of the old texts. I think Walcott is suggesting that if this is the case, the point is not to lapse into despair or mutual isolation but to find the integrity to acknowledge the violence of that history. All the same, it is significant that both Trewe and Philip (and Walcott) back off from a complete engagement with the logic and dynamics of the *power*, or more appropriately, the will-to-power, that inheres in both the constructions of Eurocentrism and the deconstructions of oppositional nativist texts, codes and languages.

The two paradigms of the interrogation and contestation of Eurocentrism that we see in *Dream on Monkey Mountain* and *Pantomime* do not by any means exhaust the range of the literary exploration of epistemologies and discourses of colonization and decolonization in contemporary post-colonial writing. Where do we, for instance, place Achebe's *Arrow of God*? Ezeulu instantly recognizes the connection between the new religion, the new teaching and the incipient reconfigurations of power relationships generated by the new colonialism and its peculiar regime of peripheral, *administrative* capitalism (as distinct from the *settler* capitalism of colonialism in other parts of Africa). Ezeulu decides to send one son into tutelage of the new 'teaching', to be on the safe side. But Ezeulu loses both ways: the new colonialism completely marginalises the great store of knowledge and wisdom that Ezeulu's priestly vocation and function draws upon (including lunar observations and calendrical calculations); it also presents him with a son, who having served his tutelage, comes with a dislocated subjectivity, an alien 'soul'. And where also, for another important text, do we place J.M. Coetzee's *Waiting for the Barbarians*? The protagonist, the Magistrate, is a scion of a humane, skeptical, courageous and conscientized rationalism. As he contemplates the present history of (a particular) Empire running to its conclusion, he also ruminates on History. He does this by trying to unravel the message or meaning of the cryptic scripts and writing that his excavations of the ruins of a previous empire have thrown up. Yes, he muses, the 'barbarians' will outlast 'us', defeat 'us' (we deserve defeat); but will 'they' have the capacity and the inclination to understand or interpret 'us' the way we have done 'our' predecessors? One wonders what Ezeulu and the Magistrate would have had to say to each other if the accidents or contingencies of history or literary creation had brought such types into direct contact.

I see the value of these two paradigms as indicating some *sub- texts* for critical theory's engagement of Eurocentrism. One can only indicate these in a very general, condensed and schematic fashion here. First, *Dream on*

Monkey Mountain suggests a nativist moralism in which the rejection of 'Europe' and Eurocentrism is taken to its extreme limit. It is perhaps not unfair to see this as analogous to certain forms of the 'Black Aesthetic' rubric of the Sixties and early Seventies in the United States, and certain expressions of the 'decolonization' poetics in Africa in the Seventies and early Eighties, especially that associated with Chinweizu, Madubuike and Jemie in their famous (or notorious) book, *Toward the De-colonization of African Literature*. The underlying impulse here is a total change of nomenclature, models, inspiration; the call for an autochthonous, pristine, originary aesthetic is so total that *any* trace or influence of European techniques and forms in literature, and any European critics and schools in literary criticism is condemned *ad initio*. I think *Dream on Monkey Mountain* effectively dramatizes the falsity and pitfalls of the 'decolonzation' claimed by this form of nativism.

Pantomime, I think, implies a radical relativism in its complete deconstruction of both Eurocentrism and nativism; this evidently recalls certain forms of post-structuralist and deconstructivist assault on essentialism and the 'metaphysics of presence' in the canons, and the celebration of indeterminacy. As analogically dramatised in *Pantomime* this position invites its own 'deconstruction' and interrogation: what is the value of a radical relativism which carries out a necessary demythologization of essentialized Eurocentrism and nativism but evades or occludes the violence of the power relations between them by tacitly assuming an equivalence of either actual power consolidation between them, or the will-to-power of their pundits and adherents? Let us reinscribe this interrogation into its concrete articulation in the global balance of forces of world literature study at the present time: what differentiated consolidations and sedimentation of power do we encounter in the world of global institutional cultural politics between, say, Derrida, de Man and the Euro-American deconstructors and post-structuralists on the one hand, and Chinweizu and his 'de-colonizing' nativists on the other?

The Texts of 'Mother India'

'For the first time in world history, mechanical reproduction emancipates the work of art from its parasitical dependence on ritual'.[1] So wrote Walter Benjamin in his brilliant essay entitled 'The Work of Art in the Age of Mechanical Reproduction'. The question of the primacy of an original fades into insignificance as a wholly new concept of 'reproducibility' comes into existence. The question is no longer one of 're-presentation' but essentially one of 're-production'. With a deft shift in emphasis Benjamin suggests that mechanical reproduction now irrevocably replaces ritual by politics. Reformulated, the mystery surrounding the original, which is traditionally conceived as shrouded, removed, in short an Other, is replaced by an involvement in the processes of reproduction and response. Where the reproduction of a painting is read through an original, perceived or absent, the filmic text is the origin of its meaning, for it represents nothing other than its own self: there is no image beyond the filmic shot, no 'real' (the authentic, ritualistic presence), no godhead or ultimate source of meaning, a perceptual signified, behind the image. It is constructed through the lens, and exists only because of it. Not surprisingly, it was seen as a travesty of art, a subversion, essentially, of the mimetic principle which gave art a point of reference and even a legitimacy. The sort of studied, careful response that art demanded is replaced now, as Benjamin argues, by an ever-changing movement. He quotes Duhamel's reactions to film as being typical of high culture's barely concealed uneasiness on the subject. Instead of that difference which marks art, the difference, that is, of historical 'placement' and detachment, the film now makes it possible for art to enter popular culture and collapse its dichotomies. Its real antecedents are not painting but architecture and the epic poem, forms which have a participatory function in culture. Their aesthetic qualities are, in short, functional. Benjamin cites Duhamel again:

> [the film is] a pastime for helots, a diversion for uneducated, wretched, worn-out creatures who are consumed by their worries ... a spectacle which requires no concentration and presupposes no intelligence ... which kindles no light in the heart and awakens no hope other than the ridiculous one of someday becoming a 'star' in Los Angeles.[2]

It is advisable to break Duhamel's criticism into three. The first thrust is clearly class orientated – those who see films are basically 'uneducated', a huge mass of humanity whose cultural antecedents remain markedly oral; the second is psychological in that it necessitates involuntary response; the third, finally, is rooted in desire, the displacement, essentially, of the filmic subject by the spectator. The last is also characteristic of the narcissistic conflation of Self and Other, that first stage in human development where the image in the mirror is still trapped within the Imaginary – the cinema, in short, is read in this instance as primarily indentificational, or in Brecht's terms 'repressive'.[3] Behind Duhamel's critique of filmic response (as basically mindless and non-intellectual) is precisely the politicisation of artistic process raised by Benjamin. In other words, Duhamel's criticism politicises the film even as it proposes to frame it within a crude aesthetics of folklore. For, in terms of Benjamin's own argument, the film is part of a new consciousness, a political democracy where the authority of the primary text (the text in fact as the ultimate source of all meaning, as a kind of an Absolute Signified) ceases to matter.

Can authentic meaning be restored once genesis is erased? Terry Eagleton, whose statement I've reformulated as a question, seems to think so.[4] The question is an important one because Benjamin's case for mechanical reproduction – idealistic, messianic as well as revolutionary as it seemingly is – is predicated upon the belief that history progresses as much from its bad side as from its good side: 'there is no cultural document that is not at the same time a record of barbarism', wrote Benjamin in another context.[5] The target of the essay is clearly the 'auratic' phenomena associated with the original, and the reactionary, aesthetic, deployment of the original towards Fascist ends. For Benjamin then, film marks a release because in film at least the question of the original cannot surface. Now the reason why Benjamin is so central to my own thinking about film is that the programme for cultural release foreshadowed by Benjamin has been a feature of Indian culture throughout its history. Since art and religion were so closely intertwined, 'auratic' value resided not in the original but in the culture's capacity to transform the original into a symbol which could then enter the domain of the popular. Thus the release of art from ritual is in the making from its very genesis because authorship (as in the epics) is socially or 'functionally' (recall Foucault's concept of the 'author-function'[6] here) defined. The result is that each work of art, as symbol, is always both original and a forgery. It could be argued, and there is enough evidence to endorse this, that the reinscription of the Indian work of art into an 'auratic economy' was the product of the Western search for and fetishisation of the original.

In literature it took the form of the search for the original text or author. Is the *Bhagavadgita* for instance, contemporary with the rest of the sixth book of the *Mahabharata*? Can we reconstruct the original poems of the medieval saint singers of India? For the Indian whose interest was in the total text as transmitted towards a given moment in history these questions were irrelevant to its total value. For the European scholar, intellectual integrity or honesty demanded that the original be established, the 'source' of the voice be found – we owe this to the 'author's' memory. Here then is our point of departure from Benjamin. In releasing art from its dependence on the 'auratic' and the original, mechanical reproduction simply advanced a process which had been at the heart of Indian culture. And since the 'aura' was never for the brilliance of the original but rather for the emotional intensity of its subject matter (*rasa* theory is crucial here), film simply intensified the audience's relationship to the symbol in Indian society.

I

Cinema in India began as a colonial business, and it has never been able to shed its colonial origins. Post-colonial cinema is thus locked into modes of representation and generic fashions begun when the colonised represented themselves through an essentially colonial machinery of mechanical reproduction. This feature is crucial to any reading of Post-colonial Indian cinema – unless it completely subverts its own cinematic history, it will always be colonial (and hence 'tame') in its overall ideology. In this respect my crucial filmic text, *Mother India*, symbolises the ambiguous stature of Indian post-colonial popular culture generally – a culture so deeply expatriate even whilst it proposes to be so defiantly non-expatriate.

Each year the statistical handbook of the Government of India devotes a number of pages of its Mass Communication section to films. The statistical information given in these yearbooks shows the Indian film industry as a profit-making industry in the general capitalist acceptation of the term and an enormous cultural artefact, both politically aware and self-reflexive, conforming indeed to the propositions about 'photographic' culture outlined by Benjamin. Ever since Dhundiraj Phalke's *Raja Harishchandra* (1913),[7] feature films have been an integral part of the political economy of India. Their mode of production and distribution to this day conforms to the classic definitions of supply and demand one generally associates with crude capitalism. In short it is a purely profit-making enterprise in which questions of art and aesthetics are subordinated to the profit-making motive – the industry as a whole has never been in the red! Statistics may be readily cited to demonstrate the resilience of this industry. Indian cinema ranks among the country's top ten industries,[8] giving the government a revenue in excess of 200 million dollars and providing jobs to between two and three million people. It is a totally private enterprise with virtually no hidden government subsidies. Beyond this, the presence of some 11,000 permanent and 'touring' cinemas[9] expands the number of people directly employed by the Indian film industry considerably. Since 1980 the number of films produced annually in the nine major Indian languages has consistently exceeded the 700 figure. The total output of feature films in all the Indian languages in 1983 was in fact 742, a figure equal to the 1980 record-breaking achievement. Though no details of export earnings are given in the more recent Indian yearbooks, a quick glance at yearbooks in which these statistics were included indicates a foreign exchange potential in excess of ten million dollars. With the video boom the figure may have to adjusted slightly, though in real terms, as John Ellis suggests in his admirable recent work,[10] it is unlikely that the video is going to radically alter the money-making capacity of the film industry. Nevertheless, the claims made by the Indian Film Producers' Guild are disconcerting. In Britain – for years the major foreign market for Indian films – the number of theatres showing Indian movies has dropped from an all-time high of 159 to 2 in recent years.[11] The probable impact of the video aside, the 'privatisation' of the Indian film into homes through the video industry is clearly contrary to the very basis of the Indian film which quite unabashedly fits into a massive Indian tradition of oral culture and folklore.

The enormity of the 1983 figure of 742 feature films may be understood better if we recall that that figure is almost as high as the combined output of Japan, the US and Hong Kong put together (748).[12] With an adult (16 and over) viewing public in excess of 400 million, the Indian film has a potential audience only slightly less than that of Hollywood! Any systematic examination of the political economy of the Indian film industry will, however, require not only a thorough-going analysis of all aspects of the film industry's financial system (including 'black-money', underhand payment to actors and so on) but also a breakdown of the social and class types who see these films. That analysis would require a paper with very different aims and must at this stage be left aside for a much more comprehensive study of the Indian film industry. Here my primary concern is not so much with Indian film (though some understanding of it is crucial for a study of this kind) but with one particular example of Bombay Film, a term I use collectively to include films which are generally produced in Bombay and whose medium is Hindi. Furthermore the term 'Bombay Film' is used for a product which is made for popular consumption. This restricted use of the term excludes from my immediate study films, though in Hindi, with an experimental dimension or artistic self-consciousness. In exploring this definition of Bombay Film I would like to postulate that *Mother India* and related films discussed in this paper belong to a single genre. I use the term genre not in the usual fashion of 'western', 'social drama', 'mythological', 'detective', 'mystery' and so on but as a term which expresses a certain fidelity to a particular formula for success. This formula, naturally, has a clearly defined narrative to which we may, after considerable distortion, give the term *grande syntagmatique*, the film, that is, as one huge narrative unit.[13] This being so, it is possible to show how every filmic text conforms, in broad outline, to a grand narrative which may, in itself, become identical with one film. Along with this narrative fidelity, the formula also demands that the film be constructed around the figure of a star-as-hero/heroine. Yet unlike the *masala* or kedgeree (*khichri*) theory put forward by many fanzies (through which in fact the cinema is partially constructed anyway: cinema is, after all, a 'construction' through a highly diversified set of responses) and approvingly cited by *Time Magazine* in an issue devoted, in part, to Asian cinema,[14] the Bombay Film is a very subtle art form which expresses a high level of consciousness about its dependence on formula. Indeed, the generic totality we give Bombay Film should not be allowed to hide the very obvious fact that it is capable of accommodating differences and contradictions.

One final look at the statistics. If we examine the figures given for 1981 we see that 206 films were certified in Bombay.[15] Since only 153 Hindi movies were produced that year, Bombay clearly produces or is the centre for the 'certification' of at least 53 movies which are not in Hindi (these would presumably be Gujarati and Marathi films). Furthermore, there is a growing Hindi film industry in Madras which has been responsible for at least a dozen or so Hindi films each year. Thus in using the generic title 'Bombay Film' I refer to a particular form or style of films made in Hindi. Except for some basic differences (Hindi movies from Madras tend to exaggerate the 'look' or 'pose' – the impact of the classical Southern dance forms is evident here), the generic specificity of Bombay Film is not altered by locality. I do, however, claim that the dominant cinematic form in India is this cinema. This may seem at first glance surprising because 153 Hindi films out of a total of 742 constitutes less than a quarter of all films produced. A quick glance at the 1981 figures once again shows the numerical strength of the Southern (Madras) cinema, notably those films produced in Malayalam, Tamil and Telegu. The total output of films in these languages amounts to 380, well over twice the number of movies made in Hindi. Yet films in none of the other Indian languages (including Bengali and Gujarati) have potentially pan-Indian audience. And often films in the other languages are no more than straight imitations of Bombay films in Hindi. I referred to a potential audience of some 400 million for Indian films generally. It is clear that the Bombay Hindi film alone commands about three-quarters of that audience. A remark attributed to Shashi Kapoor, a member of the family most commonly associated with the Bombay Film of the last three or four decades, is salutary: 'What Gandhi couldn't do for India, the Bombay cinema has successfully accomplished'.

II

One of the things about any cultural artefact is that it shows how the culture of which it is a product represents itself. Since no culture can represent the source culture better than the source culture itself, it follows that, in a way, the most authentic representations (even when these representations are ultimately distortions of that culture) and critical readings must in fact come from Indians themselves.[16] It is this question of representation, of cultural representation, of self-representation which takes me to *Mother India*, the modern epic of India for, as I have said, the real knowledge and understanding of India must come from those texts which have been disseminated into and consumed by that culture. This knowledge is not simply a matter of 'passive consumption'; it requires a sympathetic understanding of critical practices not necessarily available to the Indian him/herself.

Released in 1957 *Mother India* is a film which has probably been dubbed and subtitled more than any other film in Hindi. It was screened in London four years later; and both in Britain as well as, of course, in India it has been shown regularly in cinemas patronised by Indians. It is said that it is screened somewhere in India on every day of the year. In 1983, Channel 4 showed it on British television as part of its highly successful season of Indian Cinema. Now in its thirtieth year, it has acquired something of a cult status and in some quarters the status of the 'definitive' Indian film text. Along the way it has won many awards in India, has been widely acclaimed in the Middle East and Southeast Asia and has gained an Oscar nomination (in 1958).

Its producer and director Mehboob Khan, a Muslim, was an important figure in the Indian film industry, having produced extremely popular films such as *Aurat* (1940) (an early version of *Mother India* which was indebted to Pudovkin's socialist realist cinematic adaptation of Maxim Gorky's *Mother* [1926])., 17 *Mela* (1949), *Andaaz* (1950), and *Aan* (1951) among others. *Mother India* is in some ways more centrally diffused and contradictory than Mehboob's other films in the genre of Bombay Cinema. It is in fact not one film but a number of films, not one text but a multiplicity of texts. The first text is obviously embedded in the title itself. *Mother India* goes back immediately to Katherine Mayo's antagonistic and racist book of that name published in 1927.[18] The connection is disturbing because Katherine Mayo adopted a crudely geneticist argument (though her sensational account of sexual abuse through child marriage had some basis in fact) aimed at representing the Hindu (and not the Muslim) as both physically and emotionally decrepit and hence totally incapable of running his or her own affairs. Mayo's book was a best-seller which went into some dozen reprints in just under three years, and was used as a powerful propaganda tool by the British against the Indian Nationalists, Gandhi included.

The title also triggers a second *Mother India* text in that it forcefully reminds us that there is something motherly about India, or that motherness is India. Nevertheless there is a curious reading of 'Mother India' in this film which is perhaps much more interesting, for 'Mother India' is really an English title – there is nothing Indian about the words 'Mother' and 'India'. When you look at the credit stills of *Mother India* you find that 'Mother India' is simply transcribed into the Hindu/Sanskrit script or the Urdu/Persian script so that 'Mother India' is presented as a kind of a universal term which is not in need of translation at all. This is rather intriguing for an Indian epic (though it may be a statement about the power of colonial discourses generally) because the title therefore enters into a string of Bombay films with none of *Mother India's* totalising vision, nor its presumed universality. *Taxi Driver* (1952), *Street Singer* (1940), *CID* (1957), *Mr X* (1956) were all Indianised; they are nuanced in such a way that they become part and parcel of the sociolect. There remains, however, something terribly unusual, removed, detached, alien about *Mother India*. In short 'Mother India' is a transcendental signified. What are the connections? 'Mother India' has a certain hegemonic presence. It is a translation of *bharata mata* behind which stands the Sanskrit compound *matrbhumi*, Motherland. Through yet another system of transformations one can actually connect *matrbhumi*, Mother-earth, with the figure of Sita, the heroine of the *Ramayana*, the *dhiram bharyam* (the steadfast wife) who replaces, in Indian consciousness, 'Mother India'. There is another way in which the connection is sustained and this is through the name of Sita. Sita means 'of the furrow' and indicates through her name her own autochthonic origins. So that 'Mother India' really becomes a way of talking about Sita, the figure who is really a stand-in for India. Historically, however, Sita is not a given; she has never been there in that form all along; she had to be fought for; and Hindu cultural and Brahminical ideology had to come to terms really with what was in the epic tradition, Sita's rape and reinstitution into Rama's world. In that act of struggle a whole Sita idiom evolved; a whole set of Puranic treatises were written to make Sita other than herself. Where Rama actually became, in the later recensions of Valmiki, god-incarnate, Sita somewhat more slowly and problematically became Vishnu's consort Lakshmi. The culture invested Sita with excessive meaning, over-determined her through massive semantic and mythic overcoding, but could not quite remove her epic violation. That guilt of 'rape' led to excessive circumspection and cultural bracketing for woman generally. This congruity of Sita/Mother India/Woman thus surfaces as an artificially constructed presence which I think is culturally and ideologically rather suspect. In projecting that affinity the ruptures and discontinuities are glossed over. Instead we get an excessive insistence upon *dharma*, the Law of culture, and an excessive valorisation of genealogy so that Sita may be granted a central position in Indian consciousness. If Mother alone knows the secret of your birth (it's a lucky child who knows its father) her power within culture becomes inviolate and beyond falsification. I have spoken almost metaphorically, alluding to symptoms and possibilities rather than historical certitude and finality. *Mother India* then represents, at least as I see it, a massive problem of Motherness, Sitaness and Otherness in Indian culture. If we return to the epic formulations of Mother, we are far from satisfied with the film's presumed certainty about its version of the history of Sita. To deconstruct *Mother India*, to decentre it, to read it through a kind of negative dialectic, against the grain so to speak, is tantamount to rupturing ideological smoothing over or gloss. It is in short a recipe for the Indian return of the repressed.

What I am suggesting is that 'Mother India' is a problem and an historical compromise. Indian culture (and this culture also endorses a predominant patriarchal point of view) has countered this problem through the projection of a range of symbols which are dispersed throughout the culture. These symbols associate Mother with Goddess (here Sita is Lakshmi), with Wife (here Sita is Draupadi), with Lover (here Sita is Radha), and through the slightly contradictory iconography of Kali and Durga, as the avenger or destroyer, where Sita of course is the female embodiment of some of the characteristics of none other than Shiva. In this final historical compromise woman (femininity) is seen as a total counterpart of the two crucial masculine gods, Vishnu the Preserver, and Shiva the Destroyer. This is in fact the second major text of *Mother India*. Given its specific cultural antecedants (and readings) *Mother India* also blurs the 'feminist' distinctions between the 'feminine' (as a social construct) and the 'female' (biologically determined sexual difference). For the more adept student of gender and sex (which I

126

am not) it would necessitate a systematic and culture-based reading of the female form in India.

A third *Mother India* text requires two sets of productive activities: firstly, the manner in which the signifier 'Mother' is filled out in the film; and secondly, the manner in which a narrative is generated. This second set of productive activities – the manner in which the narrative is generated and how the viewer responds to it – may be discussed first since it is relatively straightforward. In one of the two great epics of India, namely the *Ramayana* of Valmiki, the poet Valmiki is careful to say that the epic as sung by Lava and Kusha, the twin sons of Rama, 'is replete with all the poetic sentiments: the humorous, the erotic, the piteous, the wrathful, the heroic, the terrifying, the loathsome, and the rest'.[19] These sentiments are of course straight out of Indian theories of *rasa* or emotional responses as these were advanced in the great texts of Sanskrit dramaturgical and poetic practice. The continuities between an on-going Indian cultural tradition and Indian Cinema is not lost on the viewer of the film, as Raj Kapoor (*Awaara, Jagte Raho* etc.) said in an interview:

> Where did the whole thing originate? The telling of a story, the singing of a story, came from [the] mythology, it came from the epics, it came from the Vedas. These were then portrayed in villages and from the villages they travelled with players in folk-lore, in folk music and in folk drama and then developed into theatre. Till the talkies arrived we could not bring that tradition to the public at large. And theatre had as its mainstay not only dialogue, but music. Now this is very, very important to the Indian audience – that theatre combines all different fields of fine art into one. And when we came to the medium of cinema and the talkies came in – we brought music, dialogues, and everything else to the Indian Cinema. Since then Indian Cinema has used all different facets of entertainment: it has got its magic, its thrills, its romanticism but underlying all this is *music*, which is India.[20]

No Indian film is more aware of this cultural heritage than *Mother India*. In other words, beneath *Mother India* lies a complex set of cultural practices which vie for domination among themselves, song vying for domination over dialogue, dialogue over song, filmic representation over dialogic representation (that is, visual effects over oral effects), the actors amongst themselves, personal sincerity (that is, the ability of an actor to portray a character), and generic or historical/cultural sincerity (that is, how a particular type, the Rama figure or the Sita figure for instance, has always been represented in that culture). There is thus a continuous tussle, a continuous struggle or contest going on between these various cultural practices in a movie like *Mother India*. If we want to look at the the question of difference, if we want to look at the question of where or when or at what point a film actually triumphs over the obvious, the conventional, the predictable, the routine, I think we will have to locate it at the level of a certain kind of rebelliousness within the context of these norms. The kind of rebelliousness which I have in mind may be located when actors already confined to pre-ordained rules through, for instance, their names, their roles and so on, break past these confines and momentarily rupture the text.[21] Great Bombay Film actors, and I use the word 'great' with caution, are in fact those who are aware of the weight of the tradition and their own subtle little difference from that particular tradition. In their better moments, these actors were probably actors such as K.L. Saigal (best known I think for his performance in P.C. Barua's 1935 classic *Devdas*), V. Shantaram, Dilip Kumar, Raj Kapoor, Sunil Dutt (especially the Sunil Dutt of *Mother India*) and, more recently Amitabh Bachchan, Shabhna Azmi, Rekha and Smita Patil. This catalogue of 'great actors' emphasises the extent to which popular cinema in India draws on a wealth of Indian cultural experience, understood by and shared with the audience. When cinema in India has borrowed (and which cinema has not come under the alluring and dizzying influence of Hollywood?), it has transferred its borrowing to produce specifically Indian effects – from Indian Charlie Chaplins to Indian James Bonds. *Mother India* too has borrowed from the West, and it is informed by these borrowings. But in spite of all its borrowings and the accompanying imperfections that borrowings necessarily bring to cinema of another culture, *Mother India* remains very much an Indian text.

III

I would now like to return to the question of how the signifier 'Mother' is constructed. The text is obviously held together through the figure of a woman. We are meant to identify her with *Mother India* but I suspect this is not as obvious as we think. Many viewers have seen her metonymically and not symbolically. Since neither suture nor identity is totally maintained in the way in which the heroine is represented (this is not the case with the hero as we shall see later), the metaphorical congruity so essential for absolute identification is thwarted at every stage. And, furthermore, since *Mother India* enters an already coded Bombay filmic practice, the practice which in fact endorses a mixture of dramatic and poetic properties, generic flux and open-endedness, it follows that textual production itself will be discontinuous and fractured. *Mother India*, as I have said already, is a much more contradictory text than meets the eye.

We are introduced to the Mother as 'the Mother of the village' and for this reason she is asked to open a new dam just constructed in a village in post-colonial India – remember this is 1957, ten years after independence.

[It is clear that Prime Minister Nehru supported Mehboob Khan's venture to make *Mother India* – *Mother India* begins with many shots of agricultural advances, irrigation projects, use of tractors and so forth]. The story is then unfolded as a 'memorial reconstruction'. Yet this woman through whose memory the story is enacted is not, strangely enough, named after Sita or Lakshmi or Durga or Kali or even Kunti. On the contrary she is called Radha, a choice which in itself signifies that the other names I have mentioned are not, except in mythological films, part of Bombay filmic practice. In other words, the naming of 'Mother India' as Radha signifies that Bombay Film does not like to call its heroines Sita or Lakshmi or Durga or Kunti even though these goddesses and heroines from the epics would have been seen much more naturally and readily as precursors of 'Mother India'. I am not saying that Radha belongs to a completely different system: it's just that given her special relationship with Krishna, Radha can be manipulated much more readily by Bombay Cinema. In some ways Radha is much more open-ended; Sita is obviously closed. This kind of naming takes us to the heart of Puranic India, to the heart of that India where *Mother India* is set, where the narrative of *Mother India* is unfolded; and this is of course in the heart of Krishna territory, Uttar Pradesh, where the folk deity is in fact Krishna. Stories about Krishna are the source of many of the idioms, metaphors, and rituals we find in *Mother India*.

In any artistic transformation Sita, though deeply ambiguous, remains extraordinarily stable. As a result Indian Cinema can do very little with a figure like Sita. Her field of operation is limited; her relationship with the audience carries with it such a vast repertoire of expectations and prior readings as to make her totally predictable. I think it is for this reason, among many others I am sure, that in *Mother India* the Mother, the Woman, is not called Sita, she is called Radha, Krishna's jovial consort, immortalised in Jayadeva's Sanskrit masterpiece *Gitagovinda*, the song of Krishna.

How does Radha fit in? Radha as I have said is Krishna's mistress, a cowherd whose love-longing for Krishna – at least insofar as the Vaishnavite, East Indian and especially Bengali tradition is concerned – is read as the epitome of religious devotion to God. Physical love, in other words, is read allegorically or homologously, as *bhakti* or devotion. The intensity with which that physical love is expressed (as in Jayadeva for instance) is directly proportional to the intensity with which the devotee as Radha expresses her devotion to her beloved Krishna as God. I think this is an important feature of the relationship between physical love and devotion in Indian devotional and, indeed, erotic texts as well. The connection between the *rasa* of eroticism, the *rasa* which has been given the Sanskrit name of *shringara*, and a much later *rasa*, the *rasa* of *bhakti* or devotion, is a very important connection and it is one which is probably familiar to students of Medieval European devotional texts as well.

It should be noted, however, that this figure of Radha is in many ways a later development. The great founders of Indian discursivity, the *Mahabharata* and the *Ramayana*, which are the basis of much filmic, literary, theatrical or dramatic culture of India, remain remarkably silent about Radha. She seems to have emerged much later and is chronicled extensively not so much in epic texts but rather in what are called the *Puranas*, a slightly different body of literary and religious texts. These were compilations which got under way probably in post-classical India, in the period from around the 5th or 6th century A.D. (these are very vague starting points only). So while Sita is fundamentally epic, going back to the *Ramayana*, Radha is indeed Puranic. Where Sita, as we have seen, does not have referential freedom – she is closed, she is fixed, immutable, existing only in endless replays of sameness – Radha's presence, on the other hand, enables the typically Indian concept of life as play, as a game, as ludic, to surface. As a result of this 'openness', Radha oscillates between woman, devotee and beloved. In *Mother India*, of course, she also acquires, through typically Indian processes of mediation, the qualities of the mother too.

Let's apply this information to *Mother India*. As I have said the Mother, played by the actress Nargis, is called Radha. Her husband is predictably Shamu, a diminutive of Shyam, a North-Eastern Indian name for Krishna, who is also known as Govinda, Gopala, Madhava, and so on. This Krishna/Radha relationship, written over the Rama/Sita relationship, enables the film to play with sentiments which Mother-as-Sita would have precluded. It enables precisely those sentiments, those many *rasas* whose combination, expression and manipulation make up the great text that Lava and Kusha spoke about in the *Ramayana* to surface. In *Mother India* woman is therefore represented as wife, as lover, as Mother in both her role as a preserver and destroyer and also, because she is Radha and not Sita, as a figure who is marginally comic. I say 'marginally comic' because the comic elements do not invade the total text. They simply enable the film, consciously or unconsciously, to bring in the Devaki/Krishna playfulness to the text as well as to suggest a relationship tinged probably with Oedipal longings. There is thus a conscious collusion and collision with culture taking place in *Mother India*. The film rather nervously gestures towards configurations and possibilities of meaning which go outside and beyond the basic plot of the film itself. More immediately, I have suggested that the way in which Radha enters Indian consciousness and a particular order of mythology is very crucial for any reading of this film.

I have tried to include in the overall genealogical field triggered by Radha other characters from *Mother India*. Let me now make those connections a bit more explicit. Radha and her husband Shamu connect the text to earlier, particularly literary, antecedents. The family tree that we can extrapolate from *Mother India* would go something like this. Radha marries Shamu/Krishna and they have four children, but only two survive. The first one is called Ramu who, again along the lines of Shamu, is the diminutive of Rama, the epic hero. The other son is Birju and Birju, unlike Rama the archetypal, dutiful son, is slightly different in the sense that Birju probably comes from Braj the locality in which Krishna lived and of which he is the local deity. Through this sense of 'locale', Birju, as a diminutive of Braj, in fact appropriates some of the symbolic roles of Krishna. The case might not be as simple as all that but I think that it is quite obvious that there is an underlying connection (through Braj) between Birju and Krishna. So just as Radha may be broken up into the dutiful woman and a playful mistress, so Krishna too is both god incarnate – the mediator in the ritual of battle as in the *Mahabharata* and hence a Rama figure – and the child-like mischievous stealer of honey and butter, celebrated in Puranic lore. Through this particular tradition of naming, Shamu's children make up two dimensions of Krishna himself – Krishna as Rama, the law-giver, and Krishna as the player, the mischief-maker, the stealer of butter. The composite Krishna/ Rama of Shamu, in other words, is therefore dispersed through Ramu the dutiful son and Birju the playful son. The first one is clearly epic, the second from the Puranas. In this manner Ramu enters a predictable discourse whereas Birju remains ambivalent – both the teaser of water-carrying maids, as well as, in the final analysis, the avenger. Since Birju's relationship to his first or ur-name is problematic (since its basis is really in metonymy and not in metaphor) we may fill out his existence or his character in *Mother India* in various ways, or at various levels. The Mother's love towards the younger son both conforms to cultural norms (and these are predictable cultural norms) and at the same time endows that love with a replay of the Radha/Shamu desire so cruelly brought to an end in the first hour of the film. From this possibility the older brother is excluded. Indeed those who give in to the Law of the Mother, like her husband and her older son, are symbolically castrated and made inarticulate. As a young child Ramu in fact does not say a word throughout the film except perhaps to scream 'ma' ('mother'). It becomes clear, therefore, that in naming the younger son Birju and in making the connection with Krishna, albeit the playful Krishna, and through him in making Birju more like his rebellious father Shamu before he succumbs to the mother's wish to till an unproductive piece of land, thereby losing both his arms, the film connects sexual potency with rebellion against the Mother even whilst it plays, unconsciously, with the much more frightening issue of the Oedipus complex. Birju in fact dies holding a pair of blood-soaked *kangans* (his mother's marriage bangles) he had recovered from Sukhilala. As a son's symbolic restitution of his mother's honour, it is an image fraught with inescapable sexual overtones.

IV

The *Mother India* text is also a function of filmic representation and is constructed through it. In the first half of the film at any rate, the epic form of visual representation is relatively unified. Through the obvious mediation of the technique of socialist realism, especially those techniques of film-making polished and perfected by people like Eisenstein, Pudovkin and Mayalovsky, we find a particular construction of narrative underway. There are certain classic epic shots (the long shot and the epic pose) which are favoured over others and which among many others dominate the first half of the film: the image of bullock carts being dragged across the horizon, a long shot taken from just underneath the branches of a tree, a man's gaze atop a scaffolding, Mother and Sons in profile against or together with the symbols of the hammer and sickle. These are visual images which reinforce an overall epic filmic technique of representation. *Mother India*'s epic form is thus as much filmic (through techniques of film making) as it is narrative. The ideological basis of this appropriation must be considered especially insofar as the film was clearly endorsed by Jwaharlal Nehru, the then Prime Minister of India, as indicative of the progress that India had made ten years after independence. Thus in speaking about *Mother India* as a multiplicity of texts we must refer as much to its filmic complexity as to the verbal fragments, the collage of various narratives, which underlie this particular text.

At the level of discourse, however, we find at least two narratives in *Mother India*. The first is a relatively clear-cut and sustained narrative which begins with Radha's marriage to Shamu, goes through the loss of Shamu's arms and his disappearance, and effectively ends with the growth of the two surviving sons Ramu and Birju. The second more complex narrative is probably less well sustained and the film does tend to weaken somewhat in the second half. This second narrative is all about love and hate, desire and sexuality, comic buffoonery and the tragic, where the narrative gets lost in the kinds of filmic representations selectively endorsed by the Bombay film industry. And here, in this second narrative, we have bullock cart races, banditti and a general speeding-up effect whereby the essential control of the text through the Mother is lost. In this narrative – that is in the second narrative of *Mother India* – the text acquires different centres: the Mother, Birju, the landlord Sukhilala, and the woman school teacher, who finally becomes the revolutionary intellectual and who points out the need for action after Birju fails to learn accountancy. But since this second text, the second narrative, is complex and discontinuous or fractured, its unity has to be found elsewhere, beyond the textual domain, beyond the film *Mother India* as we see it, and in the base culture itself. It is here that *Mother India*, like the genre of Bombay Cinema, requires a multiplicity of self-justifying and self-explicating discourses. In one way the semantic field of the signifier *Mother India* is a discourse (and text) of this kind.

V

An informed analysis of *Mother India*, therefore, takes us away from the surface expressions of culture to those dialectical processes in the deep structure which hold Indian society together. This is, of course, the conflict between living in this world (*pravritti*) and renunciation (*nivritti*).[22] In *Mother India* there is considerable cultural unity in the sense that Birju's renunciation from the affairs of the world (insofar as he leaves the social order of the village to become a bandit) is carefully plotted. This narrative is characteristic of one way of renouncing the world, although this is not the renunciation which is endorsed by Birju himself. But once he does become a bandit and therefore outside the social order that controls village life, he must be denied first of all love of woman and second pro-creation. In other words, the avenger must first renounce before he can upset the world order. To destroy a feudal system, the person from within must renounce its structures; onslaught is possible only by someone who has no real 'familial' constraints. This is very important for Birju. He leaves his Mother, but his departure is necessary before the so-called revolution can take place.

But renunciation and through it revolution by the free floating social agent is ultimately side-stepped by the text. If Sukhilala is the ultimate feudal lord, he is a father as well; if he wishes to defile other women, he has a daughter as well. Between the roles of feudal lord and father, between the lecher and the father it is the figure of the Father which acquires greater significance. Thus *Mother India* – ostensibly about struggle against tyranny/ feudal colonialism – cannot escape past the larger underlying categories which govern (and in turn subdue) Indian society. Thus the film can resolve (or neutralise) the urge towards revolution only by distorting the dominant epic narrative. This is done through the introduction of a sub-plot about the honour of a village girl (the landlord's daughter in fact) who is abducted, towards the very end of the film, by Birju the renouncer/revolutionary. It is this sub-plot – so far completely irrelevant to the underlying revolutionary impulse of the text – which suddenly becomes the narrative in terms of which *Mother India* resolves the terrible crisis of the Indian revolutionary in a post-colonial world.[23] Mehboob Khan's ploy here is to introduce a facet of *Mother India* we've already outlined. In the face of the 'rape' of the village girl, 'Mother India' must now be reinscribed into her role as the Law, as the upholder of *dharma*. Thus in re-introducing the notion of Law as *dharma*, the film returns 'Mother India' to the larger paradigmatic narrative, the founding narrative, which generates (perhaps illusorily so) this complex discourse. The end of the feudal world-order comes not because Birju kills Sukhilala and abducts his daughter, but because in upholding the eternal *dharma*, the Indian body politic effectively demonstrates its own moral uprighteousness.

It is this specific conjunction of Mother as upholder of the Law and Mother as the avenger which leads to the radical impossibility of action in Indian society. United India after independence needs a guerrilla war like a hole in the head. In allowing a son to be killed by a mother, *Mother India*, the epic of post-colonial India, bares open the contradictions upon which this massive civilization is based. One remembers Hegel's incisive critique of Indian society: 'The Hindoo race has consequently proved itself unable to comprehend either persons or events as parts of a continuous history...'[24] And so ritual enactment, ritual treatment replace history. Ritual overcomes the processes by which history itself can fulfil its own teleological designs. The questions we now ask are what happens to history in *Mother India*? What happens to history in Indian texts? Why is it that the details of struggle against an outmoded system of feudalism are not given their full representation? How can the Indian peasant triumph over that kind of economic exploitation? These questions are tantalisingly present in *Mother India*; they surface so many times and yet they are never really resolved, and the resolution, when it comes just before Birju's death at the hands of his Mother, remains incomplete and is not really a resolution of a massive contradiction in Indian society. The immemorial difference between the serf and his feudal lord remains virtually untouched.

VI

There are two dialogic situations, occurring within about five minutes of each other, which I should now like to examine to show the deep-seated ambiguities of Indian culture and how these ambiguities ultimately preclude the revolutionary act. In other words, popular Indian Cinema is so conservative and culture-specific as to make a radical post-colonial Indian Cinema impossible – and not only that, it tries to subvert the radical, as in *Mother India*, by drawing it into its fold and then neutralising it or reabsorbing it back into Hindu culture. The first dialogic 'moment' is the death of Sukhilala at the hands of Birju; the second is Birju's own death at the hands of his Mother.

The struggle between Birju, the renouncer/revolutionary/bandit and Sukhilala, the feudal lord, takes place in Sukhilala's house and it is about what constitutes true knowledge. Faced with Birju's hatred of the written word (Birju after all is illiterate), Sukhilala insists that his books of accountancy, his ledger books, are in fact repositories of knowledge and as knowledge they should not be defiled. To this Birju replies, 'I have no time for this knowledge (*vidya*), this is the knowledge that took my land away, this is the knowledge that took my bullocks away, this is the knowledge that led to the defilement of my Mother'. Birju declares that he will not forgive and concludes before stabbing him, 'You are a bandit, and I too am a bandit; the law (*kanun* not *dharma*) will not leave you alone, it will not leave me alone'. Birju's obsession with another version of law, colonial law (as *kanun*) as distinct from the Law (*dharma*), is raised here.

The second dialogic situation may be translated as follows:

Girl: Radha Auntie, Radha Auntie, save me!
Mother: Birju, leave Rupa alone or else I'll kill you.
Birju: You can't kill me, you are my Mother.
Mother: I am also a woman.
Birju: I am your son.
Mother: Rupa is the daughter of the entire village, she is my honour too. Birju, I can lose a son, I cannot sacrifice my honour.
Birju: If you dare, shoot – shoot, I too shall not break my vow.
(Mother screams 'Birju' and fires).

The final triumph of the Mother confuses and places into disarray the revolutionary act essential for post-colonial reconstruction. And the purely cinematic (technical) aspects of representation clearly problematises the political questions about culture-specific images and their place in a definable post-colonial discourse. In upholding *dharma* as Law (in the form of Mother as Durga), as in fact a typically Indian Androgynous Law, the film refuses to accept the concept of action based upon political (rather than cultural) necessity. Yet so far as the spectator is concerned, his or her specular identification is always with Birju. Thus in allowing this kind of identification to take place, the director's complicity in subverting the Law of the Mother (and of Culture) comes into play. In shot after shot suture is maintained; Birju's gaze *is* the spectator's gaze even whilst he denounces Hindu ideology and contradicts the spectator's age-old cultural assumptions. In the process the film is shot through with contradictions precisely of the kind endorsed by Krishna in the battle of the *Mahabharata*. Your action has a legitimacy if it has moral force – in terms of purity of action (*karmaphalatyaga*) it is Birju who triumphs and not the Mother. Perhaps it is the only way in which Mehboob Khan can make his political statement about India: let the Mother affirm the Law, *dharma*, but let the spectator *confirm* Birju's actions. Couched in such a contradictory epistemology, *Mother India* becomes so outrageously 'conforming' and yet so defiantly subversive.

NOTES

1. Walter Benjamin, *Illuminations*, ed. Hannah Arendt, trans. Harry Zohn (London: Fontana, 1973), p. 226. 'The Work of Art in the Age of Mechanical Reproduction' was originally published in 1936.
2. Quoted in Benjamin, p. 241.
3. Stephen Heath, *Questions of Cinema* (London: MacMillan, 1981), p. 9.
4. Terry Eagleton, *Walter Benjamin or Towards a Revolutionary Criticism* (London: Verso, 1981), p. 62.
5. Eagleton, p. 48.
6. Michel Foucault, 'What is an Author?', in *Textual Strategies*, ed. J.V. Harari (London: Methuen, 1980), pp. 148ff.
7. Palatal and retroflex sibilants have been transliterated as *sh*; the retroflex vowel as *ri*; and the voiceless unaspirated palatal consonant as *ch*. I have kept Bombay Film's original transliterations of films throughout.
8. 'Selling Dreams', *Asiaweek* (May 4, 1984), 38-44.
9. *India 1982: A Reference Annual* (Delhi: Ministry of Information and Broadcasting, 1982), p. 153.
10. John Ellis, *Visible Fictions: Cinema, Television, Video* (London: Routledge and Kegan Paul, 1982), pp. 270-81.
11. 'Big Budget Survivors', *India Today* (May 31, 1984), 32-40.
12. *Asiaweek* (May 4, 1984), 40.
13. Christian Metz, *Language and Cinema*, trans. Donna Jean Uniker-Seboek (The Hague: Mouton, 1974), pp. 96-105.
14. *Time Magazine* (July 19, 1976), 9.
15. *India 1982: A Reference Annual*, p. 152.
16. Edward Said, 'Orientalism Reconsidered', *Race and Class* 27 (Autumn 1985), p. 7.
17. A later film version of Maxim Gorky's *Mother*, directed by Donskoy, was released in 1956. In the Russian *Mother* (as in Gorky's original) it is the Mother who is converted to the path of revolution.
18. Katherine Mayo, *Mother India* (London: Jonathan Cape, 1927). This book went through eight impressions in six months.

19. *The Ramayana of Valmiki – Vol I Balakanda*, trans. Robert P. Goldman (Princeton: Princeton University Press, 1984); *sarga* 4, *shloka* 8.
20. Rosie Thomas *et al*, *Cinema, Cinema*, Channel 4 Television (London, 1983).
21. See Vijay Mishra, Peter Jeffery and Brian Shoesmith, 'The Actor as Parallel Text in Bombay Cinema', *The Quarterly Review of Film Studies*, forthcoming.
22. Vijay Mishra, 'Towards a Theoretical Critique of Bombay Cinema', *Screen*, XXVI, 3-4 (May-August 1985), p. 139.
23. Peter Brooks, 'Freud's Masterplot', in *Literature and Psychoanalysis*, ed. Shoshana Felman (Baltimore and London: Johns Hopkins University Press, 1982), p. 292. According to Peter Brooks, the sub-plot usually suggests 'a different solution to the problem worked through the main plot, and often illustrates the danger of short-circuit'.
24. G.W.F. Hegel, *The Philosophy of Fine Art*, trans. F.P.B. Osmaston (1835-38; New York: Hacker Books, 1975), II, p. 49.

Caligula's Horse

'Opening address delivered at Eighth Conference on West Indian Literature, Mona, Jamaica, May 1988.

If I had not been, since boyhood, sceptical of all forms of address, by which I mean prose spoken in public, I would not have been invited to address you this morning, since the honour you have paid me is the very one I have been determined to avoid because I write verse. Public prose contains in it an affability, in fact, a superiority that is political. It must contain charm, however contorted its syntax; it must communicate, however high-pitched its subject; and most horrible of all to a poet (a word that makes me nauseous when I apply it to myself), it must make sense. It is the very opposite of the perpetual ignorance of poetry, the induced chaos from which a poem begins. I am perhaps perpetuating this chaos now, because it is very difficult, almost impossible, not in my nature, to make sense. Because I do not know what sense is, certainly because I know it is not common but rare, I have avoided writing critical or philosophical prose for all of my life.

Typing this last word I made an error. I wrote the word 'love' instead of the word 'life', and have corrected it to mean what I intended. To mean what I intended is what this public prose would have me believe, but to discover, through a typographical error, what is accidental but also true is to leave in the error and write 'I have avoided writing critical or philosophical prose for all of my love'. That is one part of the poetic process, accident as illumination, error as truth, typographical mistakes as revelation. Auden once received proofs of a poem called 'Iceland', or about Iceland, in which he had originally written 'and the poets have names for the sea' but which came back from the printer as 'and the ports have names for the sea', so Auden seized on the printer's error with a spasm of revelation equal in its shock of delight to the laser beam that unhorsed Saul on the Damascus road, and kept the typo. 'And the poets have names for the sea' is very good but pompous, but 'the ports have names for the sea' is not only epical but fantastically accurate. The provinciality and hermetic variations of the separate, terrified or possessing faith of those small wharves for that eternal force outside their ragged limits, the bays like mouths all pronouncing the word sea, naming it separately and self-assuredly, thanks to the astigmatism of a printer, or thanks perhaps to Auden's calligraphy, made a line of verse that makes another poet gasp with delight.

Besides I have always thought in two margins. It has been the rigid benediction of my life, and to think in two margins – one on the right, and one on the left, obviously – is to serve a life-long sentence. To live out a pun. By a life-long sentence I mean both the sweet and chafing prison which the soul chooses and which it calls (since apparently everything must have its noun) poetry, but it is also to see poems as simply parentheses, asides of that life-long sentence, as now a phrase of Dylan Thomas's springs to mind: 'that poetry is statements made on the way to the grave'. So, you see what happens when poets are asked to think with only one margin, that of the left, unless they are Korean, or Hebrew, writing in the wrong direction, but still with the sense of that other approaching margin, that versus at the end of which the plough turns, those primary gardens always laid in squared furrows; but to be a creature who always thinks of two margins, left and right as the poem is being made, who believes as much in the right-hand margin as he or she does in the left, is more than a pun about politics. The business of politics is the business of discourse, and the language of discourse is prose, the language of one margin only, and that one margin, in politics, may be called right when it is left and left when it is right.

This is not only what confuses those who listen to political addresses but what reduces cities to rubble and incinerates generations who mistake the margins. But also, this business of margins, of making sense, of saying what one means, is the occupation of tyrants, of those who can make four-hour tirades without interruption, without self-contradiction, without that ignorance which the poet believes in, without a sense of horizon, and certainly from the conviction that the tyrant-speaker must believe that he owns both margins. If tyrants had to compose their tirade in verse, if critics had to write criticism in regular metre, we would have less argument and more accidental, even contradictory, essays. Pope said it in one couplet; but the proper study of mankind, as he points out, is an inferior occupation compared to the question of God.

Because this is an injunction to critics: that their subject is not literature but God, or the gods, that poets should be judged by their approach towards this subject, and the source of that subject is chaos, ignorance, and its emblem is (how sweet Latin sounds in such contexts) *Dominus illuminatio mea*, Lord, who art the light of my life. The moment when Auden, in a flash that is like a seam in this chaos, like a light that comes from what he had no intention of writing, wrote the word 'ports' for the word 'poets' – that is what I would be more happily engaged in this morning.

But there also comes a time when we pay for all we have tried to do by being asked to practise, to honour, its opposite, when a poet who has earned some respect from his colleagues is asked by critic-philosophers this question: 'Yes, we know you can write poetry, but can you think?' And I confess with a right-hand margin and left-hand margin combination of arrogance and humility that I do not know how to think. Not to know what to think is the bewilderment of the normal human predicament in a political context. And so we are told what to think by popes, by parsons, by lecturers, and apparently now by me. Because my position here is elective, political, with frightening dangers, the most honest posture I could assume is that of a shrug. For that shrug – whether it be the grunt of a furrowed-forehead primate or of a hermit who has taken a vow of exterior silence – is what angers systems, what infuriates the right-hand margin. The poet chooses his prison so early that it makes the prison cell of the tyrant a repetition, it makes the cell of the monk theatrical. Besides, the silence of the hermit is what makes him loquacious, garrulous in his conversations with the silent language of trees, seas, stars, crabs, his ancestors, stones and squirrels, and God.

But now it has happened: the seduction of authority. Now I am like the tyrant, the orderer, the one who says 'Listen, I will reveal, I shall guide, I shall confirm expectation, I shall play by the rules.' The tyrant mounts the platform and the hundreds of thousands in the public square are crying 'Convince me', the parson ascends the pulpit and the congregation is praying 'Convert me', the poet ascends to the lectern and the moment he is bemedalled or laurelled like a competing athlete, or some betting pool of literature's favourite horse, he becomes the pet of the crazy emperor, he becomes a critic. He has sublimated himself.

How obvious this is, that a poet should sneer at critics. You see, even in this, behaviour of a certain predictability is confirmed. Critics have their own form of masochism, because once they have elected the tyrant to pronounce, the parson to preach, the medalled and laurelled athlete or the crowned horse of Caligula to say a few words into the microphone like Mr. Ed, they are also saying with the penitential fury of their self-Inquisition 'Insult us, tell us we are dirt, preserve that sublimity to which we have elevated you once you remember that we, who supposedly speak sense on behalf of the mob, can bring you down as fervently, remember we are the ones who make sense, the ones who preferred that you think for us.'

This too is theatrical, and only part of the truth. The margin on the right has dissolved like a horizon in a fog of its own making, a required performance of a half-lie – because since boyhood I have delighted in criticism. I cherished the essays of Eliot not because of his perceptions but because of their quotations. They induced in me the truest humility: that is, the desire to imitate, to imprison myself within those margins. Since then a lot of dead fish have beached on the sand. Mostly the fish are French fish, and off their pages there is the reek of the fishmonger's hands. I have a horror not of that stink, but of the intellectual veneration of rot, because from the far-off reek which I get from the stalls of the Academy, there is now a school of fishermen as well as schools of fish, and these fishmongers are interested in examining the disembowelled entrails of poetry, of marketing its guts and its surrounding conversation of flies. When French poetry dies the dead fish of French criticism is sold to the suckers. 'Moby Dick is nothing but words, and what are words, and what do I mean when I say Moby Dick, and if I say Moby Dick what exactly do I mean?' It convinces one that Onan was a Frenchman, but no amount of masturbation can induce the Muse. What do I mean by masturbation? Well, you take your hand and you write from the left-hand margin and stop when you have achieved some spasm of self-recognition that may not breed but will appear to conceive, and that is known as literary philosophy and without any danger of arrest by the spiritual police, it is what I am demonstrating now.

I cannot think because I refuse to, unlike Descartes. I have always put Descartes *behind* the horse, and the horse is Pegasus – not the hotel I am staying in at the moment, but the other Pegasus, the one with the wings. What I believe is: I don't know how to think therefore I am. I am one who cannot accept these processes, of games of self-contradiction, of essays on poetry, any more than I can accept the right-hand margin of History, which begins, in our language, from the left and proceeds without trim, without metre, without that closing question of the couplet until it satisfies itself with cause and effect. This ignorance is old. It is the future of the Caribbean.

Historians say now, it all depends on what you mean by History. To me that is no different from saying it all depends on what you mean by prison, what you mean by church, what you mean by a cobbled alley in Lisbon, an abandoned barracoon at the back of a plantation which tourists photograph. The real question is 'What do you mean by Time?' And it is here that historians had better secure their wristwatches or sundials, because we have to be careful of blasphemy, those of us whose religion is verse. The imagination is a territory as subject to invasion and seizure as any far province of Empire, so today when the sellers of dead fish claim whatever they claim (because honestly I never think of them), and when historians are willing to join poets in defining history as one aspect of imagination – that is, memory – it is then that poets have to be mauled and abused. Tyrants are failed artists. They paint in secret, they compose verses in secret, but they sculpt their own images publicly. The last thing they have, like historians, is imagination. A historian dare not imagine, a poet dare not think, certainly not in the way that he is expected to. That is Stalin murdering Mandelstam. History is memory, but it is not creative memory.

And what is the difference between what the historian (and literary criticism is a branch of history) remembers, and what the poet remembers? Time. To the dictator time is a given period of which he is terrified – for him there is no consolation in the fact that his bronze image will be at least bad art or that the bard who sings his achievements can take permanent revenge by writing badly about him. The superficial idea of art as immortal is not what I mean: this is a prosaic idea of time, the immortality of art. To the poet, there is no word for this dimension of memory, and the wonder of poetry is that it does not mean time to be defined temporally any more than God dare be defined by that sense of moving from the left margin to the right to arrive at some proof.

The young poet is a blessed being. If there is one now in this audience, I invite him or her to sneer, to turn away from these linear pronouncements with that sacred contempt with which I refused, by the grace of God, to believe, to prefer instead the grace that waits for the accidents of the print-setter who changed poets to ports, to the earlier error I made when I wrote either life for love of love for life, I have now forgotten which, and to see, as something of a public figure but still I hope, a hermit, a hider, a protector of silences, the vow I took as a boy not to listen. I have a friend in Saint Lucia who lives in a wonderful cove over the hill from a luxury beach-hotel. He wrote poetry once, and he is also an important official in Government, and in fun once I called him the only public hermit I know. That is what, I am sure, in spite of the honour, you would have me remain. Thank you.

Reading List

Chinua Achebe, *Morning Yet on Creation Day* (London: Heinemann, 1975).

Mervyn Alleyne, *Roots of Jamaican Culture* (London: Pluto Press, 1988).

Louis Althusser and Etienne Balibar, *Reading Capital* (London: New Left Books, 1975).

Sunday O. Anozie, *Structural Models and African Poetics: Towards a Pragmatic View of Literature* (London: Routledge and Kegan Paul, 1981).

W.D. Ashcroft, 'The Function of Criticism in a Pluralist World', *New Literature Review*, no 3 (1977) pp. 3-13.

Margaret Atwood, *Survival: A Thematic Guide to Canadian Literature* (Toronto: Anansi, 1972).

M.M. Bakhtin, *The Dialogic Imagination*, ed. Michael Holquist, trans. C. Emerson & M. Holquist (Austin: University of Texas Press, 1981).

Etienne Balibar and Pierre Macherey, 'On Literature as an Ideological Form', *Untying the Text: A Post-Structuralist Reader*, ed. Robert Young (Boston and London: Routledge and Kegan Paul, 1981).

Francis Baker *et al.*, eds. *Europe and its Others*. 2 vols. Proc. of the Essex Sociology of Literature Conference, 1984 (Colchester: University of Essex, 1985).

————, *Literature, Politics and Theory: Papers from the Essex Conference 1976-84* (London: Methuen, 1986).

Krim Benterrak, Stephen Muecke and Paddy Roe, *Reading the Country: Introduction to Nomadology* (Fremantle: Fremantle Arts Centre Press, 1984).

Homi Bhabha, 'Of Mimicry and Man: The Ambivalence of Colonial Discourse', *October*, No. 28 (1984) pp. 125-33.

————, 'The Other Question', *Screen*, no 24 (1983) pp. 18-36.

————, 'Representation and the Colonial Text: A Critical Exploration of Some Forms of Mimeticism', *The Theory of Reading*, ed. Frank Gloversmith (Brighton: Harvester, 1984) pp. 93-122.

————, 'The Commitment to Theory', *New Formations* 5, (Summer 1988) pp. 5-23.

————, 'Signs Taken for Wonders: Questions of Ambivalence and Authority under a Tree Outside Delhi, May 1817', *Critical Inquiry*, vol. 12, no.1 (1982), pp. 144-65.

David T. Haberly, 'The Search for a National Language: A Problem in the Comparative History of Postcolonial Literatures', *Comparative Literature Studies*, vol. 11, no 1 (1974) pp. 85-97.

Wilson Harris, 'Adversarial Contexts and Creativity', *New Left Review*, no 154 (1985) pp. 124-28.

_____, *Explorations* (Mundelstrup: Dangaroo Press, 1981).

_____, 'The Frontier on Which Heart of Darkness Stands', *Research in African Literatures*, vol. 12, no 1 (1981) pp. 86-93.

_____, *Tradition, the Writer and Society* (London: New Beacon, 1967).

_____, *The Womb of Space* (Westport: Greenwood, 1983).

Graham Huggan, 'Anxieties of Influence: Conrad in the Caribbean', *Commonwealth*, vol. 11, no 1 (1988) pp. 1-12.

Peter Hulme, *Colonial Encounters: Europe and the Native Caribbean 1492-1797* (London: Methuen, 1986).

_____, 'Polytropic Man: Tropes of Sexuality and Mobility in Early Colonial Discourse' in Barker, *Europe and its Others*, vol. 2, pp. 17- 32.

Linda Hutcheon, *The Canadian Postmodern: A Study of Contemporary English-Canadian Fiction* (Toronto: Oxford University Press, 1988).

Abiola Irele, *The African Experience in Literature and Ideology* (London: Heinemann, 1981).

Fredric Jameson, ed., 'Third World Literary and Cultural Criticism', special issue of the *South Atlantic Quarterly*, vol. 87, no 1 (1988).

_____, 'Third World Literatures in the Era of Multinational Capitalism', *Social Text*, no 15 (Fall 1986) pp. 65-88.

_____, *The Political Unconscious* (Ithaca, N.Y.: Cornell University Press, 1978).

Abdul JanMohamed, 'The Economy of Manichean Allegory: The Function of Racial Difference in Colonialist Literature', *Critical Inquiry*, vol. 12, no 1 (1985) pp. 59-87.

_____, 'Humanism and Minority Literature: Toward a Definition of Counter-hegemonic Discourse', Boundary 2, vol. 12, no 3/vol. 13, no 1 (Spring/Fall 1984) p. 281-99.

_____, *Manichean Aesthetics: The Politics of Literature in Colonial Africa* (Amherst: The University of Massachussetts Press, 1983).

Abdul JanMohammed and David Lloyd, eds., 'The Nature and Context of Minority Discourse', Special Issue of *Cultural Critique*, no 6 (1987).

_____, eds. 'The Nature and Context of Minority Discourse II', Special Issue of *Cultural Critique*, no 7 (1987).

Biodun Jeyifo, *The Truthful Lie: Towards a Radical Sociology of African Literature* (London: New Beacon, 1980).

Barbara Johnson, *A World of Difference* (Baltimore: Johns Hopkins University Press, 1987).

Adil Jussawalla, *Family Quarrels: Towards a Criticism of Indian Writing in English* (Berne: Lang, 1985).

Bruce King, ed. *Literatures of the World in English* (London: Routledge and Kegan Paul, 1974).

Kroetsch, 'Unhiding the Hidden: Recent Canadian Fiction', *Journal of Canadian Fiction*, vol. 3, no 3 (1974) pp. 43-45.

Eva-Marie Kroller, 'Postmodernism, Colony, Nation: The Melvillean Texts of Bowering and (Boileau) Beaulieu', *Revue de l'Université d'Ottawa/University of Ottawa Quarterly*, vol. 54, no 2 (1985) pp. 53-61.

George Lamming, *The Pleasures of Exile* (London: Michael Joseph, 1960).

Charles Larson, 'Heroic Ethnocentrism: The Idea of Universality in Literature', *The American Scholar*, vol. 42, no 3 (Summer 1973) pp. 464-75.

Dennis Lee, 'Cadence, Country, Silence: Writing in a Colonial Space', *Boundary 2*, vol. 3, no 1 (Fall 1974) pp. 151-68.

_____, *Savage Fields* (Toronto: Anansi, 1977).

Jean-Francois Lyotard, *The Postmodern Condition – A Report on Knowledge*, trans. Geoff Bennington and Brian Massumi (Manchester: Manchester University Press, 1984).

Diane Macdonell, *Theories of Discourse* (Oxford: Blackwell, 1986).

Pierre Macherey, *A Theory of Literary Production*, trans. Geoffrey Wall (London: Routledge and Kegan Paul, 1978).

John Matthews, *Tradition in Exile: A Comparative Study of Social Influences on the Development of Canadian and Australian Poetry in the Nineteenth Century* (Toronto: University of Toronto Press, 1962).

_____, 'Lifeboats for the Titanic: Patterns of Identity in Commonwealth Literature', *ACLALS Bulletin*, 5th Series, No 2 (1979) pp. 223-29.

D.E.S. Maxwell, 'Landscape and Theme', in *Commonwealth Literature*, ed. John Press (London: Heinemann, 1965) pp. 82- 89.

Russell McDougall and Gillian Whitlock, eds. *Australian/Canadian Literatures in English: Comparative Perspectives* (Melbourne: Methuen Australia, 1987).

Albert Memmi, *The Coloniser and the Colonised* (New York: Orion Press, 1965).

Leslie Monkman, *A Native Heritage: Images of the Indian in English-Canadian Literature* (Toronto: University of Toronto Press, 1981).

John Moss, ed. *Future Indicative: Literary Theory and Canadian Literature* (Ottawa: Ottawa University Press, 1987).

Arun Mukherjee, *Towards an Aesthetic of Opposition: Essays on Literature, Criticism and Cultural Imperialism* (Stratford: Williams-Wallace, 1988).

_____, 'Ideology in the Classroom: A Case Study in the Teaching of English Literature in Canadian Universities', *Dalhousie Review*, 66, 1-2 (Spring/Summer 1986) pp. 22-30.

_____, 'The Vocabulary of the "Universal": Cultural Imperialism and Western Literary Criticism', *World Literature Written in English*, vol. 26, no 2 (Autumn 1986) pp. 343-52.

C.D. Narasimhaiah and C.N. Srinath, eds. *A Common Poetic for Indian Literatures* (Mysore: Dhvanyaloka Publications, 1984).

W.H. New, *Among Worlds: An Introduction to Modern Commonwealth and South African Fiction* (Erin: Porcepic, 1975).

_____, 'New Language New World' in *Awakened Conscience*, ed. C.D. Narasimhaiah (Sterling: Delhi, 1978) pp. 361-77.

Ngugi wa Thiong'o, *Homecoming: Essays on African and Caribbean Literature, Culture and Politics* (London: Heinemann, 1972).

_____, *Decolonising the Mind: The Politics of Language in African Literature* (London: James Currey, 1986).

_____, *Barrel of a Pen: Resistance to Repression in Neo-colonial Kenya* (London: New Beacon, 1983).

Walter J. Ong, *Orality and Literacy: The Technologising of the Word* (London: Methuen, 1982.

Craig Owens, 'The Discourse of Others: Feminists and Postmodernism' in *The Anti-Aesthetic: Essays in Postmodern Culture*, ed. Hal Foster (Port Townsend, WA: Bay Press, 1983) pp. 57-81.

Benita Parry, 'Problems in Current Theories of Colonial Discourse', *Oxford Literary Review*, vol. 9, nos 1-2 (1988) pp. 27-58.

Michel Pecheux, *Language, Semantics and Ideology*, trans. Harbans Nagpal (New York: St. Martins, 1982).

Kirsten Holst Petersen and Anna Rutherford, eds. *A Double Colonization: Colonial and Post-Colonial Women's Writing* (Mundelstrup, Denmark: Dangaroo Press, 1986).

Mary Louise Pratt, 'Margin Release: Canadian and Latin-American Literature in the Context of Dependency', in *Proc of the Xth Congress of the International Comparative Literature Association*, 1982, vol. 2, ed. Anna Balakian (New York: Garland, 1985) pp. 247-56.

John Press, ed., *Commonwealth Literature* (London: Heinemann, 1965).

Russell Reising, *The Unusable Past: Theory and the Study of American Literature* (New York and London: Methuen, 1987).

Dieter Riemenschneider, ed. *History and Historiography of Commonwealth Literature* (Tübingen: Gunther Narr, 1983).

Edward Said, 'Intellectuals in the Post-colonial World', *Salmagundi*, no. 70-71 (1986) pp. 44-64.

_____, *Orientalism* (New York: Vintage, 1979).

_____, Orientalism Reconsidered' in *Literature, Politics and Theory: Papers from the Essex Conference 1976-84*, ed. Francis Barker *et al.* (London: Methuen, 1986).

_____, *The World, the Text and the Critic* (Cambridge: Harvard University Press, 1983).

Kumkum Sangari, 'The Politics of the Possible', *Cultural Critique*, 7 (Fall 1987) pp. 157-86.

Mineke Schipper, 'Eurecentrism and Criticism: Reflections on the Study of Literature in the Past and Present', *World Literature Written in English*, vol. 24, no 1 (Summer 1984) pp. 16-26.

Gregory Shaw, 'Art and Dialectic in the Work of Wilson Harris', *New Left Review*, 153 (Sept-Oct 1985) pp. 121-28.

Stephen Slemon, 'Post-colonial Allegory and the Transformation of History', *The Journal of Commonwealth Literature*, vol. 23, no 1 (1988) pp. 157-68.

_____, 'Allegory and Empire: Counter-Discourse in Post-colonial Writing'. Dissertation. University of Queensland, 1988.

_____, 'Revisioning Allegory: Wilson Harris's *Carnival*', *Kunapipi*, vol. 8, no 2 (1987) pp. 1-16.

_____, 'Monuments of Empire: Allegory/Counter-discourse/Post-colonial Writing', *Kunapipi*, vol. 9, no 3, pp. 1-16.

Wole Soyinka, *Myth, Literature and the African World* (Cambridge: Cambridge University Press, 1976).

Gayatri Chakravorty Spivak, *The Other Worlds: Essays in Cultural Poltics* (New York & London: Methuen, 1987).

_____, 'Three Women's Texts and a Critique of Imperialism', *Critical Inquiry*, no 12 (1986) pp. 243-61.

_____, 'Can the Subaltern Speak? Speculations on Widow Sacrifice', *Wedge*, no. 7/8 (Winter/Spring), 1985. pp. 120-30.

Robert Stam and Louise Spence, 'Colonialism, Racism and Representation: An Introduction', *Screen*, Vol. 24, No 2 (1983) pp. 2-20.

Subramani, *South Pacific Literature: From Myth to Fabulation* (Suva: University of South Pacific Press, 1985).

Richard Terdiman, *Discourse/Counter-Discourse: The Theory and Practice of Symbolic Resistance in Nineteenth Century France* (Ithaca: Cornell University Press, 1985).

John Thieme, 'Scheherazade as Historian: Rudy Wiebe's "Where is the Voice Coming From?" ', *Journal of Commonwealth Literature*, vol. 17, no 1 (1982) pp. 172-81.

Helen Tiffin, 'Commonwealth Literature: Comparision and Judgement' in *History and Historiography of Commonwealth Literature*, ed. Dieter Riemenschneider. (Tübingen: Gunther Narr, 1983) pp. 19-35.

_____, 'Post-Colonialism, Post-Modernism and the Rehabilitation of Post-Colonial History', *Journal of Commonwealth Literature*, vol. 23, no 1 (1988) pp. 169-81.

_____, 'Comparative Literature and Post-colonial Counter-discourse', *Kunapipi*, vol. 9, no 3 (1987) pp. 17-34.

_____, 'Rites of Resistance: Counter-Discourse and West Indian [Auto]Biography', *Journal of West Indian Literature*, vol. 3, no 1 (January 1989) pp. 28-46.

Tzvetan Todorov, *La Conquête de l'Amérique: La Question de L'autre* (Paris: Editions de Seuil, 1982). (*The Conquest of America*, trans. Richard Howard (New York: Harper & Row, 1984).

Derek Walcott, 'The Muse of History', in *Is Massa Day Dead?*, ed. Orde Coombs (New York: Anchor, 1974).

Renata Wasserman, 'Re-Inventing the New World: Cooper and Alencar', *Comparative Literature*, vol. 36, no 2 (Spring 1984) pp. 815-27.

R.E. Watters, 'Original Relations: A Genographic Approach to the Literature of Canada and Australia', *Canadian Literature*, no 7 (1961) pp. 6-17.

Cornel West, 'Minority Discourse and the Pitfalls of Canon Formation', *The Yale Journal of Criticism*, vol. 1, no 1 (Fall 1987) pp. 193-201.

Hayden White, *Metahistory: The Historical Imagination in Nineteenth Century Europe* (Baltimore: Johns Hopkins University Press, 1973).

James Wieland, *The Ensphering Mind: History, Myth, and Fictions in the Poetry of Allen Curnow, Nissim Ezekiel, A.D. Hope, A.M. Klein, Christoper Okigleo and Derek Walcott* (Washinton D.C.: Three Continents, 1988).

Denis Williams, *Image and Idea in the Arts of Guyana*. Edgar Mittelholzer Memorial Lecture (Georgetown: National History and Arts Council, Ministry of Information, 1969).

Chantal Zabus, 'A Calibanic tempest in Anglophone and Francophone New World Writing', *Canadian Literature*, 104 (Spring 1985) pp. 35-50.

NOTES ON CONTRIBUTORS

BILL ASHCROFT teaches at the University of Papua New Guinea. He has published articles on Australian and South Pacific writing and on literary theory and linguistic philosophy.

DIANA BRYDON is Professor of English at the University of Guelph, Canada. She has published a book on the Australian writer Christina Stead, and numerous articles on post-colonial literatures and literary theory.

CAROLYN COOPER teaches in the Department of English, University of the West Indies, Jamaica. She has published articles on Black American and Caribbean writing and on feminist literary theory.

MICHAEL DASH is Professor of French at the University of the West Indies, Jamaica. He has published numerous articles of French and French Caribbean writing and literary theory, and two books on Haitian literature and culture.

GARETH GRIFFITHS is Professor of English at the University of Western Australia. He has published a book on African and West Indian literatures, and numerous articles on post-colonial literatures and literary theory.

GRAHAM HUGGAN teaches in the English Department, Harvard University, Boston. He has published on post-colonial literatures and literary theory.

BIODUN JEYIFO was born in Ibadan, Nigeria. He has taught at the universities of Ibadan and Ife and now lectures at Cornell University. His publications include *Contemporary Nigerian Literature* and *The Truthful Lie: Essays in a Sociology of African Drama*.

WIJAY MISHRA teaches at Murdoch University, Western Australia. He has published numerous articles on film, on Indian literature and culture, and on Indian and European literary theory.

DAVID MOODY lectures in drama at Murdoch University. He has published articles on African drama, African literature, and Marxist literary theory.

MEENAKSHI MUKHERJEE is Professor of English at Jawanarlal Nehro University, Delhi. She has published books and articles on Indian literature in English, and on post-colonial literatures generally.

ALAN RIACH is a lecturer in English at Waikato University, Hamilton New Zealand. His writing has appeared in many journals in Scotland and New Zealand and he has contributed to Scottish Television's poetry series *In Verse* and the Aberdeen University Press *History of Scottish Literature* (volume 4: the Twentieth Century).

STEPHEN SLEMON teaches at the University of Alberta, Canada. He has published articles on post-colonial literary theory, magic realism, and allegory.

CRAIG TAPPING has taught in Nigeria and Ireland and is now teaching at the University of British Columbia, Canada. He has published articles on African and other post-colonial literatures.

HELEN TIFFIN teaches at the University of Queensland, Australia. She has published numerous articles on post-colonial literatures and post-colonial literary theory.

DEREK WALCOTT is an internationally known and highly acclaimed poet and playwright from St. Lucia in the Caribbean. He teaches at Boston University and now divides his time between Trinidad and Boston.

MARK WILLIAMS teaches at the University of Waikato, New Zealand. He has published numerous articles on New Zealand writers and on the work of Wilson Harris.